DISCARDED

# Burmese Politics

# Burmese Politics
## *The Dilemma of National Unity*

JOSEF SILVERSTEIN

Rutgers University Press
New Brunswick, New Jersey

Library of Congress Cataloging in Publication Data

Silverstein, Josef.
　Burmese politics.

　Bibliography: p.
　Includes index.
　1. Burma—Politics and government.   2. Burma—Ethnic relations.   I. Title.
DS530.4.S56　　959.1′04　　　80–200
ISBN 0-8135-0900-9

Copyright © 1980 by Rutgers, The State University of New Jersey
All rights reserved
Manufactured in the United States of America

*To my wife, Lynn
and to my sons, Frank and Gordon
who know, love, and share Burma with me*

# Contents

|     | Preface | ix |
|-----|---------|-----|
|     | Map | xii |
|     | Introduction | 1 |
| 1   | The Peoples of Burma | 6 |
| 2   | The Consequences of British Rule | 26 |
| 3   | World War II | 50 |
| 4   | The Struggle for Political Unity, 1945–1946 | 64 |
| 5   | The Struggle for Political Unity, 1946–1948 | 93 |
| 6   | Aung San and U Nu | 134 |
| 7   | The Anti-Fascist People's Freedom League, 1945–1948 | 162 |
| 8   | The Constitution of 1947 | 185 |
| 9   | The Politics of Contradiction | 206 |
| 10  | Military Rule and the Future of National Unity | 230 |
|     | Selected Bibliography | 250 |
|     | Index | 254 |

# Preface

This study grew out of a long association with Burma and a deep interest in the problem of unity, which began with my first visit to the country in 1955. Over the next twenty-five years I returned as often as I could to gather data and information and to keep alive my contacts with scholars, journalists, government servants, and friends, who shared their thoughts and ideas with me.

One need only be in Burma for a short time and read a few things to discover that for the Westerner there is a problem with names. Burmese do not have family names. Individuals are named according to the day and time of birth and the advice of the astrologer. Since certain names are associated with particular days, many people have identical names. Therefore, in order to differentiate between individuals with the same name, some people add prefixes to their given names. The prefixes may be drawn from the town in which one lives, an office one has held, or a movement in which one has participated. Thus, Tharrawaddy Maung Maung, a prominent person, adopted the name of his home town as a prefix to his given name so that he could be distinguished from other Maung Maungs. The earning of a doctorate, the holding of a high position, or participation in the nationalist movement during the 1930s have provided a variety of prefixes. Ba Maw, the wartime leader in Burma, earned a doctorate in philosophy, and people who knew him and people who wrote about him always called him Dr. Ba Maw. Aung San first and Ne Win later, as generals in Burma's army, were known as Bogyoke Aung San and Bogyoke Ne Win. Men who were active in the pre-war nationalist movement called themselves *Thakins* or masters to emphasize that they and not the British were the masters of Burma. Thus, the first prime minister of Burma, Nu, called himself Thakin Nu until independence and then dropped the prefix in favor of a traditional one in common usage throughout the country. Where prefixes are used in this study they correspond to common usage for the time being discussed for that particular individual.

Among Burmese, men are addressed or call themselves either *Ko* or *Maung*. Others address them by these two salutations, but should they be older than the person addressing them or prominent in some way, they might be addressed as *U*. *Ko* usually means "older brother" or refers politely to someone older than the speaker. *Maung* usually means someone younger than the speaker. *U* is a salutation used to address an older, prominent, or venerated person. That person will never call himself *U*, but instead will identify himself either as Maung or Ko. Thus, Nu dropped *Thakin* in favor of *Maung* and everyone called him U Nu.

There are two salutations among women, *Ma* and *Daw*. The former is used by a younger woman, usually unmarried; the latter is used to address an older woman or someone who either is married or has achieved prominence.

The narrative should clarify further the conventions of Burmese naming.

This study could not have been done without the financial help I received over a long period of time from the following sources: the Ford Foundation Foreign Area Fellowship Program; the United States Educational Foundation in Burma; the Social Science Research Council–American Council for Learned Societies; the Institute of Southeast Asian Studies (Singapore); and the Lee Foundation (Singapore).

Over the years I have enjoyed the friendship and advice of many scholars, administrators, and friends, both in Burma and the United

PREFACE                                                            xi

States, who have helped me in a variety of ways. Although they are too many to name in this short statement, a few deserve to be singled out: George McT. Kahin for his wisdom, patience, and good counsel; the late J. S. Furnivall for his advice both as a visiting lecturer at Cornell University and later in Burma; the late U Thant, who while serving as the secretary to the prime minister of Burma was never too busy to see and talk to me about Burma, my studies, and my writing; U Htun Myaing of the United States Educational Foundation in Burma, for the countless ways he helped my family and me during our two long visits and several short ones during the last quarter of a century. Although they and others helped me to understand Burma, I alone am responsible for the information and interpretations expressed in the following pages.

I wish to thank the Cornell University Southeast Asia Program for permission to use some of the material I published earlier in the introduction to my *Political Legacy of Aung San*. I also want to thank the Rutgers University University Research Council for its financial aid in the preparation of the manuscript for publication.

Finally, I would like to thank Phyllis Moditz for her patience in typing the final drafts.

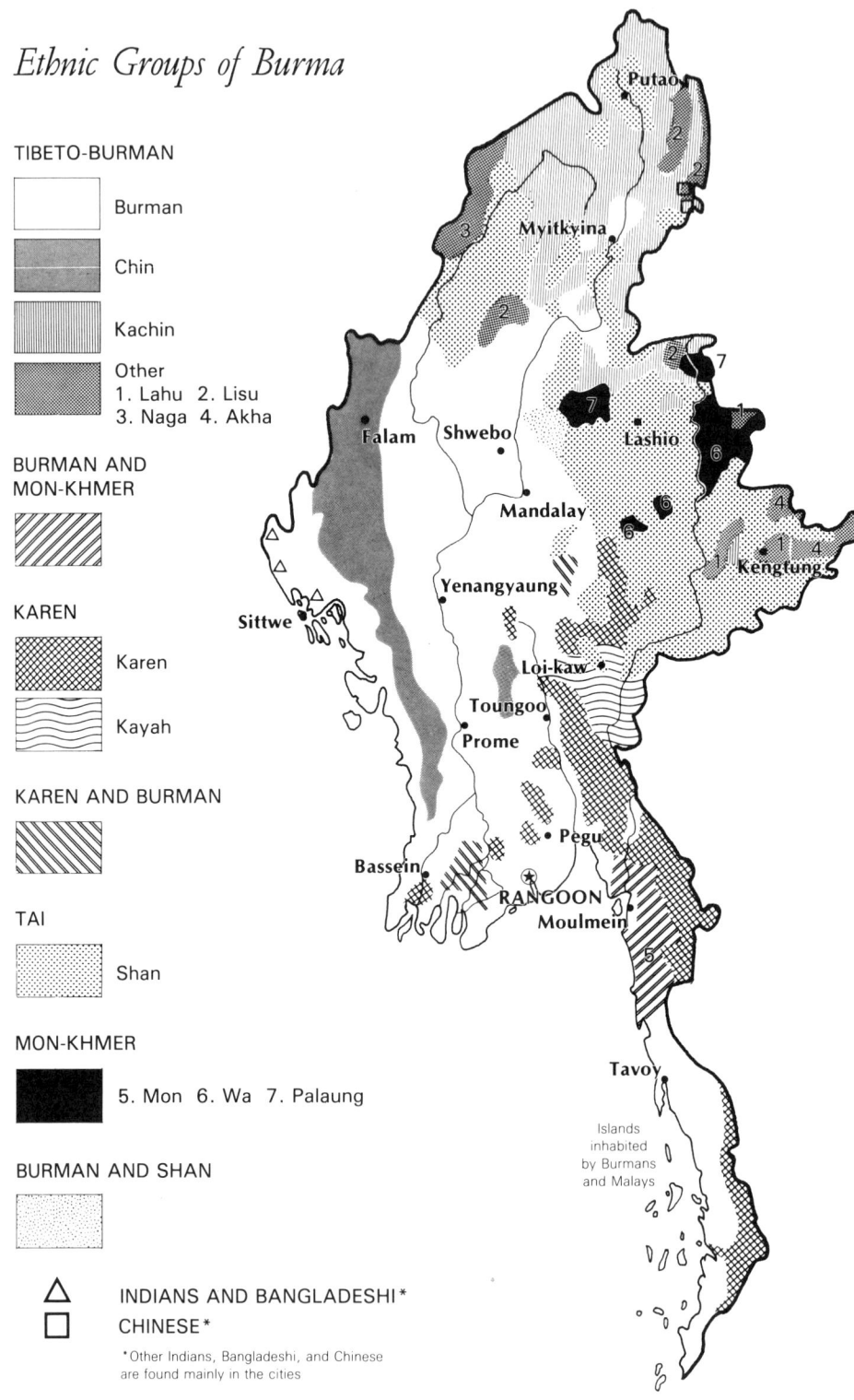

# Introduction

In the history of modern Burma, the date September 24, 1947 is all but forgotten. It deserves a better fate because on that day the delegates to the Constituent Assembly, representing all the major ethnic and political groups, unanimously adopted a new constitution by which independent Burma would be governed. The document was as remarkable as the event. Within its few chapters the authors sought not only to define the national goals, the limits of government, and the rights of the people but to construct a political union in which formerly separated peoples could be joined together to benefit from unity yet continue to enjoy a considerable degree of cultural, ethnic, and political diversity. The success of the assembly prompted its president, Sao Shwe Thaike, to comment that "the unity of the indigenous peoples shattered by . . . the loss of freedom has . . . been restored again, this time so firmly forged that slight shocks will no longer inflict appreciable damage on the solid and strong unity that is now ours."[1] A more cautious note was struck by Thakin Nu, who would become the first prime minister under the new constitution: "The unity

---

1. Burma, Ministry of Information, *Burma's Fight for Freedom* (Rangoon, 1948), p. 96.

among the indigenous races is only in the initial stages and it is still tender and frail. We shall have to strain every nerve to make this unity stand firm as a pillar of rock unshakable."[2]

The disagreement between the two leaders on the nature and strength of ethnic and political unity was not without precedent. Historians, too, have disagreed on the extent of ethnic and political unity in past and present Burma. John Furnivall argued that prior to British rule separate national feelings held by the ethnic groups in Burma proper were "fast disappearing" and "a national consciousness" under Burman rule was in process."[3] This development, he wrote, was arrested by the British; and cultural and ethnic particularism was encouraged by the alien rulers.[4] Discussing the peoples of Burma proper, Geoffrey Harvey wrote in a similar manner; but on the relationship between the peoples of the hill territories and those of Burma proper, he wrote, unlike Furnivall, that it was the British and not the Burmans who were instrumental in uniting the two areas and creating the political boundaries of modern Burma.[5] Kyaw Thet, formerly of the University of Rangoon,

---

2. Ibid., p. 95; *New Times of Burma*, September 26, 1947, p. 2.
3. John S. Furnivall, *Colonial Policy and Practice* (New York, 1956), p. 17; idem., *The Governance of Modern Burma* (New York, 1958), p. 21. In the contemporary literature of Burma, there is a great deal of confusion in the use of the terms *Burman* and *Burmese*. British writers usually employ *Burman* as a political term incorporating all the indigenous inhabitants of the country and *Burmese* as an ethnic term to identify the major group in Burma. See idem., *Colonial Policy and Practice* p. 11, n. 1, as an example of such usage. In 1922, the government of India adopted as its official definition of *Burman*: "Any person born of parents both of whom at the date of birth were domiciled in Burma and who is not an Anglo-Indian or an Indian . . . it will be observed further that the definition of a Burman will include men of all indigenous races. It will, for example, include a Karen, as in these urban constituencies the Karen electors will be included as in the general electorate" Great Britain, *Accounts and Papers*, vol. 16, "Colonies and British Possessions: East India, 1922" (Correspondence), Cmd. 1671, 1922, p. 21. In Burma the terms are currently used generally in reverse; *Burman* is used in an ethnic sense and *Burmese* in a political sense. In this study, the terms are used in the latter way.
4. Furnivall, *Governance of Modern Burma*, op. cit., p. 22; idem. *Colonial Policy and Practice*, op. cit., pp. 105–109, 142 ff.
5. Geoffrey E. Harvey, "The Conquest of Upper Burma," in H. H.

## INTRODUCTION 3

argued that "historically the problems of political integration have existed and never been adequately solved in Burma."[6] Sao Saimong Mangrai, writing from the perspective of the hill minorities, argued that Shan–Burman relations from the earliest times were characterized by separate identity, territory, and traditions.[7] John Cady and Frank Trager tend to agree with Kyaw Thet and Sao Saimong, whereas Htin Aung supports Furnivall's thesis.[8] More recently, Victor Lieberman put forth an argument about race and politics in eighteenth-century Burma based on his study of the Mon–Burman War of 1740–1757. He argues the insignificance of "national" or "racial" struggle as an explanation for that internal conflict. Instead he suggests that "the correlation between cultural, i.e., ethnic, identity and political loyalty was necessarily very imperfect, because groups enjoying the same language and culture were fragmented by regional ties, and because the dominant modes of political organization . . . were essentially indifferent to cultural distinctions."[9] Applying his theories to the period following World War II, he seems to return to the thesis of Furnivall when he suggests that his findings lead him to "suspect that the colonial period introduced a basic discontinuity into the structure of Burmese ethnic relations."[10]

Anthropologists too have contributed to the discussion. In his classic study of the Kachins, Edmund Leach devoted a great deal of discussion to the manner and extent of Kachin adoption and assimilation of Shan language, culture, and institutions, even to the

---

Dodwell (ed.), *Cambridge History of India*, vol. 6 (London, 1932), p. 447; idem., *British Rule in Burma: 1824–1942* (London, 1946), pp. 84–86.

6. Kyaw Thet, "Burma: The Political Integration of Linguistic and Religious Minority Groups," in P. Thayer (ed.), *Nationalism and Progress in Free Asia* (Baltimore, 1956), p. 157.

7. Saimong Mangrai, *The Shan States and the British Annexation* (Ithaca, 1965), pp. 47–80.

8. John F. Cady, *A History of Modern Burma* (Ithaca, 1958), pp. 39–44; idem., *The United States and Burma* (Cambridge, 1976), pp. 7–12; Frank N. Trager, *Burma: From Kingdom to Republic* (New York, 1966), pp. 79–81; Htin Aung, *A History of Burma* (New York, 1967), pp. 280–297.

9. Victor B. Lieberman, "Ethnic Politics in Eighteenth-Century Burma," *Modern Asian Studies* 12(3) (1978): 480.

10. Ibid.

point of becoming Shan.[11] Frederick Lehman in his study of the Chins noted that where they lived in close proximity to Burmans they borrowed and assimilated the values and ways of the more advanced Burmans.[12]

Whatever perspective one takes, there are in contemporary Burma numerous identifiable ethnic groups with long histories as residents in the area; with distinct political, cultural, and social characteristics; and with mutual desires and who were encouraged during British rule to maintain their separate identities. Thus when Great Britain decided to transfer power to an indigenous independent government, the local leaders were hard pressed to find a satisfactory solution to the problem of creating political and ethnic unity among the separate groups.

Although historians have taken note of the multiplicity of races, they have ignored to a large degree the problem of national unity. Instead they have concentrated on the political and cultural history of the dominant Burmans as conquerors, culture borrowers and bearers, and empire builders. As a result, current publications about Burma give readers inadequate background on and analysis of the nation building of the Burma nationalists in the present century. In this manner historians have overlooked the historic decisions taken at the Constituent Assembly and embodied in the constitution; and they have treated the postindependence problems of internal rebellion, the demand for statehood both in and out of the Union, the threat of secession, and the military coup of 1962 as isolated or exotic issues not truly rooted in the multiracial political soil of Burma. If the whole record of Burmese history is to be written, it is necessary to examine and unite an important strand—ethnic relations and the problems of national unity—with the record of the Burmans.

The place to begin is not the Constituent Assembly but an earlier point. It is not necessary to go back to the earliest relationships

11. Edmund R. Leach, *Political Systems of Highland Burma* (London, 1954).
12. Frederick K. Lehman, *The Structure of Chin Society: A Tribal People of Burma adapted to a Non-Western Civilization* (Urbana, 1963). For a brief but excellent general discussion of this question, see Peter Kunstadter, "Introduction," in Peter Kunstadter (ed.), *Southeast Asian Tribes, Minorities, and Nations*, vol. 1 (Princeton, 1967).

among ethnic groups, but it is helpful to know the background and political history of the major groups and their interaction both under Burman and under British rule. The point of concentration, however, must be World War II and the immediate postwar period, when the historic patterns were shattered, when new leadership arose and new ideas took over, and when the basis for Burman–minority relations in a future independent Burma was created. The constitution embodied some untried solutions, and its adoption marked the end of one period and the beginning of another.

It could be argued that with the abrogation of the constitution following the military coup of 1962 and its ultimate replacement with a far different one in 1974 such an examination is moot. This is not so because the new one embodies principles and ideas at variance with its predecessor and alters both the form of government and the relationships among the racial groups. The military government has used its monopoly of the means of communication to obscure or rewrite the past to be consistent with its own ideas. But the revisionism of the men in power deceives no one concerned with the problem of relations between races in Burma. Ethnic revolts and insurgency continue now as in the past. Those who fight on do so not because their memory is faulty or their aspirations are at variance with what they remember being promised but because they believe the agreements they or their fathers entered into with the Burmans in 1947 are still valid.

This study attempts to draw together the many threads that formed the unity expressed at the Constituent Assembly. It identifies the important ethnic groups; examines their relationships before World War II; and reviews in detail the issues, episodes, and ideas that inform the historical record of the relations between the Burmans and the minorities from World War II to independence. It examines the leadership, the dominant political party, and the constitution, and then looks at the contradictory politics that characterized the period of civilian rule. Finally, it looks briefly at the ideas, policies and practices of the military since they seized power in 1962 and their failure thus far to find permanent and lasting solutions to the problems of national unity. Because the issue of national unity is fundamental to an understanding of contemporary Burmese politics, this analysis is intended to provide a new approach to its study.

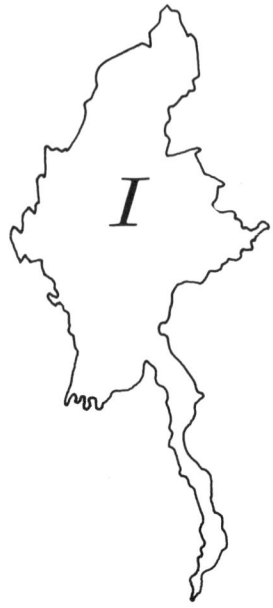

# *I*

# The Peoples of Burma

It may be true, as John Furnivall has suggested, that in Burma "a promise of national unity was foreshadowed from before the dawn of history because the major racial elements are akin, peoples fundamentally the same racial and cultural kind."[1] It is a fact, however, that the promise was never realized. Beginning with the old Burman Empire, there was no nation in the sense that all the people shared a common loyalty as well as a territory, used a single language, and enjoyed a sense of unity and identity. Society was sharply divided; people thought of themselves as members of their ethnic group rather than as subjects of the Burman kings. There was no political concept of citizenship to make it possible for non-Burmans to adopt a national loyalty. The Burmans were numerically and militarily superior—the only ethnic group able to weld the peoples of Burma into a political unit. Despite their attitude of superiority toward other peoples, they were not averse to borrowing and adapting the religious and cultural practices of their neighbors.

1. John S. Furnivall, "Historical Setting," in Frank N. Trager and Associates (eds.), *Burma*, vol. 1 (New Haven, 1956), p. 3. Furnivall's ideas were expressed by an earlier writer and friend of Burma: J. George Scott, *Burma: A Handbook of Practical Information* (London, 1911), p. 61.

## THE PEOPLES OF BURMA

Some assimilation and integration with members of the other ethnic groups in Burma took place through intermarriage and intermingling. The social and political pattern of ethnic pluralism in precolonial Burma continued throughout the period of foreign rule and became part of the tradition of the peoples of contemporary Burma.

To date, no authoritative history of the peoples of Burma has been written. Most modern historians accept the theory that the descendants of the present inhabitants of Burma migrated to the area from the north and gradually fanned out and settled widely in the territory. From stone inscriptions and royal chronicles, it has been possible to identify the more important ethnic groups and learn something of their way of life and their relations with the dominant Burmans.[2]

The first modern effort to gather ethnic data over a wide area was undertaken in 1872, when the British authorities took their first census of Lower Burma. Nine years later the effort was repeated; subsequently a new census was taken and reported every ten years (the 1941 census was taken but not reported because of the eruption of World War II in the Far East). Each report differed from its predecessor in a number of important ways: the area, the methods of identifying and classifying people, and the auxiliary data included.

The last complete census—1931—gives a limited view of the heterogeneous population of modern Burma. It attempted to determine ethnic identity by the mother tongues of those enumerated.[3] In the previous census a different criterion had been used, the language "ordinarily used in the home."[4] Thus it is impossible to compare

---

2. Gordon H. Luce, "Note on the Peoples of Burma in the Twelfth and Thirteenth Century A.D.," in India, *Census of India, 1931*, vol. 11, *Burma*, pt. 1, Report (Rangoon, 1933), app. F, pp. 296–302 (hereafter the census is cited *Census of Burma 1931*); Pe Maung Tin and Gordon H. Luce, *The Glass Palace Chronicle of the Kings of Burma* (London, 1923), p. 6 and passim; Luce, "Burma's Debt to Pagan," *Journal of the Burma Research Society* 22 (1932): 120–127; Saimong Mongrai, *The Shan States and the British Annexation* (Ithaca, 1965).

3. *Census of Burma, 1931*, p. 143.

4. Ibid.

accurately the results of the last two prewar census reports. Both reports employ the same broad language categories, making it possible to use this source as a point of departure.

According to the census of 1931, there were fourteen identifiable language—racial groups (Table 1). Grouped in this manner, the data only partially reveal the ethnic diversity. Using language as the sole basis of ethnic identity, the report ignores other means of identification and classification used by anthropologists and by the Colonial Service in Africa. The authors of the census report of 1931 were aware of this problem. In the body of the report they warned the reader that "this classification of languages is only tentative and that many of the languages which are regarded as distinct are only dialects of other languages"; in another place they note that there is "extreme instability of language and racial distinctions in Burma."[5] The report enlarges on these two themes in an essay by J. H. Green included in the appendix. Green disagreed with the methods of racial classification and argued that "linguistic evidence . . . when used as the sole basis is liable to lead, and in the case of the races of Burma, has, I think, led to many errors in our racial classifications." In the same note he argued further that "some of the races or tribes change their language as often as they change their clothes."[6]

The inadequacy of the language-racial method is clear from an examination of any of a number of language subgroups in the Burma census, for example, the Arakanese. In the 1921 report the speakers of Yanbye were grouped together with those who spoke Arakanese;[7] in the 1931 report the two language groups were separated. The latter report also notes that Burmans who have lived among the Arakanese for a long time and have intermarried "probably prefer to be known as Arakanese."[8] Further examination of the report reveals the tenuousness of the results included.

Green concluded his criticism of the language-racial method by proposing that the census of Burma adopt new categories for racial

---

5. Ibid., p. 174.
6. J. H. Green, "A Note on the Indigenous Races of Burma," in ibid., app. C, p. 245.
7. Census of Burma, 1931, p. 178.
8. Ibid., p. 179.

Table 1. Burmese Language–Racial Groups

| Language family | Group | Subgroups | Number |
| --- | --- | --- | --- |
| Tibeto-Chinese | Burma | 16 | 9,627,196 |
| | Lolo-Muhso | 12 | 93,214 |
| | Kuki-Chin | 45 | 348,994 |
| | Naga | 2 | 4,224 |
| | Kachin | 9 | 153,345 |
| | Sak (Lui) | 6 | 51,820 |
| | Mro | 1 | 13,766 |
| | Tai | 11 | 1,037,406 |
| | Chinese | 4 | 193,594 |
| Austric | Malay | 2 | 8,323 |
| | Mon | 1 | 336,728 |
| | Palaung-Wa | 11 | 176,382 |
| Karen | Karen | 17 | 1,367,673 |
| Man | Man | 2 | 951 |

Census of Burma, 1931, pp. 173, 202–204.

analysis. He suggested it would be more meaningful to group people according to physical appearance, body measurement, culture, customs, technology, and temperament.[9] To understand the growth of political and ethnic consciousness among the peoples of Burma, it is necessary to look to the reports of the ethnographers, anthropologists, and British civil servants who have lived among the various peoples of Burma and who have tried to describe the differences in character, appearance, and culture that distinguish one from the other.

The dominant ethnic group in Burma is the Burman. Geoffrey Harvey estimated that at the time of the First Anglo-Burmese War they numbered between two and three million.[10] Historians are uncertain when the first Burmans settled in the plains area of

9. Green, op. cit., p. 246.
10. Geoffrey E. Harvey, History of Burma from the Earliest Times to 10 March 1824: The Beginning of the English Conquest (London, 1925), p. 333.

Upper Burma. D. George E. Hall says that it probably was between the ninth and eleventh centuries, whereas Gordon Luce gives A.D. 839 as the approximate date.[11] By the middle of the eleventh century they had established their hegemony over the other peoples of the land and created their first empire. Under their early, vigorous kings they conquered the Mons, who lived in the delta region of Lower Burma;[12] adopted the Buddhist faith; built a great city at Pagan; erected countless pagodas reflecting Indian influences; and adapted the Pali script to their language. The Pagan period is the golden age of Burman tradition, customs, and ideas.

The Burmans were an agrarian people. Living in small, relatively self-sufficient villages, they raised their food staple, rice, and engaged in home crafts, which they traded with their neighbors. J. George Scott in his classic study of Burman life in the late nineteenth century describes it:

> The Burman is the most calm and contented of mortals. He does not want to grow rich. When he does make a large sum of money, he spends it all on some pious work, and rejoices in the thought that this will meet with its reward in the next existence. . . . A bountiful soil will not let its children starve; and so the Burman jogs on through a cheerful existence, troubled by no anxious cares and free from all the temptations of ambition.[13]

Furnivall in his later study of the precolonial economy described social life in rural Burma as organized to provide "a comfortable life for all the people of the village" and not "as in a mill or factory where the object is to produce the largest outturn at the lowest cost."[14]

Authority in rural Burma was personal and was exercised by a hereditary leader called the *myothugyi* or *taikthugyi*. The *myothugyi*

---

11. D. G. E. Hall, *Burma* (London, 1950), p. 11; Luce, "Burma's Debt to Pagan," op. cit., pp. 120–127.

12. Pe Maung Tin and Luce, op. cit., pp. 70–79.

13. Shway Yoe [J. George Scott], *The Burman: His Life and Notions*, vol. 1 (London, 1882), p. 78.

14. John S. Furnivall, *An Introduction to the Political Economy of Burma*, 2nd rev. ed. (Rangoon, 1938), pp. 43–44.

ruled over a group of villages that "were not separated by definite territorial boundaries."[15] Men were graded in rank and permanently attached to a hereditary leader. Regardless of where a man lived, it was to his captain he paid his taxes and for his captain he performed his service. "So long, however, as they remained subjects to the jurisdiction of their chief they were 'his men' such as feudal tenants were the men of the feudal lord."[16] Those who bore arms and served in the army were of a higher class than those who performed other sorts of public service. Together these two classes were called the *ahmudan*; and they enjoyed social superiority to the *athi*, men who paid taxes in lieu of service. The class structure was not rigid, and men and women could easily move up or down.[17] Furnivall notes that the *athi* were more homogeneous than the *ahmudan* and were mainly cultivators.

Atop this peasant-rural base existed the royal household and the semidivine king. According to Daw Mya Sein "he was the absolute lord of the lives, property and personal resources of his subjects, exercising all the normal attributes of sovereignty. . . ."[18] Patterned on the Hindu concept of kingship, the king was believed to be a descendant from Manu. Hidden from view in his palace and supported in office by the royal regalia, he performed certain rituals connected with agriculture, defended the Buddhist faith, protected his people, and governed them with the advice of Brahman priests and Burman bureaucrats.[19]

Burman character has prompted many studies.[20] Scott suggested

15. Ibid., p. 40.
16. Ibid., pp. 38–39.
17. Ibid., pp. 37–39.
18. Mya Sein, *The Administration of Burma: Sir Charles Crosthwaite and the Consolidation of Burma* (Rangoon, 1938), p. 18.
19. John F. Cady, *A History of Modern Burma* (Ithaca, 1958), pp. 4–11.
20. Shway Yoe, op. cit.; H. Fielding Hall, *The Soul of a People* (London, 1917); for more recent studies that draw on the preceding two sources as well as on empirical evidence, see Geoffrey Gorer, *Burmese Personality* (Washington, 1943) (mimeo); L. M. Hanks, "The Quest for Individual Autonomy in Burmese Personality," *Psychiatry* 12 (1949): 285–300; Sein Tu, *Ideology and Personality in Burmese Society* (n.p., n.d.) (mimeo); idem., "The Psychodynamics of Burmese Personality," *Journal of the Burma Research Society* 47(2) (1964): 263–285.

that the long history of military struggle was the result of two inherent characteristics of the Burmans: bellicosity and pride of race.[21] More concerned with the religious beliefs and practices of the Burmans, H. Fielding Hall suggested that the historic tendency to live by fighting came from the Burman characteristics of personal courage and religiosity.[22] Hall, aware of the apparent inconsistency between warfare and the teachings of the Buddha, concluded

> Wars of invasion, the Burmese have waged. . . . They are but men and men will fight. If they were perfect in their faith, the race would have died out long ago. . . . Whatever the Burmese have done, they have kept their faith pure. . . . They have known the difference between good and evil, even if they have not always followed the good.[23]

From the eleventh century on, religion has been a major source of social cohesion among the Burmans.[24] Every male Buddhist at some point in his life enters the religious order and, clothed in the symbolic yellow robe with head shaven clean, temporarily loses his secular identity and becomes a novice. While a member of the *sangha* he is treated by the lay community with all the respect and reverence of a lifetime member. As a novice he studies and memorizes the teachings of the Buddha, becoming fully indoctrinated with the moral precepts by which Burman Buddhists try to live.

Besides inculcating moral and religious values, the religious order fulfills another social function: educating the youth of the community. The children are taught to read and write at a very young age, making literacy widespread among the Burmans.

---

21. Shway Yoe, op. cit., 2:153–165.
22. H. F. Hall, op. cit., pp. 51–78.
23. Ibid., pp. 77–78.
24. Harvey, op. cit., p. 4; three excellent studies of Buddhism and society and Buddhism and politics are Melford E. Spiro, *Buddhism and Society: A Great Tradition and Its Burmese Vicissitudes* (London, 1971); Donald Eugene Smith, *Religion and Politics in Burma* (Princeton, 1965); and E. Michael Mendelson, *Sangha and State in Burma*, ed. John P. Ferguson (Ithaca, 1975).

Three minority groups shared Lower Burma and parts of Upper Burma with the Burmans: the Arakanese, the Mons, and the Karens. Of these, the Arakanese were closest in kinship to the majority Burmans. According to Scott, D. G. E. Hall, Harvey, and other historians, the Arakanese were part of the Burman migrations into the area, became separated from the mainstream, and settled in semi-isolation in the Southwest in an area that came to be known as Arakan.

The Arakanese claimed a longer history of rule by their own kings than did the Burmans.[25] Like the Burmans, their culture and traditions were influenced by their close proximity to the superior culture of India, their western neighbor. Unlike the Burmans, they developed an interest in seafaring, trade, export of rice, and the use of money.[26] They enjoyed a long separate and independent existence, which lasted from the end of the Pagan dynasty in the thirteenth century to 1784–1785, when the Burmans defeated and destroyed the Arakanese kingdom, exiled the Arakanese king along with 20,000 of his subjects, and appointed a governor to exercise local authority over those Arakanese who remained.[27] According to A. Phayre, thousands chose to "abandon their country and took refuge in British territory" rather than live under Burman rule.[28]

By the beginning of the First Anglo-Burmese War in 1824, two developments were taking place among the Arakanese: Those forced to leave their home and live in Burma among the Burmans were assimilating and being integrated into local society; those who continued to live in the depopulated area of Arakan or in India kept their nationalist and anti-Burman sentiments alive, perpetuated their separate identity, and helped precipitate the first war between Britain and Burma.[29] At the beginning of the twentieth century, Scott said of the Arkanese identity:

25. Scott, op. cit., p. 66; Harvey, op. cit., pp. 137–149.
26. Scott, op. cit., p. 66.
27. Harvey, op. cit., p. 268.
28. A. Phayre, *History of Burma* (London, 1883), p. 220.
29. Harvey, op. cit., pp. 201–221; D. G. E. Hall, *Europe and Burma* (London, 1945), pp. 86–99.

The Arakanese are proud of their assumed superior antiquity, but consider themselves Burmans; the Burmans look upon them as uncouth talkers and accomplished liars, but do not deny the kinship. The separation of the two is a matter of sentiment and is likely gradually to disappear.[30]

The Mons, or Talaings, are historically and ethnically distinct from the Burmans, the Karens, and other indigenous groups in Burma. Their migration into the area is believed to have preceded that of most of the other peoples in the land.[31] Having settled in the South along the seacoast, they were among the first to come into direct contact with Indian civilization, adopt Theravada Buddhism, develop an alphabet and a written script, and adapt Indian law to their local needs.[32] The Burmans, under the leadership of Anawratha about A.D. 1067, conquered the Mons and transported their king, scholars, religious leaders, and "an entire population numbering 30,000."[33] According to the *Glass Palace Chronicle of the Kings of Burma*, the Burmans assimilated Theravada Buddhism and other aspects of Mon culture following their victory over the southerners.[34] The war between the Burmans and the Mons initiated a long history of strife between the two groups, which lasted until the eighteenth century, when Alaungpaya and his successors finally defeated the Mons and then consciously sought to assimilate the two groups. Furnivall makes a point of the fact that under the

30. Scott, op. cit., 67.
31. Harvey, op. cit., p. 3; John S. Furnivall, *Colonial Policy and Practice* (New York, 1956), p. 12; Scott, op. cit., pp. 61, 130; Luce, "Notes on the Peoples of Burma," op. cit., p. 299, explains the name *Talaings*: "The Burmese name for the Mons is Talaings [*Tauluin*]. . . . Phayre's and Yule's derivation of the word from *Telinga*, a variant of *Kalinga*, a vague term for east and south of India, still holds the field; the same word *Keling, Kaling, Kling*, is used to denote Indians generally in Malaya, Siam and Cambodia. *Tauluin*, we must assume, was a word used at first indiscriminately by the Mramma [Burmans] of Central Burma for inhabitants of Lower Burma, whether indigenous or settlers from India; and as the alternative word, *Kala*, attached itself more particularly to the latter, the meaning of *Tauluin* would seem to have been limited to the former."
32. Harvey, op. cit., pp. 4–5, 29; Scott, op. cit., pp. 129–130.
33. Harvey, op. cit., p. 28.
34. Pe Maung Tin and Luce, op. cit., pp. 77–80, 86–92.

last Burman dynasty "Mons were eligible for the highest offices."[35] Although the two communities were thoroughly mixed during a long period of intermarriage and intermingling and of adherence to and acceptance of the same culture and social values, Mon identity persisted; and their ancient history as a separate kingdom still prompts a few descendants to aspire to a separate and autonomous state.

The minority that suffered most at the hands of the Burmans and was afforded the least opportunity to intermarry and associate with them was the Karen. The Karens are among the oldest inhabitants of Burma, having come originally from what is now southern China during the sixth or seventh century.[36] One of the earliest descriptions of the Karens is found in the journal of Father Sangermano written in the last quarter of the eighteenth century:

> A good and peaceable people, who live dispersed through the forests of Pegu in small villages consisting of four or five houses. . . . Although residing in the midst of the Burmese and Peguans they not only retained their language, but even their dress, houses and everything else are distinguished from them. . . . They are totally dependent upon the despotic government of the Burmese.[37]

The name Karen includes a number of different tribes, of which the Pwo, Bwe, and the Sgaw are the most numerous. According to

---

35. Furnivall, *Colonial Policy and Practice*, op. cit., pp. 16–17; he gives no examples to support this observation. It is the argument of Victor B. Lieberman, "Ethnic Politics in Eighteenth-Century Burma," *Modern Asian Studies* 12(3) (1978), that during the long war Burmans and Mons changed sides and loyalties and manifested these changes in personal appearance, language, and behavior. He also points out, however, that Alaungpaya was able to rally support to his cause by appealing to Burmans to unite against the Mons; he reports that, at the battle of Prome, Alaungpaya's supporters "unfurled their topknots to show soldiers with whom they could not communicate verbally that they were comrades" (p. 473).

36. John F. Cady, "The Karens," in Trager and Associates, op. cit., 2:826; Harvey, op. cit., p. 13; Harry Marshall, *The Karens of Burma* (Calcutta, 1945), p. 2. Following the contemporary political split between delta Karens and hill Karens, each is treated as a separate group in this discussion.

37. Father Sangermano, *A Description of the Burmese Empire* (Rangoon, 1924), pp. 36–37.

John Cady, the Pwo were the earliest Karen settlers, and they eventually established their home among the Mons in the area around the present-day cities of Thaton and Amherst. The Sgaws first settled in the watershed between the Sittang and Salween Rivers but were eventually driven west and south by the more powerful and aggressive Burmans.[38] The Bwe, who settled in the area lying east of Toungoo, were the only Karen group that never fell under Burman domination. Thus, according to both Cady and Harry Marshall, the area inhabited by the Bwe is the only one entitled to be called Karen territory.[39] Although the majority of Karens lived among the more dominant and aggressive Mons and Burmans, the close proximity did not lead to widespread assimilation; only a subgroup of the Pwo, the Toungthus or Pa-O, adopted Theravada Buddhism and developed a written script.[40]

The Burmans treated the Karens as inferiors and discouraged them from intermingling. Those Karens who lived under direct Burman rule were forced to labor and pay heavy capitation taxes.[41] Throughout the pre-British period many Karen tribes moved into the hills and remote areas of the plains and delta to avoid persecution.[42] Marshall suggests that their timidity and the Burman exploitation and oppression together form the basis of the current antipathy between the two groups.[43]

The Karens never organized politically beyond the level of the village. According to a British official who was one of their strongest admirers, the Karens had no feeling of nationhood; they were a

38. Cady, "The Karens," op. cit., pp. 826–828.
39. Cady, ibid.; Marshall, loc. cit.
40. Cady, "The Karens," op. cit., p. 827; Marshall and Cady disagree as to which of the two larger Karen groups were the more resistant to Burmanization. Marshall suggests that the Pwo dialect was less persistent than the Sgaw among those living close to the Burmans, whereas Cady suggests that the Sgaws occupied the bridge position between the delta Karens, who were more or less Burmanized, and the primitive Karen groups living in the hills. Harry I. Marshall, "The Karen Peoples of Burma," *Ohio State University Bulletin* 26 (13) (1922): 3; Cady, "The Karens," op. cit., p. 832.
41. Cady, "The Karens," op. cit., p. 832.
42. Marshall, *The Karens of Burma*, op. cit., p. 1.
43. Harry Marshall, *The Karen Peoples of Burma* (Columbus, Ohio, 1922), p. 304.

"mixed horde of aboriginal savages."[44] Leadership in a Karen village usually went to the person who asserted his authority, and he retained it until he lost it in a challenge or passed it at his death to a son or nephew. Sometimes rival leaders arose, split the village, and each took their followers away to found a new community.[45] In areas where the Burmans asserted their authority, Karen villages were administered by a special Burman official, not part of the imperial system, who was empowered to collect a capitation tax, exact gifts in kind, and demand corvée labor from the people.[46]

During the Anglo-Burmese wars, the British benefited from the deep cleavage between the Burmans and the Karens. The invaders found the latter able and willing guides; after the war the British cited the Karens for their service.[47] In addition, during the First Anglo-Burmese War, the delta-dwelling Karens fought alongside the Mons against the Burmans.[48]

The Karens were alienated from the Burmans in still another way. The American Baptist missionaries who came to Burma in the early nineteenth century played no small part in arousing the Karens and educating them in the Western tradition. The Karens of the delta and the plains warmly received the missionaries because their appearance and their religious mission seemed to fulfill the prophecy of an ancient Karen myth that predicted the return of a white brother bearing the lost book. The Karen identification with the Baptists and the British further widened the gulf between the Karens and the Burmans.[49]

---

In the oval-shaped ring of hills and mountains surrounding Upper Burma lived numerous ethnic groups that either recognized the suzerainty of the Burman kings or accepted nominal authority pro-

44. D. Smeaton, *The Loyal Karens of Burma* (London, 1887), p. 29.
45. Marshall, *The Karens of Burma*, op. cit., p. 29.
46. Cady, "The Karens," op. cit., p. 832.
47. Marshall, *The Karens of Burma*, op. cit., p. 32.
48. Cady, "The Karens," op. cit., p. 847–848.
49. Kyaw Thet, "Cultural Minorities in Burma," in H. Passin (ed.), *Cultural Freedom in Asia* (Rutland and Tokyo, 1956), pp. 229–231; Furnivall, *Colonial Policy and Practice*, op. cit., pp. 16, 23–24.

vided it did not bear down too hard on their traditional independent social and political structure. British sources noted that there were more than one hundred distinct tribes in the area. "The great majority, however, are too small to be of political importance and the four largest, Shans, Kachins, Chins, and Karens dominate more than 95 per cent of the frontier area between them."[50]

Of the four largest groups, the most numerous is the Shan. It is generally believed that the Shans entered the hill fringe and the plains of Upper Burma in the seventh century, after Nanchao (which was located in what is now known as Yunnan) was overrun by the Chinese. As part of the Tai migrations southward into the Indochina peninsula, they spread throughout the northern region of Burma and settled among the various indigenous groups that had preceded them into the area. According to Sir Charles Crosthwaite, those Shans who settled in the plains area among the Burmans tended to merge with the latter, "but those on the high plateau to the east continued to be governed by their own chiefs according to their own customs, subject to the suzerainty of Burma."[51] For a short while after the fall of the Pagan dynasty in 1287, the Shans overran Upper Burma and established a temporary hegemony over the other ethnic groups.[52] The Shans were direct political rivals of the Burmans for control of the entire area from that period until 1604, when they ceased resisting and accepted indirect rule by the Burmans.[53]

Despite Burman conquest, the Shans maintained their separate political identity. Internally, the Shans had their own social and political organization, which differed from those of the Burmans or the other groups in the territory. Like the peoples of the plains and the delta, the Shans had their own language, written script, history, and a centuries-old literature.[54] Whenever the Shans came

50. Burma, *The Report of the Frontier Areas Committee of Enquiry, 1947*, pt. 1, Report (Rangoon, 1947), p. 6.
51. Charles Crosthwaite, *The Pacification of Burma* (London, 1912), p. 133.
52. Harvey, op. cit., pp. 73–122; Saimong Mangrai, op. cit., pp. 47–51.
53. J. George Scott and J. T. P. Hardiman, *Gazetteer of Upper Burma and the Shan States*, vol. 1. (Rangoon, 1900), pt. 1, p. 199.
54. H. N. C. Steavenson, *The Hill Peoples of Burma* (Calcutta, 1944), p. 13.

in close proximity to the Burmans, they tended to merge with them through assimilation of customs, traditions, and social values.[55] Those Shans who remained separate were organized in numerous subgroupings each under the absolute authority of a hereditary chief or *sawbwa*. Because of the hostility, mistrust, and jealous rivalry between these chiefs, the Shans were unable to unify into a single nation as the Burmans had done.

The Burman policy toward the Shan States was to govern them indirectly and to leave their traditional social and political organizations intact. A resident advisor was attached to the courts of the larger states; a resident-general or *bohmu-mintha*, stationed in Mongnai with a large force of armed men under his command had general responsibility in the entire area.[56] Only when a Shan chief refused to adhere to advice or attempted to forward revolutionary activity was he interfered with or removed by the Burman overseer. The Shan chiefs showed their loyalty to the Burman kings by sending their sons to the royal court, ostensibly to become imbued with respect and loyalty to the Burman king but in reality as hostages for their own behavior and loyalty. In addition the Shan chiefs usually sent a daughter as a bride for the much-married Burman king. Both Crosthwaite and Scott—two British government servants who played an active part in bringing the Shan States under British rule—agree that the Burman policy was to keep the Shan chiefs divided and, at the same time, dependent on the power and authority of the Burman Empire.[57] To the Shan peoples, their chiefs appeared to be great and independent leaders because there was little or no physical evidence of any power superior to them.[58]

The Shans were united with the Burmans by nonpolitical bonds such as religion; their Buddhism, like that of the Burmans, was accommodated to and blended with the deeper and older religious practice of spirit or *nat* worship.[59] In transition areas where the two

---

55. C. Brant, "The Shans," in Trager et al., op. cit., 2:628; Steavenson, op. cit., p. 12.
56. Crosthwaite, op. cit., p. 135.
57. Scott and Hardiman, op. cit., p. 41; Crosthwaite, op. cit., p. 135.
58. Crosthwaite, op. cit., p. 135.
59. R. G. Brown, "The Pre-Buddhist Religions of the Burmese," *Folklore*

groups met and intermingled, other ties such as common dress, language, and agricultural practices were evident. Nonetheless the Shans as a group never lost their culture, their political organization, nor most definitely their sense of identity.

Among the other hill peoples inhabiting the upland fringes separating Burma from its largest neighbors, India, China, and Siam, the three most important in the light of contemporary development were the Kachins, the Chins, and the Kayahs or Karenni.[60] In political organization, historical origin, customs, and traditions, they too were distinct from the plains and delta dwellers. In general, while acknowledging the nominal suzerainty of the Burmans, especially in the transitional zones between the plains and the hills, they were indifferent to the life of the plains peoples. For the Burman Empire, these peoples and their hilly homeland served as a shield against potential invaders from the west, north, and east. Most historians recounting the long history of Burma pay scant attention to them because of their late arrival and their lack of contribution to the culture and general development of the area. Harvey, for instance, records little more than the fact that they served as warriors in the Burman armies.[61]

The political relations between the three and the Burman Empire were neither formal nor regular like those between the Burmans and the Shans. Only among the Kayah was there any real challenge to Burman nominal authority. An intense quarrel between the chiefs of Western and Eastern Karenni erupted in 1863; the British deputy commissioner of Toungoo proceeded to the area to restore peace and while there found occasion to renew the "contract of friendship" between Great Britain and Western Karenni originally

---

32 (1921): 79–89; Shway Yoe, op. cit., pp. 276–289; Luce, "Notes on the Peoples of Burma," op. cit., pp. 298–299 also points out that even the Mons did not practice pure Theravada Buddhism.

60. *Karenni*, or Red Karens, is the term by which the Burmans called this particular group of people; the people, however, called themselves the Kayah. The British followed the practice of the Burmans. After the establishment of the Union of Burma, the Kayahs formed one of the states and insisted that it be called the Kayah State, the name made official in 1951 by an amendment to the constitution (Amendment Act 62, 1951).

61. Harvey, op. cit., pp. 3, 4, 228, 236.

signed in 1857.[62] Beginning in 1873, reports of Burman efforts to extend their suzerainty over Western Karenni brought a protest from the British. The Burmans, weakened by two wars with the Westerners and incapable of asserting their authority over the Kayahs, settled the matter by signing a treaty with Great Britain on June 21, 1875, that said that "the State of Western Karenni shall remain separate and independent and that no sovereignty or governing authority of any description shall be claimed or exercised over that State."[63] No such problem ever arose with the Chins or Kachins; both were content to accept nominal Burman authority so long as there was no attempt to interfere with their internal affairs nor force them to accept direct rule.[64]

All three groups were less politically developed than the plains people. Kachin social and political organization differed from that of the Chins and Kayah. Edmund Leach suggests that two patterns of political organization existed among the Kachins: *gumsa* villages ruled by hereditary chiefs and village councils and the more democratic *gumlao* villages in which residents selected headmen and councils of elders, rejecting a rigidly graded society and hereditary status.[65] The *gumsa* pattern was predominant in the northern area and the highlands, whereas the *gumlao* was found mostly in the west. Both patterns were unique to the Kachins. As a hill people, the Kachins practiced *taungya* or "mountain dry field" rice cultivation, which conformed to their semimobile way of life and which distinguished hill people generally from those on the plains. Their religion, like that of other hill peoples, was spirit or *nat* worship.

*The Report of the Frontier Areas Committee of Enquiry, 1947* notes that in the pre-British period the relation between the Kachins and Burmans "was less than close."[66] The report takes note

---

62. C. U. Aitchison, *A Collection of Treaties, Engagements and Sanads Relating to India and Neighboring Countries*, 3rd ed., vol. 1 (Calcutta, 1892), p. 263.
63. Ibid., p. 284.
64. Burma, op. cit., pp. 8–9.
65. Edmund R. Leach, *Political Systems of Highland Burma* (London, 1954), p. 198; R. E. Huke, "The Kachins," in Trager et al., op. cit., 2: 699; Scott, op. cit., p. 93.
66. Burma, op. cit., p. 8.

of the fact that Kachin levies were used in the Burman army as early as 1551–1581, during the reign of King Bayinnaung. It concludes its remarks about Kachin–Burman relations with:

> The Burmese were not interested in the internal administration of the Kachins and the suzerainty exercised did not mean much more than occasional presents or tributes from the Kachins and their occasional service in the Burmese armies.[67]

The Chins, living in the northwestern hill area of Burma, are believed to be an offshoot of the original Burman settlers; because of their subsequent isolation, their customs "give a probable picture of the pre-Buddhistic Burman usages."[68] Like the Kachins, the Chins had no concept of a nation-state and were divided into numerous warring tribes and subdivided into numerous clans. They are reported "to have had social intercourse with the Burmese at the time of the kingdom of Pagan (1044–1287)"[69] and to have provided soldiers for the armies of King Bayinnaung (1551–1581) and King Alaungpaya (1752–1760). Chins who lived in regular contact with the Burmans adopted their language, customs, and religion, whereas those living in the remote hill areas retained the traditional Chin social and political pattern, animistic faith, and local dialects.[70] The Chins continued to practice slavery until the twentieth century, when the British forced them to cease. The Burmans never exercised direct authority over the more primitive Chins nor sought to assimilate them into their society.

The Kayah, or Red Karens, inhabit an area in eastern Burma, sharing borders with the Shans of Burma and the Tai of Siam. They enjoy the distinction of having been one of the few hill peoples to free themselves from Burman hegemony (which dated back to the time of the reign of the Burman king Minkyinyo, 1486–1531)[71] before the British replaced the Burmans as the country's rulers.

The Kayah are smaller in size than their plains and delta-dwelling

67. Ibid., p. 9.
68. Scott, op. cit., p. 105.
69. Burma, op cit., p. 10.
70. C. Hobbs, "The Chins," in Trager et al., op. cit., 2: 721–777; Frederick K. Lehman, *The Structure of Chin Society* (Urbana, 1963).
71. Burma, op. cit., p. 12.

cousins, more backward in their cultural development, and more aggressive in guarding and protecting their semi-independent status. Living in the hills apart from the main body of Karens, they developed a distinguishing set of local characteristics in language, dress, customs, and mores. Their close proximity to the Shans influenced their pattern of tribal organization and the names they adopted for their petty chieftains.[72]

In contemporary terms these four groups of hill peoples are the most articulate and politically mature ethnic groups in Burma. They still cling to their ethnic identity despite the present government's efforts to unite them with a higher loyalty and a broader identity as citizens of the Union of Burma.

---

The existence of a plural society for ten centuries or more raises an important historical question: Why was it that the Burman kings did not seek to assimilate and integrate the many peoples under their rule in order to give strength and stability to the empire? Part of the answer lies in the attitude of the Burmans toward the minorities, part, in the relationship of the political and social institutions of the empire to the population.

During the period of recorded history the Burmans, through force and conquest, created three separate empires. The first two each lasted for approximately two centuries, and the third enjoyed a lifetime of slightly more than one century. Between the periods of unification, what is now modern Burma was the scene of constant warfare between the largest ethnic groups. Burmans, Shans, Mons, and Arakanese. Despite their military prowess the Burmans failed to establish internal peace and security because they did not create the political machinery necessary for stable government, orderly administration, and peaceful succession to the royal throne. Neither was there a concept of nationhood that included all the ethnic minorities nor any theory that supported the idea of assimilating them.

The Burman kings, thought to be semidivine and entitled to command the absolute obedience of their subject-slaves, employed

---

72. C. Hobbs, "The Kayah," in Trager et al., op. cit., 2: 778–822; Scott, op. cit., pp. 119–123.

a dual system of governance: direct rule in Burma proper over the Burmans, Mons, and Arakanese; indirect rule over the Karens and the hill peoples. Neither system brought the majority of people into direct contact with the person of the king nor contributed to the Burmanization of the subject minorities.

Unlike China in the same period, the Burman Empire did not have a bureaucratic class or any rational system of producing and educating the men who manned the imperial hierarchy. Bureaucrats and administrators were recruited from the loyal and trusted friends and servants of the monarch. They were his personal appointees, their commissions lasting until he recalled them or until his death caused them to seek reappointment by the new king. Frequent upheavals at the throne, mainly caused by the absence of an accepted, stable order of succession, resulted in a constant reshuffling of administrators, thus making royal rule ineffective and preventing the establishment of enduring, stable government.[73]

Under such circumstances real power over the people gravitated to and located itself in the hands of the *myothugyis*, the local hereditary leaders, among the Burmans. Living in relatively homogeneous communities and under the protection of the local leaders, the people living away from the royal capital were fairly insulated from the wrath and power of the king. Unless captured in war or subjected to service as corvée labor, the people carried on in their traditional ways without significant interference.

If the direct impact of the king on the peoples of Burma proper was relatively mild, on the hill peoples it was even more so, living as they did under the authority of their own chiefs, largely unaware of the representative of the Burman king. The indirect system guaranteed the continuation of ethnic, social, and political diversity among the hill peoples and protected them from Burmanization and integration.

The royal policy of forming military and service units from among both the Burman population and the hill peoples did not promote integration because the units were kept separate. A by-product of military activity that had more effect on assimilation was

73. J. Nisbet, *Burma under British Rule and Before*, vol. 1 (Westminster, 1901), pp. 150–170; Harvey, op. cit., pp. 181–182, 209–210; Cady, *History of Modern Burma*, op. cit., pp. 9–33.

the common practice of capturing the civilian population of the enemy state, transporting it to the homeland of the victors as spoils of war, and absorbing it through intermarriage and intermingling with the home population. For example, under the Konbaung, the last Burman dynasty, Arakanese, Manipuris, and Tais were deported after battle to central Burma, where the deportees gradually adopted the language, customs, and dress of their conquerors while contributing their own arts and skills to the Burmans.[74] This practice, uncivilized by Western standards, was probably the most significant way diverse groups were absorbed. The Arakanese, Mons, and Tais were more affected than the hill peoples. Clearly the political institutions and policies were developed not for nation building but to establish an empire in which Burman dominance would be recognized, feared, and respected.

Among the social institutions, religion had the greatest potential for creating an integrated Burman society. From the eleventh century on, the overwhelming majority of the peoples in Burma were Buddhists.[75] In theory, when they entered the *sangha*, all men were one regardless of ethnic origin; but because the religion was localized through the establishment of a monastery in every village, there was little intercourse between monks of different ethnic origins. For most men the robe and the order marked a temporary interlude in their lives; when they returned to secular life they resumed their ethnic identities as Burmans, Mons, Arakanese, or Shans with the passions, fears, and stereotypes common to their groups. Whatever leveling effect the religion may have had in theory, it proved in practice a weak bond between the coreligionists of conflicting groups.[76]

The political and social institutions of the Burman Empire never created a united society. The plural society of the Burman era carried over into British rule, there to be institutionalized and perpetuated until the indigenous people regained their independence in 1948.

74. Harvey, op. cit., pp. 347–350.
75. Ibid., pp. 4–7; *Census of Burma*, 1931, p. 207, reports that out of a total population of 14.6 million, 12.3 million were Buddhists.
76. Shway Yoe, op. cit., pp. 16–45; H. F. Hall, op. cit., pp. 116–143.

# 2

# The Consequences of British Rule

To understand the political and social basis of the movement for national unity and independence after World War II, it is necessary to review some aspects of British policy and practice and the response of the indigenous population during the last sixty years of colonial rule.

Beginning after the end of the Third Anglo-Burmese War of 1885, the British authorities embarked on a series of administrative and political changes that had a major impact on Burmese society. The government did not treat the whole territory as a single administrative unit; instead it loosely followed the policy of its predecessor, the Burman kingdom, and administered Burma proper directly and the Frontier Areas indirectly.

One of the first and most significant changes made by the British was the adoption and implementation of the Village Regulation Act of October 1887, under which the power of the *myothugyi* was ended and the *thugyi*, or village headman, was raised in stature to become the agent in the village for the central administrative system.[1] The *thugyi* was directly responsible to the deputy commissioner, who in turn provided the administrative link between

---

1. Charles Crosthwaite, *The Pacification of Burma* (London, 1912), p. 81; Hugh Tinker, *Foundations of Local Self-government in India, Pakistan*

the indigenous leaders and the colonial administration. Although the act was not immediately applied in Upper Burma, there, too, it eventually became the basis for local administration.

At the national level, the first significant political change, which occurred in 1897, was the elevation of the chief executive officer from chief commissioner to lieutenant governor with a legislative council of nine members, of which four were officials and five were nominated nonofficials. The change reflected the growth and complexity of services and activities carried on in the Burma Province.

In 1909, the famed Morley-Minto Reforms for India were applied to Burma. The lieutenant governor's legislative council was enlarged to fifteen, with two of the members elected.[2] The Reformed Legislative Council of 1909 created a very restricted electorate composed of the members of the "Burma Chamber of Commerce, the representative organizations of European business and by the Rangoon Trade Association, the organization of the European Retail Trade."[3] The council included in addition one nominated member each from the Indian community and from the Shan chiefs. This marked the real beginning in Burma of special political representation for economic and political interests through the creation of special and restricted electorates.[4]

On August 20, 1917, E. S. Montagu, secretary of state for India, issued the following statement:

---

and Burma (London, 1954), pp. 56–57; John F. Cady, A History of Modern Burma (Ithaca, 1958), pp. 142–143.

2. The object of the reforms was not to establish democratic government in Burma. Lord Morley said the reforms were not intended to lead to a parliamentary system in India; H. T. White, in A Civil Servant in Burma (London, 1913), p. 25, went further and wrote, "Do not let us try prematurely to impose representative institutions on the people who neither demand nor understand them. Above all, let us avoid the pernicious cant of thinking that our mission in Burma is the political education of the masses. Our mission is to conserve, not to destroy their social organizations; to preserve the best elements of their national life; by the maintenance of peace and order to advance the well being of the Burmese people."

3. F. S. V. Donnison, Public Administration in Burma (London, 1953), pp. 38–39.

4. Great Britain, East India, Constitutional Reforms, 1929, "Report of the Indian Central Committee," Cmd. 3451, 1930, p. 20. An example of

The policy of his Majesty's Government . . . is that of the increasing association of Indians in every branch of the administration, and the gradual development of self-governing institutions, with a view to the progressive realization of responsible government in India as an integral part of the British Empire.[5]

Although this declaration was intended primarily for India, the political leaders in Burma demanded the inclusion of their province in any changes that might be contemplated for India. After much discussion both in Burma and Great Britain and after an official inquiry into the problem, Burma, like India, received parliamentary and administrative reforms in its government.

In the newly created Parliament of 1922, the practice of communal representation and separate electorates was continued and enlarged. Both were justified on two grounds: that economic activity and enterprise must be given special political representation and that large indigenous minorities scattered throughout the country and hence unable to insure the election of their own representatives, must be guaranteed representation.[6] On the former ground, Europeans, Anglo-Indians, and Chinese were granted special treatment; on the latter ground, the Karens were guaranteed seats. In both cases well organized minority pressure groups worked in behalf of their special interest and won these concessions.[7]

---

British rationalization for their actions twenty years before: "The next landmark of importance was the Morley-Minto Reforms of 1909. The principal features of institutional change were the definite introduction of the elective principle based on representation by classes and interests: the official recognition of the claims of Muslims to separate electorates and the acceptance of the principle of indirect election by municipalities and district boards as the method of selection of the majority of the unofficial members of the legislature."

5. Great Britain, *Parliamentary Debates* (Commons), 5th ser., 97 (1917): 1695–1696.

6. Great Britain, *Parliamentary Papers*, vol. 35, 1920, "Proposal of the Government of India for a New Constitution for Burma," Cmd. 746, 1920, pp. 17–18; idem., *Accounts and Papers*, vol. 16, "Colonies and British Possessions: East India 1922" (Constitutional Reforms: Burma Correspondence), Cmd. 1671, 1922, p. 19.

7. Great Britain, *Parliamentary Papers*, vol. 3, 1919, "Report of the Joint Select Committee on the Government of India Bill," Appendices (1920),

In the Act of 1935, which established a separate government for Burma, the communal concept was restated. The "Instrument of Instruction" prepared by the British Parliament for the governor-general's guidance made specific that he had "special responsibilities to protect the legitimate rights of the minorities."[8] It may be argued that the British motive for this line of development was to insure the protection and existence of ethnic minorities, but the evolution of self-government in Burma helped to foster and intensify ethnic pluralities and national disunity by emphasizing differences and by reducing the natural power of the majority through artificial institutional devices.

In the Frontier Areas, a different kind of administrative development took place. At the close of the Third Anglo-Burmese War, the British administrators moved to bring the hill peoples under their authority. Charles Crosthwaite records five objectives the British had for their campaigns in the Shan States: to force the Shans to acknowledge British supremacy in the area, to establish and preserve peace, to interfere as little as possible with internal local affairs, to reopen trade routes, and to save money and manpower by ruling the area indirectly.[9] To implement these objectives the British created a separate administrative system of local Residents who were responsible directly to the chief commissioner, or highest administrative officer in Burma. The system permitted the local chief to administer civil, criminal, and revenue matters with a minimum of interference.[10]

In the territories that later came to be identified as the Kachin State and the Chin Special Division, the British were unable to win the allegiance of the local residents by persuasion; only after military expeditions were dispatched and engagements fought did the majority accept British authority. Having done so, Kachins and Chins were then permitted to live under their own leaders in accordance

---

contains all the memorials presented to the British government by the various interest groups.

8. Great Britain, Accounts and Papers, vol. 20, 1936–1937, "Instrument of Instruction," Instruction no. 10, 1938, p. 4.

9. Crosthwaite, op. cit., pp. 21, 148–174.

10. J. George Scott and J. T. P. Hardiman, Gazeteer of Upper Burma and the Shan States, vol. 1 (Rangoon, 1900), p. 313.

with their own laws, customs, and traditions so long as they gave up such traditional practices as slaving and war making.[11]

The relationship between the Karenni (the Kayah according to contemporary terminology) and the British differed from that which existed between the other hill peoples and the Westerners. Because of their contract with the States of Western Karenni and their treaty with the former Burman government regarding the independence of the Karenni peoples of that area, the British treated the territory and its people as a separate feudatory state. Crosthwaite explained this unique arrangement as the result of British experience with legal and semantic difficulties in dealing with the Shan States. The chief commissioner in Burma thought it better to follow an earlier British precedent with Indian states and keep the Karenni states outside the colonial administrative structure.[12]

The administration of the Frontier Areas remained unchanged until 1897, when the British recognized the politically advanced development of the Shans and included one of their chiefs in the new lieutenant governor's council. The Shan representative was appointed to serve at the governor's pleasure and participated in all the council's deliberations. Then in 1922, the British made a major change in their pattern of administering the Shan States; they created two federations of Shan States and the Federal Council of Shan Chiefs. This development took place at the same time that the British were introducing dyarchy, parliament, and popular elections in Burma proper. The new Federal Council of Shan Chiefs provided a forum for the chiefs to debate general subjects as well as their budgets. In 1935, the system was further refined by the creation of the Standing Committee of the Federal Council composed of six chiefs, elected from the council at large, whose function was to deal directly with the British governor on all subjects.[13] Simultaneously the British Parliament approved a new constitution for Burma proper that institutionalized the separation of the Shan States and provided Burma proper with a system of respon-

11. Crosthwaite, op. cit., pp. 312, 350.
12. Ibid., p. 203; Burma, *The Report of the Frontier Areas Committee of Enquiry, 1947, pt. 1, Report* (Rangoon, 1947), pp. 11–12.
13. Burma, op. cit., pp. 13–14.

sible parliamentary government. Burma proper took a progressive step toward becoming a modern political state, while the Shan States remained a feudal, backward area.

The hill peoples outside the Shan States were considered less advanced than the Shans and not granted parallel privileges and reforms; instead they remained under the general supervision and authority of the governor.[14] In 1922 when the British colonial government in Burma was instituting major changes in its adminstrative system, it created the Burma Frontier Service as a separate entity from the established administrative hierarchy; no longer were civil servants eligible for duty both in Burma proper and the Frontier Areas. This proved to be another divisive measure insuring the separation of the two areas.

The 1935 constitution provided further changes that strengthened the division between the Frontier Areas and Burma proper (or as it was then called, Ministerial Burma).[15] In addition, it established two categories of territory within the Frontier Areas. Part I Areas remained under the direct control of the governor and were administered at his discretion; they were identified as "excluded

14. Ibid., p. 12. The belief that certain areas of Burma were not ready for Western-style political institutions existed for a long time prior to the 1922 Act. An example is found in Great Britain, *Parliamentary Papers*, vol. 35, 1920, op. cit., p. 15: "While it is not proposed finally and entirely to exclude any particular districts from participation in the scheme of local self-government, it is obvious that there are certain areas which are . . . in the particular state, and where the conditions have not yet developed as to warrant the introduction of self-governing institutions. . . . As in course of time these areas progress and develop, the extension to them of local self-government, either complete or in a modified form, can be considered. The Shan States have already been regarded and administered as an entity separate from the rest of Burma, and they too could be excluded from the purview of the scheme. The inhabitants of these States speak a different language, are of a different race and at a different stage of political development. Their inclusion therefore in a constitution devised primarily to suit conditions in Burma proper would not be acceptable either to them or to their chiefs."

15. The most thorough analysis and discussion of the 1935 constitution is contained in John L. Christian, *Burma and the Japanese Invader* (Bombay, 1945), pp. 77–105 (originally *Modern Burma*, Berkeley, 1942).

areas" outside the jurisdiction of the Burma Parliament.[16] Part II, or "partially excluded," Areas enjoyed some of the same privileges held by residents of Burma proper but were excluded from the provisions of the Rural Self-Government Act.[17] Under the new constitution, Part II Areas were under the jurisdiction of the Parliament, but the governor had the right to veto any legislation passed for this territory.

Part II Areas were further subdivided into two groups, one with the right to elect members to Parliament and the other without this privilege. The constitution established as an ultimate goal that Part I and II areas could eventually merge with Ministerial Burma after their inhabitants had advanced enough politically to be considered coequal.[18] The constitution, while offering promise of real political unity and an end to the historic pattern of separation, failed to win the approval of many of the younger nationalists because it provided neither a timetable nor a terminal date for this objective. World War II intervened before British tutelage could make much headway toward realizing this goal.

---

The uniting of Burma with India made it possible for the peoples of both countries to move freely between the two; the Indians took advantage of this, but the Burmese did not. The sudden influx of an alien group added to the existent ethnic and social problems. During the first hundred years of British rule in Burma, no barriers were erected to limit or discourage the influx of Indian laborers, peasants, merchants, and professionals. According to the first population census in 1872, there were 136,504 Indians in Lower Burma,

16. Christian, op cit., p. 101: "Excluded areas are those whose inhabitants differed from the other peoples of Burma in kind of civilization, and where an almost complete reversal or abandonment of tribal customs would be necessary before they could be incorporated into the political life of the remainder of Burma."

17. Ibid.: "Partially excluded areas are those which have accepted to a greater or lesser degree the same general type of civilization found in the other parts of Burma."

18. Great Britain, The Government of India Act, 1935, 26, Geo. 5, chap. 3 (London, 1936), sec. 473.

constituting 4.9 percent of the total enumerated population. By 1931, their number had grown to 1,017,825, or 6.9 percent of the total population.[19] This steady inflow of Indian workers led to a popular belief among the Burmans that their country would soon be swamped and they would become a minority in their own territory. Communal antipathy grew with the establishment of communal seats and special Indian electorates in the reformed parliaments of 1922 and 1937.[20]

Although the record of Indian–Burman relations under British rule was a long one of antipathy and occasional violence, there is scattered evidence that numerous Indians settled among the local population; changed their names, religion, and way of dress; married local women; and managed to merge with the indigenous people. There is stronger evidence that some Indians, who were born in Burma, identified themselves with the indigenous population at an early period in their lives and actively led or participated in the milestone activities of the nascent nationalist movements of Burma. In the famed student strike of 1920 and again in 1936, Indians were leaders and supporters of the strikers.[21] There is evidence also that the young nationalist leaders of Burma looked to the Indian Congress Party for guidance and advice and considered it a model

19. Burma, *Report on Indian Immigration* (Rangoon, 1941), pp. 4–11; *Census of Burma, 1931*, pp. 228–230. The figures are inaccurate, first because people were identified by the language they spoke and their birthplace, not by citizenship. Second, the census, often as not, was taken at periods after the normal agricultural and milling seasons, when numerous Indians had returned to India for short visits, so that census rolls reflected the low, not the high, count.

20. N. V. Rujkumar, *Indians outside India* (New Delhi, 1954), p. 55. The Indian Congress Party in its 1924 meeting held at Belgaum passed a resolution opposing "the tendency among Indian settlers in Burma to claim communal representation and strongly advised them not to make any such claims as such separatist tendency is bad in principle."

21. Two examples stand out. In the 1920 movement, N. C. Sen, a leading student and debater, was one of the original committee to call the strike. Later he changed his mind and left the strikers; yet in so purely a nationalist movement, he was an important leader. See Publicity Bureau of the University Boycotters, *Voice of Young Burma* (Rangoon, 1922), passim. In 1936, Maung Raschid, a future cabinet member in postindependence Burma, was one of the leaders along with U Nu and Aung San.

for their own activities.[22] Thus, although communal antipathy between Burmans and Indians was widespread among the masses, a small degree of harmony and assimilation was also evident.

---

Under British administration the local armed forces were radically changed both in ethnic composition and in mission. In place of the once-feared Burman armies the British created new units recruited almost exclusively from the minority and alien segments of the population. The new army was based on the Indian pattern of organization, "and the military tradition was of close identification of the soldier with his tribe or community rather than with the nation at large."[23] Ethnic units recruited from the Karens, the hill peoples, and the Indians composed the major portion of the local armed forces. During World War I an all-Burman unit was organized, but after the war it was disbanded. The reserves in the Burma Auxiliary Force were recruited from among the Anglo-Burmans.[24] The main mission of the army was also changed. After the British established law and order throughout the nation, the army was reduced in size and its new objective was to participate in the defense of India and the British Empire. Thus the army was not representative of the majority of peoples in Burma and was alienated by its official role from the country of its origin.[25]

The British attempted to alter this situation after Burma was separated from India, but the outbreak of World War II in 1939 prevented the new plans from being fully implemented. Both Geoffrey Harvey and Hugh Tinker call attention to the fact that the Burmans were unsympathetic to the new plans because all the higher

22. Aung San, *Burma's Challenge* (Rangoon, 1946) (mimeo.), p. 2.
23. Hugh Tinker, *The Union of Burma* (London, 1957), p. 315.
24. Christian, op. cit., pp. 313–315.
25. Geoffrey E. Harvey, *British Rule in Burma, 1824–1942* (London, 1946), pp. 40–42. Speaking of the British policy, he writes, "But sociologically it was disastrous; it deprived the less martial races of great experience. History shows that the Burmese were not unfit; and the failure to recruit them may be one of the causes underlying the increase in crime, for instincts which can be sublimated in the army must find an outlet."

ranks were slated for the professional soldiers—the minorities—so that their own chances for promotion did not appear favorable.[26]

These are but a few of the political and social changes under British rule in Burma. John Furnivall sums them up:

> British rule did nothing to foster national unity. On the contrary, both directly and indirectly, it stimulated sectional particularism. It separated Burma proper from the frontier peoples by practicing direct rule in the former and indirect rule in the latter; and it divided the frontier peoples from one another by leaving them under their own local chieftains. Also, by opening the armed forces to the minority peoples and barring them to the Burmese, it fostered racial antagonism and subverted the internal balance of power, rendering it unstable.[27]

The reaction of the peoples of Burma to British rule and their relations with one another can best be seen in the rise of Burmese and Karen national movements. Both communal groups reacted in an opposite manner and both entertained conflicting ideas about the future of Burma after independence was granted. Their activity and aspirations provide a microcosm of the ethnic disunity in Burma under British control.

The Burmans never accepted the idea that colonial rule was a blessing or an unlimited benefit for their country. Psychologically they resented their conquest by a stronger foreign power, the political rise of the minorities, and their own failure to unite and restore Burman leadership and prestige. The full development of an exchange economy, with increased economic competition with the Indians, both in agriculture and in the new and expanding cities, caused the Burmans to associate their misfortunes and their inability to recover power and leadership with colonial rule. Their reaction to the British went through numerous stages; from hostility it gradually changed to peaceful coexistence and eventually became bitter and hostile again; it manifested itself in abortive

---

26. Ibid., p. 42; Tinker, *The Union of Burma*, loc. cit.
27. John S. Furnivall, *The Governance of Modern Burma* (New York, 1958), p. 22.

revolts, racial riots, and the mushrooming of a multiplicity of political parties and movements ranging from peaceful and conservative to violent and revolutionary. The reforms the British offered failed to win their total support because they saw them as partial measures that favored the minorities.

Prior to the Montagu announcement in 1917, there was not a significant political nationalist movement among the Burmans. After the collapse of their monarchy and the defeat of the royal pretenders, dacoits, and others who rose to challenge the British between 1885 and 1895, the Burmans withdrew from political activity and concerned themselves with their historic pursuits, agriculture and religion. The first real nationalist stirrings came after the turn of the century, when a nonpolitical religious movement developed. The Young Men's Buddhist Association (Y.M.B.A.), modeled after the Young Men's Christian Association, was founded to look after the religious, educational, and social needs of the people.[28] It served as the training ground for future national leaders and as the formulator of issues that stimulated the people to common action.[29]

The political changes that followed the Montagu declaration in 1917 took numerous forms. Between 1917 and 1922, the Burmans attempted to organize an all-embracing nationalist movement. The General Council of Burmese Associations (GCBA), which succeeded the Y.M.B.A., attempted, by changing its name and activity, to represent all the peoples in Burma.[30] It failed for two reasons: It did not attract the minorities who gave their support to the British, and it could not contain the politically articulate Burmans who were divided on goals and tactics.

In kaleidoscopic fashion the GCBA gradually fragmented and reassembled as many groups. One of the most significant offshoots was the *Wunthanu Athin* movement in the villages of Burma. Created initially to bring national issues and politics to the villages

---

28. Great Britain, East India, *Constitutional Reforms*, 1918 "Addresses Presented in India to His Excellency the Viceroy and the Right Honorable Secretary of State for India," Cmd. 9178, 1918, p. 32.

29. Ba U, *My Burma* (New York, 1958), pp. 3–7.

30. John S. Furnivall, *Colonial Policy and Practice* (New York, 1956), p. 144.

and thus widen the political participation of the people, the *Wunthanu* gradually degenerated into extremist organizations that opened their ranks to criminals and charlatans as well as to dedicated political leaders. It sided with the extremists on religious and ethnic issues, and from its ranks sprang many of the leaders and followers of the Saya San revolt in 1930–1931.[31]

Closely associated with the GCBA and the *Wunthanu* organizations were the Buddhist monks, who placed their interest in worldly affairs ahead of their religious vows. Two of the monks, U Ottama and U Wisara, won countrywide fame for their political activity. Both suffered arrest and incarceration and one, U Wisara, died in jail as a martyr-hero. Under their aggressive leadership, the *Wunthanu* organization and the other nascent Burman-led nationalist organizations became firmly linked with the Buddhist religion.[32] During the nineteen-twenties and nineteen-thirties, the politically oriented monks became major participants in the political process.

The students were another important element in the Burman nationalist movement. Beginning in 1920 with the university students' strike against the British-sponsored University Act, the students entered Burmese politics and provided an important element of leadership and active participation. The student movement was broadly based and like the GCBA, sought the support of young people from all ethnic groups. The 1920 strike is of key importance, not only because it was the most aggressive anti-British act undertaken to that date, but because it marked the beginning of a Burman-led effort to create an indigenous school system in which the language of instruction and the teachers were Burmese and the subjects were selected by their importance for the inculcation of a truly nationalist spirit.[33] The national schools movement was supported by the people throughout the country. Buddhist monks and university students were recruited as teachers, and the people at

---

31. Great Britain, *Parliamentary Papers*, vol. 12, 1931/1932, "Report on the Rebellion in Burma up to May 3, 1931," Cmd. 3900, 1932, pp. 11–12.

32. Maung Maung Pye, *Burma in the Crucible* (Rangoon, 1952), pp. 11–16; Furnivall, *Colonial Policy and Practice*, op. cit., p. 143.

33. N. C. Sen, *Peep into Burmese Politics* (1917–42) (Allahabad, 1945), p. 12. The subjects taught were Burmese language, literature, history, and the development of home industries.

large were asked to give both moral and financial support to the movement. Although the movement failed to establish a permanent national school system, it did play a vital role in awakening the people to the nationalist cause and providing a training area for the next generation of political leaders.[34] The date of the beginning of the university strike, December 4, 1920, was memorialized and is still celebrated as National Day. It also marked the entry of students into the nationalist movement and politics, both as leaders and as agitators.

The aggressive nationalism that developed in the nineteen-thirties can be traced to many causes. The reforms of 1922 did not provide the Burmans with greatly added prestige or actual power in their own country. The economic depression that gripped Burma in 1930–1931 drove the peasant deeper into debt and forced him to lose his land; it also crystallized his grievances against the colonial system and led him to take violent action and to support anti-colonial movements. Both the publication of the Simon Report, which investigated the operation of the 1922 reforms, and the Burma Round Table discussions with the British government on the future political development of Burma focused the public's attention on local grievances, discontent, and frustrations. The direct results of these and other causes were the ill-conceived and badly executed revolts and the rise of new, aggressive political national movements whose goal was independence and whose tactics were a mixture of parliamentarianism, direct action, and propaganda.

Of these movements the earliest and the most significant for the future was the *Dobama Asiayone*, or "We Burman Society." Organized chiefly by university students and supported by the young men and women of the country, the members called themselves *Thakins*, or Masters; their goal was independence.[35] As dedicated

---

34. Publicity Bureau of the University Boycotters, op. cit., pp. 26–28, 41–42, 102–103; Cady, op. cit., pp. 217–221.

35. Burma, *Interim Report of the Riot Inquiry Committee* (Rangoon, 1939), p. 43; Ba Khaing, *History of Burmese Politics* (Rangoon, 1937), in Burmese, pp. 174–176. Furnivall believes that Maung Ba Thaung was the first Burman to adopt the name *Thakin*: "It was about that time that Maung Ba Thaung came into the office one morning and announced that in

nationalists their initial objective was to combine a revival of indigenous language and literature with the study of Western thought and technology. The *Dobama Asiayone* drew its ideas from Marxism, the Sein Fein movement of Ireland, and the fascist movements of Italy and Germany. Its chief model for local politics and tactics was the Indian Congress Party.[36] When the new constitution for Burma was granted in 1935, the *Dobama Asiayone* sponsored a parliamentary party called the *Komin Kochin* ("one's own king—one's own kind") whose objective was to elect members to the legislature with the explicit purpose of wrecking the new political institutions. The policy of the *Thakins* called for the uniting of all the indigenous groups and the creation of a Burman nation. Their first manifesto was issued in the memory of the Burmans who lost their lives during the Indian–Burman riots of the nineteen-thirties. Their slogan was

> Burma is our country; Burmese literature is our literature; Burmese language is our language. Love our country, raise the standards of our literature, respect our language.[37]

Although they accepted the support of the monks, religion was important to their movement only in the sense that it was part of their nation's heritage and provided emotional stimulus for ethnic unity. In the war years beginning in 1939, they allied themselves with other extremist organizations and were outlawed as seditious and a threat to colonial rule.

Other parties rose in the nineteen-thirties that were similar to *Dobama Asiayone*, such as the *Sinyetha* ("Poor Man's") Party, and the *Myochit* ("Love of Country") Party. Each strove to win the support of the Burman people and to stimulate their national aspirations. The political developments of this period accentuated

---

the future I was to address him as Thakin Ba Thaung. He was, I believe, the first Thakin" "Introduction," in Thakin Ba Thaung, *A Thousand and One Nights* (Rangoon, 1950), p. h.

36. Maung Maung Pye, op. cit., pp. 17–22; Burma, *Riot Inquiry Committee*, loc. cit.

37. Ba Khaing, op. cit., pp. 176–178; Kodaw Hmaing, *Book about Thakins* (Rangoon, 1938), in Burmese, pp. 119–121.

communal tensions and isolated the various groups from each other. For most politically conscious Burmans, self-rule meant Burman rule, and the minorities were expected either to assimilate or to accept a reduced social and political status. The Burmans found in the Arakanese and the Mons strong political allies for their violent attacks on the Indians and for all their religious endeavors.

Three issues exercised the Burmans and stimulated them to organize, agitate, and even rebel: the place of the Indian in Burma, communalism in politics, and physical unification of Burma—the unification of the Frontier Areas with Burma proper. Clearly the most important of these was the Indian issue. Initially the Burmans and Indians were not in direct competition because the latter settled in the cities and took various occupations not desired by the indigenous population. In time, however, the Indians came to threaten the Burman peasant through their rising power as money lenders and eventually as landowners. The worldwide depression of the nineteen-thirties heightened the problem as many indigenous farmers were forced to leave the fields and seek employment in the cities.[38] The resulting direct economic competition between Burmans and Indians helped precipitate the anti-Indian riots of that decade.[39]

The Burmans expressed their resentment toward the Indians in the Simon Commission hearings:

> The so-called development of Burma by Indian capital and Indian labor has practically meant the exploitation of Burma's resources and has hardly brought any benefit to the sons of the soil. On the other hand, a big slice of Burma's earth has already passed into the hands of Indian capitalists. . . . While the uninterrupted flow of Indian capital tends to "dispossess the swain," the uninterrupted flow of Indian labor, however advantageous it may be to the foreign capitalist carrying on business in Burma, tends to oust indigenous labor from the field.[40]

38. Great Britain, *Report of the Royal Commission of Labor in India*, Cmd. 3883, 1931, p. 440.
39. Maurice Collis, *Trials in Burma* (London, 1953), pp. 143–148.
40. Great Britain, *Indian Statutory Commission Report, 1929–1930*, vol. 3, Cmd. 3568, 1931, p. 511.

The dispossession of the Burmans from their land by alien moneylenders was recognized by the British as a potential cause of political trouble. The 1937 reports of the Burman–British Land and Agriculture Committee noted that "conditions in lower Burma are nearing the danger point and that the continual transfer of land from the agriculturalist to the non-agriculturalist is likely to result in violent agitation for the ousting of foreign owners."[41] The Riot Inquiry Committee in 1938, which studied the violent anti-Indian riots of that year, agreed with the Land and Agriculture Committee's conclusions and added that the riots were antigovernment, "and to some extent at least, anti-Government meant in the context, discontent by the agriculturist with his conditions."[42] As long as British rule remained in Burma, the Indians provided a living symbol of what foreign domination was capable of imposing on a subject people.

On the question of communal representation, the nationalists were divided. The older leaders accepted the communal idea and supported the position taken by a majority of the members of the Burman Legislative Council, whose representatives before the Simon Commission argued that communalism should be continued "until conditions alter to justify their abolition, even at the risk of slower progress toward the realization of common citizenship."[43] In addition they favored increased representation for Indians, Karens, and Anglo-Indians. They accepted communal representation in the belief that all elements of society were entitled to a voice in a democratic government. They refused to recognize that communal seats were divisive and that progress toward unification of the peoples would be slowed down.

Opposing this line of thought were the younger political leaders, especially those who came to maturity during the latter half of the nineteen-twenties. U Ba U expressed their view when he, as a member of the Burmese Legislative Council, dissented from the majority report:

41. Burma, *Report of the Land and Agriculture Committee*, pt. 2, *Land Alienation*. Reprint (Rangoon, 1949), p. 58.
42. Burma, *Riot Inquiry Committee*, op. cit., p. 11.
43. Great Britain, *Indian Statutory Commission Report*, op. cit., p. 512.

The general constituencies, where the Burmese Buddhists dominate things . . . have also returned an Anglo-Indian, a Karen and many non-Burmese Muslims and many Burmese Chinamen. They generally work together to further the national cause. The special constituencies of Karens, Anglo-Indians and Indians, however, return their own men, and the national members of the special constituencies do not mix as freely as those of the general constituencies with the rest of the elected members. I should therefore say that the existence of special constituencies tends to divide up the members into racial groups, generally viewing the questions of importance from racial angles, instead of fostering a national unity of purpose. A healthy and vigorous public opinion is not possible of formation so long as the system of religious and racial representation maintains.[44]

At the Burma Round Table Conference held in London in 1931–1932, the anticommunal position was argued by U Pu, who declared that the Burmans were practically ruled by the minorities, "who indeed, were like guests in our house." He observed that the minorities such as the Karens were "legally, socially, and morally, no other than Burmans and they are one of the chief indigenous races." He also considered the Shans as Burmans but argued that under British influence they "have been made to identify themselves as a minority party."[45] To him, the only real minorities were the aliens—the Indians and the Europeans—and he and those he represented thought that these minorities ought to be made subject to the indigenous peoples of Burma.

The question of alien minorities became an increasingly important one as political reforms were instituted. Under the 1935 constitution, the nine European votes were crucial in making and breaking cabinets because no one party held a majority. By winning the support of the Europeans and the communal representatives, Dr. Ba Maw was able to form a government in 1937; when this support was withdrawn, his government fell. The influence of these minority representatives insured conservative government

---

44. Ibid., pp. 518–519.
45. Great Britain, *Burma Round Table Conference*, Cmd. 4004, 1932, pp. 52–59.

despite the radical promises and programs of the local politicians.[46] This was clearly demonstrated when the Europeans refused to support the Burmans on the important question of whether or not to Burmanize the Burma Frontier Service. In his letter about the vote to the secretary of India, the reform secretary for the government of Burma wrote that "it is quite clear that the Bill was thrown out not on its merits, but on entirely irrelevant political considerations."[47]

Political unification of the Frontier Areas with the rest of Burma did not become a nationalist issue prior to 1930.[48] Until that date nationalists did not challenge the British argument that historically the areas were separate from Burma proper and that only British rule had joined them under a single government with power to act anywhere in the territory. The Simon Commission and the Burma Round Table Conference offered the radicals in the Burman nationalist movement the opportunity to introduce this issue to the world public. No longer were the radical leaders content to see British dominance in areas that had historically been both nominally and actually under the Burman kings. U Pu and U Bu both argued that the Shans and the Burmans were one race.[49] U Pu said the Burmans did not consider the Shan chiefs parallel to the Indian princes, and he threatened therefore that the Burmans

> will not be able to remain indifferent if the welfare of the masses of the Shan State is to be sacrificed for the maintenance of the present bourgeoise government.[50]

46. Ba Maw's *Sinyetha* policy called for Burma's independence, the equalization of privileges of rich and poor, the reduction of taxes for the poor, compulsory free education, land reform, protected inexpensive farm loans, and agricultural debt relief. Ba Khaing, op. cit., pp. 265–266.

47. Great Britain, *Accounts and Papers*, vol. 20, 1936/1937, "Letter of Transmission from R. G. McDowall to Secretary of State for India," March 23, 1937, #138 Reforms 3 J, p. 38.

48. See the limited recommendations made by U Ba Pe, U Pu, and U Tun Shein on August 9, 1919: Great Britain, *House of Commons Sessions Papers*, "Joint Select Committee of Government of India Bill," vol. 3, app. Q, London, HMSO, 1919, p. 88.

49. Great Britain, *Burma Round Table Conference*, loc. cit.

50. Ibid., p. 77.

The nationalist argument for ethnic and geographic unity was based on the assumption that British conquest and British hold on the country stemmed in large measure from its success in dividing the peoples of Burma and using each against the other. The argument took on new meaning during the war, when conditions changed and it became possible for Burma proper and the hill areas to unite.

---

Unlike the Burmans, the Karens looked upon the Westerners as teachers and protectors. Having lived for centuries in a degraded status under Burman domination, the Karens won sympathy and understanding first from the American Baptists who came to Burma early in the nineteenth century and later from the English. The delta-dwelling Karens accepted conversion to Christianity and were willing students in the mission-founded schools. Their identification with the Westerners intensified their division from the Burmans. When the British replaced Burman authority in Lower Burma, the Karens received treatment equal to that of other indigenous peoples. Because of their loyalty to the new rulers, they were drawn into the ranks of the military, the police, and the bureaucracy. By 1880, the more articulate among the Christianized Karens organized the National Karen Association (NKA) to try to unite all Karens regardless of their religion, cultural development, and location. The NKA's immediate objectives were to develop leadership, to provide higher education for gifted young Karens, and to foster and protect Karen identity and writing.[51] As a pro-British organization, the NKA approved the British campaign of pacification after the Third Anglo-Burmese War and helped enlist volunteers for the British during World War I.[52]

Also unlike the Burmans, the Karens did not fragment politically under British rule. The NKA remained the leading and respected

---

51. D. Smeaton, *The Loyal Karens of Burma* (London, 1887), pp. 201, 223–224.
52. Crosthwaite, op. cit., p. 8; John F. Cady, "The Karens," in Frank N. Trager and Associates (eds.), Burma, vol. 2 (New Haven, 1956), pp. 865–868; Harry I. Marshall, "The Karen Peoples of Burma," *Ohio State University Bulletin*, 26(13) (1922): 314.

organization of the Karens. Its spokesmen, such as San C. Po and Sidney Loo-Nee, were well educated in the Western tradition and lost no opportunity either in Burma or in England to present the case of their people.

The ideas and goals of the Karens modified with changing conditions. Just as the early Y.M.B.A. movement was nonpolitical until the Montagu declaration provided a stimulus for Burman political action, so too the NKA was originally a nonpolitical organization but altered its tactics and objectives as political reforms were introduced in Burma. The Karens were less excited than the Burmans over the prospect of self-government. In response to the Montagu statement they sent a memorial to the secretary of state saying that "the country is not yet in a fit state for self-government."[53] The memorialists argued that because Burma was "inhabited by many different races, differing in states of civilization, differing in religious and social development" it would require "many years of strenuous training under British governance before this boon can be conferred on it with security and success."[54]

Two years later the Karens altered their position. They had come to believe that the alien minorities might get better treatment under the proposed reforms than they were then enjoying. Acting as spokesman for the NKA, Loo-Nee submitted a criticism of the 1920 Craddock scheme of reforms in which he argued that the Karens, as an indigenous race second in number only to the Burmans, "should not only precede the aliens in Burma, but also progress and advance step by step along with the Burmans"; and further, that the Karens—believers in the doctrine of self-help—had served bravely in the army, proving their loyalty to the British government, so their interest should be protected and their identity maintained through separate electorates and special or communal seats.[55]

In order to test the sentiment of the people on the question of reforms, the British government appointed a committee of inquiry

53. San C. Po, *Burma and the Karens* (London, 1928), p. 66. Po was the author of the memorial and at the time the acknowledged leader of the Karens.
54. Ibid.
55. Great Britain, *Government of India Act*, 1919, op. cit., app. N, p. 82.

known as the Whyte Committee to take testimony. Dr. San C. Po, named as one of its members, recorded in his memoirs that the Karens received support for their communal representation demands from such British civil servants as Chief Secretary Lewisohn and Sir Charles Webb. When the question was raised before the committee whether a Karen might be elected from a predominantly Burman district, the answer was no. Po's comment on this point was that

> it was obvious to all that no Karen candidate would ever be elected, since no district in the province has a Karen population anywhere near as large as that of the Burmans.[56]

The Karen demands were satisfied when the reforms were finally announced; they were granted five seats in a legislature of 130 members.[57]

After a few years of working within the new political framework, the Karen leaders came to realize that communal seats and special electorates were not real safeguards in the face of an overwhelming Burman majority in the Legislative Council. In spite of the fact that real improvement was taking place in the social relations between Karens and Burmans, the Karen leaders sought a new goal: their own separate state. In their proposal to the Simon Commission in 1928, they asked that the British create a Karen state in the territory known as the Tenasserim Division. The Karens disregarded the demographic fact that they were outnumbered in almost all the districts in the division either by the Burmans alone or by the Burmans and Mons combined. Po, the father of the scheme, summed up his argument for a separate state as follows:

> It is their desire to have a country of their own, where they may progress as a race and find the contentment they seek. It is this contentment which gives a man or a nation that satisfaction and good will and creates that patriotic feeling so essential to the well being of the nation. . . . What a grand thing the achievement

56. Po, op. cit., p. 9.
57. Only eighty seats in the new Legislative Council were filled by popular elections; the remainder were appointed by the government.

of their ambitions will be for the Karens and what praises and blessings will be showered upon those who shall have made it possible.[58]

He argued further that the Karen people's future was linked with British rule; the Karens, he said, "still prefer to work hand in hand with the British as they fully admit their superior capacity and their magnanimous spirit of 'give and take' as now modified by present conditions and manifested the world over."[59] Although his plan was not developed in detail, it was believed that Po and the NKA visualized their future state as a separately administered area in a British-ruled Burma.

Communal antagonism between Karens and Burmans never reached the same proportions as between Indians and Burmans. Both John Cady and Po have written that Burman–Karen relations in the nineteen-twenties and the nineteen-thirties were steadily improving.[60] Ba Maw's appointment of a Karen to his cabinet in 1937 and Karen and Burman college and university students sharing adjoining school grounds and living in close and friendly relations were evidence of this improvement. Both writers noted that this communal cordiality was an urban phenomenon and did not extend to the rural areas, where historic antagonisms and fears still dominated the local populations. Cady notes that the Burmans looked upon Karen aid to the British during the Saya San revolt in 1930 "as gratuitously offensive, in the pattern of 1852 and 1886."[61]

By the beginning of World War II, the Karen and Burman nationalist movements were moving in opposite directions.[62] The

58. Po, op cit., p. v; see also his further discussion on pp. 77–79.
59. Ibid., pp. 73–74. Cady argues that Po made the proposal to offset the more radical element among the Karens who demanded a "Karenistan," or a partitioned Burma; see Cady, "The Karens," op. cit., p. 877, n. 102.
60. Cady, "The Karens," op. cit., pp. 879–883; Po, op. cit., pp. 11–18.
61. Cady, "The Karens," op. cit., p. 880.
62. The divergence of the two can be clearly seen in the positions taken by the Burman and Karen members in the Report of the Committee on Expenditure of the Public Services: Loo-Nee argued in a dissent for the continued use of British civil servants in the Class I category because of the possibility of continuing communal clashes. The majority report argued that there was no longer any need for the continuance of the existing policy

Karens were seeking their own state under British protection, whereas the Burmans had hardened in their determination to unite the peoples in British Burma and create an independent state, whether in or out of the British Empire is not clear from the existing literature.

---

Because of their political backwardness and isolation from affairs in Burma proper, the hill peoples did not participate in political activity and made no real effort to counter British plans for their area. During the nineteen-twenties and nineteen-thirties they provided the government of Burma with a stable element that could be relied on to accept its guidance and authority.

Minorities living in Burma proper—the Arakanese and the Mons—were caught in the middle of the struggle between the Burmans and the British. They were too few to organize an effective lobby as the Karens had done and make themselves known. The British treated them as Burmans and ignored their limited claims to separate identity. Nonetheless, the accident of location gave the Arakanese special consideration, for a majority of them lived in the Arakan Division and were able to elect their own representatives and participate in Burma's political development.[63] According to Cady, the Arakanese "under-scored periodically the reality of their own local patriotism" and they "wanted no Burman bureaucracy to replace the white one."[64]

The Mons were less fortunate than the Arakanese, for they, like the Karens, were completely intermingled with the Burmans in the delta, and no significant area could claim to be a strictly Mon community. Unlike the Karens, their intermarriage and common outlook with the Burmans on such matters as religion and political activity caused both the English and the Burmans to look upon them as

---

of importing high-price British officers to do jobs the people of Burma were equipped to handle. See Burma, *Report of the Committee on Expenditure of the Public Service, 1939–1940* (Rangoon, 1940), pp. 4, 87.

63. See the statement of the government of Burma in Great Britain, *Parliamentary Papers*, vol. 35, op. cit., p. 17; Po, op. cit., p. 77.

64. Cady, *A History of Modern Burma*, op. cit., p. 413.

a part of the majority group. Because the Mons generally accepted Burman leadership and nationalizing, Burman nationalists resented the European attempts to revive a separate and distinct Mon culture.[65]

The advent of war in Burma in 1942 and the evacuation of the British found Burma still a divided society in which ancient antagonisms, fears, and identifications had been revived and intensified. No real unity existed either among the peoples themselves or between the government and the majority of the residents.

65. Ibid.

# 3

# World War II

The personal and communal relations that led Burma to independence in 1948 had their real origin in World War II. Because of the limited amount of reliable data on what took place inside Burma during the Japanese occupation, it is impossible to reconstruct with any certainty the events and developments of that period. Yet what is known sheds a great deal of light on the antecedents to the postwar development and must be considered even though its authenticity cannot be verified in all cases. World War II is significant, not only because it marked the temporary suspension of British rule in Burma, but because it created new conditions that made it possible for the socially and politically divided peoples to come together and lay the foundations for a new, united society.

The transition from communal antipathies to national unity was neither planned nor smooth in its progression. During the period of lawlessness that followed in the wake of the British evacuation from Burma, the extremists and the opportunists among the Burmans and the Karens sought to settle long-smoldering hostilities by force of arms. Youthful Burman nationalists loosely attached to the Japanese-sponsored Burma Independence Army attacked the Karens at Papun in the Salween District on April 4, 1942;[1] a similar outbreak occurred a few weeks later, on May 26, at Myaungmya in the delta area.[2] The resulting violence and death alarmed the members of both communities, and the gap dividing them widened to an almost insurmountable gulf. Only the determined efforts of the newly emerging nationalist leaders in 1944 and 1945 made it possible to relax the tensions and hostilities between the communities and for the leaders of both groups to build communal unity based on mutual trust.

The same period saw the Burmans commit brutal excesses against the Indians trapped in Burma by the sudden defeat of the British. British intelligence reports tell of communal riots even before the fall of Rangoon on March 7, 1942, and of Burman attacks on Indians that "amounted to a massacre" after the British withdrew.[3] Abandoned by the British, countless thousands of Indians walked out of Burma across the Arakan Mountains and returned to India. The emigration helped to dampen Burman hostility. Japan's support of the overseas Indians' nationalist movements also helped bridle the Burmans, and communal tension between these two groups diminished as the war progressed.

The national unity that eventually developed during the war can be traced to three sources: the policies of the Japanese, the activities of Dr. Ba Maw's puppet government, and the work of the Resistance Movement. The Japanese sought to win the outright support of the Burmese by exchanging their support for local nationalists for the latter's cooperation in Japan's war with the West.[4] Early in the war the Japanese attempted to replace the British as the necessary counterweight in the delicate balance of forces and peoples in Burma; once the Burman nationalist movement found momentum, leadership, and widespread support, the Japanese could not recreate prewar Burma with themselves in the

1. Ian Morrison, *Grandfather Longlegs* (London, 1947), pp. 67–73. This is the most complete published account available. Other accounts may be found in Burma, *Burma during the Japanese Occupation*, vol. 1 (Simla, 1943), pp. 25–26.
2. Morrison, op. cit., pp. 186–189.
3. Burma, op. cit., p. 23.
4. Ibid., p. 18.

role of the British. As the war progressed and the Burmans asserted their leadership over the other indigenous peoples, the Japanese gradually withdrew from the internal struggle; by the end of the war they lost nearly all control over the developing social and political situation.

Japan's initial efforts to win Burman support came in the period preceding the actual invasion of the country.[5] By training thirty young Burmans to lead a future nationalist army, the Japanese hoped to capitalize on the anti-British sentiments of the majority group in Burma and win favor as their liberators.[6] The young Burman nationalists left Burma between February and June 1941 and went to Japan and Hainan Island for training; from there they went to Thailand, where they recruited the first elements of their Burma Independence Army (BIA).[7] This army entered Burma in the van of the Japanese armies and served both as scouts and troop auxiliaries for the invaders. Once inside Burma the BIA openly recruited local adherents, established temporary administration and government in areas behind the actual battlegrounds, and fought along with the Japanese.

After the violent excesses committed on the Karens and Indians by some of its units, the BIA sought to keep its members out of politics and administration. On June 5, 1942, Aung San (Boh

---

5. During the nineteen-thirties the Japanese were believed to have provided funds to U Saw and Thein Maung to establish nationalistic, pro-Japanese newspapers in Burma. See Cady, *A History of Modern Burma*, (Ithaca, 1958), pp. 366, 417–418; Maung Maung, *Burma's Constitution* (The Hague, 1959), pp. 49–51; Frank N. Trager (ed.), *Burma: Japanese Military Administration Selected Documents, 1941–45* (Philadelphia, 1971), pp. 27–36.

6. Maung Maung, op. cit., p. 51; the author drew his information from M. Sugii, *A History of the Minami Organ*, the diary of a Japanese attached to the group responsible for recruiting Burmese supporters for the invasion. For a more complete picture of the Minami Organ and its role in training the Burmans, see Won Z. Yoon, *Japan's Scheme for the Liberation of Burma: The Role of the Minami Kikan and the "Thirty Comrades"* (Athens, 1973).

7. Aung San, "The Resistance Movement," in Aung San, *Burma's Challenge* (Rangoon, 1946?) (mimeo.), pp. 9–12; Morrison, op. cit., pp. 62–68.

Teza), commander of the army, issued an order declaring that it "will not interfere with the government of the country." Officers and men were to leave political parties alone and not interfere with the administration of the government, for the objective of the army was to help establish unity throughout the country.[8]

Once actual fighting between Japan and the Allies came to an end in southern and central Burma, the Japanese reorganized the BIA by reducing it in size, training some of the officers and men recruited in the earlier days of fighting, and renaming it the Burma Defense Army (BDA). British Intelligence reported that most of the new recruits were "ex-sepoys of the Burma Rifles and the British Military Police."[9] Following the establishment of the nominally independent government of Burma on August 1, 1943, the army's name, mission, and composition changed again. At the war's end this Japanese-sponsored Burma National Army revolted, joined forces with the Allies, and participated in the expulsion of the Japanese.

Japan's policy of support to local nationalists was also expressed in its approval of the establishment of nominal self-government. The first government under Burman control, called the Burma *Baho* government, was located in and confined to Rangoon. The majority of offices went to *Thakins* and members of the *Dobama Asiayone*. Because of its inability to establish law and order, the Japanese replaced it with a new government under Ba Maw, called the Burmese Executive Administration, that came into effect on August 1, 1942.[10] It was permitted to organize a more complex system with departments for finance, agriculture, forestry, justice, and education. It was supervised closely by the Japanese military administration on matters of policy and finance. "All the Burman

---

8. Burma, op. cit., pp. 5–6.

9. Ibid., p. 58. Prior to the war, the British army in Burma was composed of three battalions of Burma Rifles, each battalion formed with two companies of Karens, one of Chins, and one of Kachins. After the war began, two new battalions were raised, and in each a company of Burmans was included for the first time; see Morrison, op. cit., pp. 212–215.

10. Burma, op. cit., p. 6. The government included ten ministers in addition to Ba Maw, among them, one Karen, U Hla Pe, from Thaton; the remainder were Burmans. Trager, op. cit., pp. 129–144.

executives had to take an oath of allegiance to the Japanese authorities in Burma."[11]

British Intelligence reports noted that, despite Japan's efforts to control all of its activity, the Burmese government was granted a relatively free hand in such matters as education, reconstruction, and justice. During this period the government was successful in implementing the Burman nationalists' objective of making Burmese the language of instruction in all schools.[12] The importance of this action should not be underestimated because it provided for widespread instruction in Burmese and gave encouragement to its common use in society, business, and politics. This had a favorable effect on those who wished to see the local culture and traditions revived in order eventually to replace those imported from the West during colonial rule.

The next step in the conversion of Burma's government to "guided" self-rule occurred on May 8, 1943, when the Burma Independence Preparatory Committee was established. It included all the members of the enlarged Burmese Executive Administration (Aung San held a seat as commander of the BDA and Sir Mya Bu held one as chief justice); six leading politicians, one of whom was Dr. San C. Po, a Karen leader; and four distinguished Burman citizens.[13] On August 1, 1943, Burma became an independent state under the protection of and in alliance with the Japanese.[14]

Like their British predecessors, the Japanese attempted to keep the Frontier Areas separate from Burma proper. When the BIA attempted to enter the Shan States in May 1942, the Japanese blocked its entry. A month earlier the Japanese transferred two of the Shan States—Kengtung and Mongpan—to the government of Thailand. In December 1942, all of the Shan chiefs were summoned to Rangoon and required to take an oath of allegiance to

---

11. Burma, op. cit., p. 7; for an account by a participant in the government, see Nu, *Burma under the Japanese* (London, 1954), pp. 19–70.

12. Burma, op. cit., pp. 46–50; Burma, Ministry of Finance, *Financial and Economic Annual of Burma* (Rangoon, 1943), p. 66.

13. Burma, op. cit., pp. 9–10; Nu, op. cit., pp. 62–69; Trager, op. cit., pp. 145–158.

14. Burma, op. cit., vol. 2 (1944), pp. 10–173; apps. 1–4 provide the most complete description in print of the government during this period.

Japan and give their promise to cooperate wholeheartedly with the new colonial authorities.[15] The Japanese, like the British, did not interfere with the local administration of the Shan States and gave the chiefs a large measure of freedom in their own territories.

Japan's policy of isolating the Shan States from Burma proper did not satisfy the nationalist aims of the Burmans, who were especially dissatisfied that their army was prevented from entering the Shan States and their political workers were barred from undertaking political activity there. The Burman demand for physical unification of the Frontier Areas with Burma proper persisted until it was rewarded on September 25, 1943, with the Japanese signing of a treaty transferring authority in the Shan States to the new Burma government and marking the end of political isolation between the two areas.[16]

Japan's authority had little or no effect on the peoples living in the area of the present Kachin and Chin states because the Japanese never established full control of the territory; lying close to the Indian and Chinese borders, it was the first area recaptured by the Allies when they went onto the offensive in 1944/1945. The British reported that the Kachins remained pro-British and that "it was their refusal to cooperate with the Japanese, to supply them with food and labor which finally forced the Japanese to abandon their position in the hills." The same report also notes that "most of the Chins remained loyal though the Japanese tried hard to win them over with propaganda."[17]

In their relations with the Indians, the Japanese were faced with a more difficult problem than with any other group in Burma. Because the Japanese supported the Free Indian Movement of Subhas Chandra Bose in the other Southeast Asian countries, particularly Malaya, they were forced to protect the Indians from the hostility of the Burmans. In addition to this, they encouraged the government of Ba Maw to recognize the Bose movement and allow his Indian army to recruit and train in Burma.[18] At the same time,

15. Burma, op. cit., 2: 79.
16. Ibid., 1: 28.
17. Ibid., 1: 27.
18. Ibid., 1: 23–25; Nu, op. cit. pp. 83–84.

the Japanese tried to satisfy the anti-Indian sentiments of the Burmans by permitting "the government [of Burma] to issue an ordinance in October, 1942 forbidding any Indian immigration."[19] Later in the same month, the new colonial rulers forced the Burman government to rescind the law because of the military need for more Indian laborers than could be recruited in Burma. Although the Japanese never satisfied either side, they did maintain a tentative peace between the two and provided the conditions for Burmans and Indians to find a means of working together.

To win the support of the youth in Burma, the Japanese sponsored a Burma branch of the East Asiatic Youth League. Under the leadership of U Ba Gyan, U Ba Shin, U Kyaw Myint, and seven other people trained at Judson College or Rangoon University, the league came into existence on June 28, 1942.[20] It was open to "anyone domiciled in Burma," but there are no reports of its ethnic composition or its success in recruiting among the non-Burmans.[21] The purpose of the league was to enlist the youth of the country in such nation-building processes as physical fitness, education, public health, sanitation, and the operation of dispensaries. The league's first president, U Ba Gyan, reported that it engaged in such constructive work as aiding in the Post Office, digging wells, and even digging a full-length canal in Henzada District.[22]

The political significance of the league lies in the fact that it remained semiautonomous, under the direct control of neither the Japanese nor Ba Maw. When the anti-Japanese underground movement developed in 1944, the league took an active part in its affairs.[23] British Intelligence reported that the league helped recruit members for the Burma National Army and that its work and general activity won wide approval throughout the country. Ba Maw looked upon it as a rival to his own organization and, in his first review of the New Order Plan, concluded his statement on youth organizations by saying that

19. D. Hinners, *British Policy and the Development of Self-government in Burma*, unpublished doctoral dissertation, University of Chicago, 1951, p. 171.
20. Ba Gyan, "The All-Burma Youth League," *Burma* 3(3) (1953): 56.
21. Burma, op. cit., 2: 139.
22. Ba Gyan, op. cit., p. 57.
23. Ibid., p. 58.

talks with the League have practically led to an understanding but the matter must be brought to a conclusion and youth's work undertaken by the State directly or indirectly.[24]

Because the league refused to participate as an adjunct of the Ba Maw government, it was officially banned in August 1944. It reorganized as the All-Burma Youth Organization and participated in the Resistance Movement and in the Burma National Army.

The contribution of Ba Maw's government to the establishment of genuine national unity among the peoples of Burma is difficult to assess; he was in office only briefly before his government was swept aside by the Allies in the wake of their victory over the Japanese in 1945. Even so, several things suggest its importance to the struggle for national unity. To begin with, his concept of nationalism included all the people of Burma. From the language of the Declaration of Independence, proclaimed on August 1, 1943, his principle of national unity was embodied in the idea of "one blood, one voice, one leader."[25] Although clearly reflecting the current fashion in Japan, Germany, and Italy, this wording also meant more than the idea of a master race; as stated in the declaration, it meant that "it was national disintegration which destroyed the Burmese people in the past and they are determined that this shall never happen again."[26]

In 1942, Ba Maw attempted to win national support for his struggle for power by creating an all-inclusive nationalist movement. With the backing of the Japanese he organized the *Dobama-Sinyetha* Party as the only legal political party in Burma. He sought to eliminate political rivalry between his prewar *Sinyetha* Party and the *Dobama Asiayone* in order to prevent the Japanese from using one against the other. His architect of political unity was

---

24. Ba Maw, "A Review of the First Stage of the New Order Plan," Burma 1(1) (1944): 116. According to U Ba Gyan, Ba Maw, fearing the competition of an organization not under his control, tried to create a rival youth organization, the Bama Wundan Movement. Its failure to displace the East Asiatic Youth League led Ba Maw to seek to merge his organization with its rival. See Ba Gyan, op. cit., p. 58.

25. Burma, op. cit., app. 2, "Declaration of Independence of Burma," 2: 255.

26. Ibid.

Thakin Mya, a leader of the *Dobama Asiayone*. The new party differed from previous political parties in Burma by opening its membership to all indigenous ethnic groups and accepting membership on an individual basis and, in addition, organizing sections for monks, women, and youth.[27] No figures are available to attest to its effectiveness in attracting members from the ethnic minorities. In April 1943, Ba Maw, in a speech in Myaungmya, the scene of one of the worst Burman–Karen riots, said that the *Dobama-Sinyetha* "is formed in order to banish party feelings and to create unity among the peoples."[28] British Intelligence reports indicated that the party had branches at all levels from the district to the village. As the only legal party in Burma, it provided a good cover for the Resistance once it became active after 1944.

Ba Maw was deeply concerned about Burman–Karen relations. In 1942, he organized a government department called the Burman–Karen Central Organization whose function it was to "bring about a speedy solution to all problems connected with the Karen citizens of Burma." Its methods of operation were personal contact, lecturing, and pamphleteering; its immediate objective was to establish a better understanding "between the Karens and the other citizens in the country." It also served to recruit Karen youths as interpreter trainees for the Japanese and as laborers in the *Heho* (the labor force attached to the Japanese army) and the Service Corps. It was abolished just before the establishment of the nominally independent government in August 1943.[29] In its place the new government of Ba Maw organized the Central Karen Board under the supervision of the forestry minister, U Hla Pe (a Karen), who was instructed to "maintain the closest contact with this Central Karen Board with the view of dealing with the Karen question successfully."[30]

In "A Review of the First Stage of the New Order Plan," Ba Maw noted that the Japanese had organized Karen associations, and he condemned this action "as something which is likely to keep

27. Burma, op. cit., 2: 135–136.
28. Ibid., p. 135.
29. Burma, Ministry of Finance, op. cit., pp. 9, 20.
30. Ba Maw, op. cit., p. 117.

the Burmans and Karens apart in the old communal way." Ba Maw concluded by saying the Burmese government must help "to abolish these organizations," and he informed the Central Karen Board's president, Saw Ba Maung, that his organization must work among the Karens in Bassein, Kawkareik, and Papun and remove the fears and suspicions harbored by the people in those areas.[31] On November 1, 1943, Thakin Mya, the deputy prime minister in the independent government of Ba Maw, restated the latter objective in his address to the Privy Council.[32] The board remained in existence throughout the life of the government and drew support from such Karen leaders as Dr. San C. Po, a Privy Council member, and San Po Thin, a rising young Karen leader from the delta area. The same period saw other efforts made to heal the breach between the two communities. Thakin Nu wrote of the determined efforts of Gen. Aung San, Than Tun, and himself to win Karen trust and support by visiting Karen areas in the delta and making personal contact with the people.[33]

The Ba Maw government sought to draw the Shan States together with Burma proper through legal and political means. There were indications that prior to the Japanese transfer of the Shan States to the Burma government the Japanese had not been successful in winning the loyalties of the Shans so were not too reluctant to grant this change.[34] Under the Burmese government, the home minister was appointed high commissioner for the area, and overall local administration was entrusted to a deputy, U Khin Maung Pyu, a Shan and former member of the Indian civil service.[35] Local administration remained in the hands of the Shan chiefs. Also under the Ba Maw government two Shans were appointed privy councillors in January 1944; one represented the chiefs and the other, the peoples of the states.[36] This was a radical departure

31. Loc. cit.
32. "The Address of his Excellency Thakin Mya, the Deputy Prime Minister at the Second Session of the Privy Council on Monday, November 1, 1943," *Burma* 1(1) (1944): 125.
33. Nu, op. cit., pp. 98–102.
34. Burma, op. cit., 2: 79–80.
35. Ibid., p. 81.
36. Ibid., p. 79.

from the experience of prewar government because for the first time the people of this area had representation in the highest council of government. Another change of equal importance took place in November 1943, when it was reported that some 5,000 Shans had been recruited into the Burma National Army. In addition Burma-sponsored organizations were opened to Shans, for example, the East Asiatic Youth League in November 1943 and the National Service Organization in January 1944. The Japanese and the Burma government also allowed the Indians to organize branches of the Indian Independence League in the Shan States.[37] The Burma government announced in August 1943 that there would be freedom of travel and trade between the Shan States, Karenni, and Burma proper; imports between areas were not to be taxed and Burmese currency was to be used throughout.[38]

To promote national culture, the Burma government under Ba Maw established the Literature and Translation Committee to create a national dictionary and a national encyclopedia. Ba Maw remarked that the committee's work was of major importance and therefore it had been included in the first part of the New Order Plan.[39]

Because the evidence is scanty and unreliable it is impossible to say with certainty how effective Ba Maw's efforts were. What can and must be said is that he made a number of positive efforts to create national unity and provided an official atmosphere that allowed and encouraged the peoples of Burma to come together for common purposes. This marked a radical departure from the official policy of the former government in Burma.

From the evidence available, it appears that the most successful means of unification was the Resistance Movement headed by Aung San, Than Tun, and Thakin Mya. Thakin Nu reports that the movement began almost as soon as the Japanese gained control of the main parts of Burma,[40] although it did not grow in size and activity until 1944, when the nationalist leaders were certain that Burma's independence under Japanese hegemony was bogus.

37. Ibid., p. 81.
38. Ibid., p. 18.
39. Ba Maw, op. cit., p. 121.
40. Nu, op. cit., p. 21.

According to the officially published version of the beginning of the Resistance Movement, the army, the Communist Party, the People's Revolutionary Party, the East Asiatic Youth League, the Karens, the Shans, the Kachins, the Chins, and the Arakanese communities began in 1942 and 1943 "to struggle each in its own way, against the Japanese fascists."[41] Aung San was more specific in his speech of August 20, 1945. He declared that, although he sought to organize an uprising against the Japanese after he returned to Burma from Japan in March 1943, conditions were not ripe for such a movement. It was not until August 4–7, 1944, that he met with Than Tun and other Communist Party members in Pegu, and there they agreed to join him in the formation of the Anti-Fascist People's Freedom League (AFPFL) and accepted the manifesto he had brought to the meeting. At Pegu the leaders also agreed on plans for broadening and coordinating the movement, adopted the tactics to be employed, and outlined the common goals.[42]

The clandestinely circulated manifesto informed the people that the movement had two major objectives: to expel the Japanese and to draw up a constitution that guaranteed, among other things, (1) equal opportunity for all citizens, irrespective of race, religion, sex, or social status, to receive education; (2) freedom to follow and develop one's own language and culture; and (3) adequate protection for the economic, social, and political interests of minorities, such as the Karen, Shan, Palaung, Taungthu, Chin, Kachin, Chinese, and Indian. The manifesto also included a program of action that called for unity among the various parties and racial groups in the country.[43] Unlike Ba Maw's Declaration of Independence, which spoke of the principle of Burmese unity as one blood, one voice, and one leader, the AFPFL manifesto appealed for support of the indigenous peoples as members of separate ethnic, religious, and political groups and not as Burmese. The Resistance leaders chose this tactic to induce the widest possible support, and they

41. Anti-Fascist People's Freedom League, *From Fascist Bondage to New Democracy: The New Burma in the New World* (Rangoon, 1946?), p. 2.
42. Aung San, op. cit., p. 16.
43. AFPFL, op. cit., pp. 15–16.

emphasized that no individual or group need fear losing identity or purpose.

The National Army demonstrated its trust in the Karens by giving their members important offices. Ian Morrison relates that the Karen leader San Po Thin asked for and received a commission in the army and induced the Burmese leaders to commission a Sandhurst-trained Karen, Kya Doe, as a colonel. Both were ushered into the inner councils of the Resistance Movement and served to link the Karens with the nationalist uprising.[44]

The Anti-Fascist People's Freedom League—the official name of the Resistance Movement—organized guerrilla forces to coordinate with the army. Louis Mountbatten notes, in his final report on the war in Southeast Asia, that he instructed his men to give arms and supplies to individuals in the Resistance. His purpose was to support local indigenous opposition to the Japanese.[45] When the Burma National Army revolted against the Japanese on March 27, 1945, it was supported by the guerrilla forces, and together they coordinated their efforts with the invading Allies.

Although the objectives and methods of the Resistance Movement differed from those of Ba Maw's government, the two must be considered as parts of the same movement in any discussion of national unity. The Burma government provided the initial stimulus for ethnic and political cooperation under indigenous leadership. The Resistance converted this united spirit into a military effort in which all, regardless of race, religion, or political party, could participate in liberating their country. The difference between the Burmese government and the Resistance was in their approach to the national question. The Burma government proclaimed that all the people of Burma were really one and their separation was artificial; the Resistance accepted the view that the peoples of Burma were ethnically and socially different with a right both to protect their uniqueness and to participate together in liberating their country from foreign rule.

---

44. Morrison, op. cit., pp. 197–201.
45. Louis Mountbatten, *Report to the Combined Chiefs of Staff by the Supreme Allied Commander South East Asia, 1943–1945* (London, 1951), p. 143.

On politics and parties the government of Ba Maw and the AFPFL also differed. Ba Maw, fascinated by the experiences of the Nazis in Germany and the Communists in Russia, sought to submerge political differences and create a single party as the expression of the people and as a symbol of their unity. The AFPFL also formed a single organization to carry out its primary objectives, but it gave each unit within its organization the right and opportunity to retain its identity, leaders, and ultimate goals. The league promised to protect both the parties within its ranks and the identity of the minorities that supported it.

The disagreement between the two over the meaning of national unity was not solved in the war years or in the decade that followed. Nonetheless the experiment in self-government and organizing a resistance movement provided the conditions for the indigenous population of Burma to be forced to work together. This experience helped eliminate and destroy some of the age-old communal barriers and erect new bridges of unity.

# The Struggle for Political Unity 1945-1946

The unity forged in the war was severely tested in the three years that followed Burma's liberation. The return of British rule relaxed the urgency that had drawn many of the conflicting groups together. The British attempt to restore the old order with its divided administration, differing degrees of political self-government, and protection of the smaller and weaker ethnic groups at the expense of the largest groups directly challenged the aspirations and goals of the newly created nationalist movement, the Anti-Fascist People's Freedom League. The league's immediate postwar objective was to convert the bonds of unity born in war and under stress into a solid band of political unity that could promise self-government and protection for the cultural, religious, ethnic, and regional diversities that characterize modern Burmese society. The differences between the British and the Burmese objectives created a stalemate not broken until the British gave way and accepted the idea of Burmese participation in the immediate governing of the country and in planning its political future.

During this brief period both the British and the Burmese leaders struggled to win and hold popular support. The British failure to present an imaginative program with a specific date for the establishment of self-government doomed the official policy even before it was implemented. An examination of British and Burmese policies and tactics during this critical period shows why the AFPFL won national support and acclaim as the party of liberation and independence.

---

The initial postwar British policy for Burma—the White Paper of May 17, 1945—called for eventual self-government within the British Commonwealth as an equal member with the other dominions. To realize this objective, it would first be necessary to undertake economic reconstruction and restore the political pattern that existed on the eve of the war. Further, the governor should exercise the emergency powers delegated to him under Section 139 of the constitution until such time, probably three or four years, as it was possible to hold a general election, transfer political responsibility to the people of Burma, and write a new constitution. While exercising emergency powers the governor could create small executive and legislative councils to give advice on economic and social reconstruction. The Frontier Areas were to continue to be treated as a special responsibility of the governor until such time as the inhabitants signified their desire to join their territory to Burma proper.[1]

There are several reasons why this policy was unacceptable to the new generation of Burmese leaders. In the first place, it was written in London by men with little or no knowledge of the changed conditions in Burma and the current popular sentiments about the political future. The authors were interested in recreating the Burma of 1941 with its foreign-dominated economic and commercial life and its position in the Commonwealth as a leading producer of food and raw materials. These goals caused them to write a policy based on a faulty assumption: that because Britain had failed to protect Burma from foreign invasion and physical destruction it was necessary to rebuild and reconstruct the shattered economy before resuming its prewar self-appointed task of guiding the Burmese to self-government.[2]

---

1. Great Britain, *Burma: A Statement of Policy by His Majesty's Government*, May 1945, Cmd. 6635, 1945.
2. These ideas are to be found either implicit or explicit in ibid., pt. 1; Louis Mountbatten, *Report to the Combined Chiefs of Staff by the Supreme*

The second reason the policy failed was that it could not be implemented immediately. Instead there was a delay of five months between Burma's liberation and the reestablishment of civil authority. During this time of military government political decisions were avoided unless directly connected with maintaining law and order, giving needed economic aid, and prosecuting the war. This hiatus provided the Burmese nationalist leaders in the AFPFL and the indigenous army, now called the Patriotic Burmese Forces (PBF), the opportunity to publicize their ideas and goals and perfect their tactics. When the military formally transferred power to the civil authorities on October 16, 1945, the peoples of Burma supported the AFPFL's criticism of the British White Paper, its leadership, and its goals.

Like the British, the AFPFL prepared and published a manifesto outlining its main objectives, and it was circulated as early as August 1944. The two major objectives were to expel the Japanese and to win genuine independence for Burma.[3] It also set forth basic ideas for independent Burma's constitution. In addition to the traditional liberties of Western democracy, the AFPFL added the right of everyone "to obtain free supply of timber and bamboo for the construction of one's own dwelling house"; the equality of opportunity for all citizens to receive an education "regardless of race, religion, sex and social status; freedom to follow and develop one's own language and culture"; and State protection of the economic, social, and political interests of the minorities, both in Burma proper and on the frontier.[4] In the program of action incorporated in the manifesto, the AFPFL called for unity of the parties and racial groups in the country: "Everybody should work in cooperation."[5]

---

*Allied Commander, South East Asia, 1943–1945* (London, 1951), pp. 200, 230; Maurice Collis, *Last and First in Burma* (London, 1956), pp. 210 ff; Burma, *Some Public Utterances 1942–1945 of His Excellency, the Governor of Burma, Sir R. H. Dorman-Smith* (Rangoon, 1945), pp. 5 ff.

3. AFPFL, *From Fascist Bondage to New Democracy: The New Burma in the New World* (Rangoon, 1946?). This small volume is a documentary history of the AFPFL to 1946. It contains copies of documents unavailable in any other printed source. The writer has checked those items that were otherwise available and found them to be accurate.

4. Ibid., pp. 14–15.

5. Ibid., p. 16.

The sentiment of the Burmese nationalists in the AFPFL was clearly expressed by a leader of the PBF on the occasion of the fall of Rangoon to the Allies. In a radio broadcast on May 7, 1945, carried throughout liberated Burma, Col. Naywin said,[6]

> You have known by now with what aims the Burmese Army has come into existence and of what stuff it is made. The one and only aim is to fight for Burmese freedom and it is to that aim that practically the whole of Burmese youth have dedicated their lives. You have seen also that it is a united front put up by all the indigenous races that call themselves Burmese. Thus it is that the Burmese Army which is composed of the Burmese, Shans, Kachins and Karens have been looked upon by all as not only the hope of the country but also as its very life and soul.[7]

At a news conference in Rangoon May 14, 1945, the AFPFL discussed the nature of its organization and the diversity of its membership. The spokesman said that "it is not a party organization—it is a combination of various political groups and organizations and communities." In addition to such new Burmese parties as the Communist Party of Burma and the People's Revolutionary Party, the league included nonparty organizations such as the Burma National Army, the Women's League, and the Youth League and ethnic groups such as the Arakanese National Congress, the Karen Central Organization, and the Shan Association.[8] The spokesman estimated the membership at two hundred thousand. He also revealed his familiarity with the policy recommendation of the Imperial Affairs Committee of the Conservative Party, which called for a period of reconstruction before the reestablishment of political life.[9] To this suggestion he replied that "there should be no fixed

---

6. This is the same Ne Win—the current anglicized way of spelling his name—who headed the government of Burma from October 1958 to April 1960 and seized power through a military coup on March 2, 1962.

7. AFPFL, op. cit., p. 30.

8. Ibid., p. 39; Nu, *Burma under the Japanese* (London, 1954), pp. 98–110; Aung San, "The Resistance Movement," in Aung San, *Burma's Challenge* (Rangoon, 1946?) (mimeo.), pp. 3–20.

9. This recommendation was embodied in a document called *A Blueprint for Burma*, published in November 1944 and debated in the House of Commons on December 12, 1944. Although not adopted, many of its ideas

period for reconstruction which can be done at any time. We want to satisfy our political aspirations first and then we will carry on the reconstruction. That is the opinion of the whole of Burma I should say."[10]

On August 19, 1945, the AFPFL expressed its immediate postwar objectives at a mass meeting where the delegates approved four resolutions calling for the end of military rule, the formation of a new Burma army with both enlisted men and officers from all the indigenous ethnic groups, the immediate formation of a national government to exercise authority in the interim preceding the election of a constituent assembly, and the continued effort to foster national unity.[11]

The ideas of the AFPFL and its criticism of the White Paper were sent directly to the governor in Simla on September 22, 1945.[12] Its argument began with reference to the Wavell plan for India under which Indians would take charge immediately of all government portfolios with the exception of defense. This proposal was viewed by the Burmese as more liberal and progressive than those offered to them under the White Paper.

> It will be seen at once that the offer is much more liberal than what Your Excellency has so far proposed in as much as the portfolio of External Affairs hitherto reserved to the Viceroy-in-person would also be transferred to Indian heads and there does not appear to be any reason why Burma should be treated less liberally than India in this or any other respect.[13]

The AFPFL also noted that the Wavell plan, which reserved the defense portfolio for the commander in chief, was formulated

---

were embodied in the White Paper of May 17, 1945. The British special operatives in Burma learned that the Burma nationalists had heard of the document from a message they received from Thakin Than Tun saying, "Don't like Blueprint for Burma," Collis, op. cit., p. 231.

10. AFPFL, op. cit., p. 44.
11. Ibid., pp. 57–62; as early as June 20, 1945, the Burmese Resistance leaders expressed their ideas and criticisms of the White Paper to the governor-in-exile, Dorman-Smith, when he visited Rangoon unofficially aboard a warship. See Mountbatten, op. cit., p. 205; Collis, op. cit., p. 245.
12. "Letter to the Governor," in AFPFL, op. cit., pp. 63–68.
13. Ibid., p. 64.

during the war. Now that the war was over, "there has been a complete change of circumstances and there does not appear to be any valid reason for not transferring the portfolio of Defense into Burmese hands."[14] The letter went on to say in unmistakable terms that "the demand for the formation of a National Government is really a demand for transfer of all power into Burmese hands."[15]

On the issue of the representatives in the future executive council, the AFPFL compared the political situations in India and Burma, two national organizations competing for power, and concluded:

> Burma is much more fortunate than India in this respect. She has only one national organization. It is the Anti-Fascist Peoples Freedom League which embraces all major political parties and indigenous racial groups of Burma and therefore is fully representative of the country. . . . Your Excellency can safely follow Lord Wavell's Plan as a precedent and appoint members of the Executive Council on the recommendation of the Anti-Fascist Peoples Freedom League.[16]

On policy and appointments the league asked that it be consulted on appointments to the legislature and the judiciary. The governor, it recommended, should choose Burmese advisors and enter into no long-term finance and reconstruction arrangements. The letter closed by pointing out that the AFPFL's demands were "comparatively moderate" in view of the fact that other colonial areas were in the process of receiving their independence or had already received it.[17]

By the time the governor returned to Burma on October 16, 1945, it was clear to everyone, both inside the country and abroad, what the Burmese nationalist leaders wanted: independence. To achieve that goal as soon as possible, they wanted to put political

---

14. Ibid.; John Cady, in his book, *A History of Modern Burma* (Ithaca, 1958), p. 522, interprets this letter to mean that the Burmese were willing to join the governor's Executive Council if all but foreign affairs and defense were transferred to the local leaders. The above passage together with others quoted in the narrative suggest that the AFPFL wanted these offices as well.
15. AFPFL, op. cit., p. 64.
16. Ibid., pp. 65–66.
17. Ibid., p. 68.

matters ahead of economic ones and make arrangements to call a constituent assembly to draft a constitution on democratic-socialistic lines with protections for cultural, religious, and ethnic diversity. During the period prior to the assembly, they wanted a national government composed of Burmese that would have real powers and collective responsibility. Their territorial demands were nothing less than the whole of British Burma. The AFPFL called on the minorities for support and promised them full participation in governing and in writing the new constitution. They advocated reserving for the people of Burma the decision of whether to remain in the British Commonwealth.

Although the positions of the British and the Burmese were in opposition, they were not completely irreconcilable. Governor Dorman-Smith, as the British representative, was free to give the White Paper a broad interpretation. With London's approval he flew to Burma on June 20, while the war was in progress, and talked with Burmese leaders who could be gathered together and who represented the new and old generations in local politics. As the military was still responsible for Burma, the governor met the local leaders aboard the H.M.S. *Cumberland* while it lay at anchor in Rangoon Harbor. According to Maurice Collis, who had access to Dorman-Smith's papers in the preparation of his book, the governor was not informed of the AFPFL demands and program until the morning of this meeting.[18]

The *Cumberland* speech given by the governor began with a restatement of British objectives in Burma: to reconstruct the economy and the society and then guide the country to self-government within the Commonwealth.[19] But, he said, it must be recognized that it was not the intention of the British "to reestablish the old regime"; instead it was their object to create a new one "without one moment's unnecessary delay." How long would this take? he asked rhetorically; his answer was that it would depend on the cooperation of the Burmese people—"obviously it will take a much shorter time than if no such support is forthcoming." The requirements for the establishment of self-government, he said,

18. Collis, op. cit., p. 245.
19. Burma, op. cit., p. 35.

were three: to create a freely elected legislature with a council of ministers, to achieve agreement among the peoples of Burma on the types of institutions they wished to establish, and to "clarify beyond all doubt her [Burma's] future relations with Great Britian by the conclusion of a freely negotiated agreement on such matters as defense, commercial relations, finance . . . Burma must know just where she stands before she starts off her new career." [20] To hold national elections it would be necessary first to reconstruct the electoral rolls, to have Parliament approve a new election law, and to establish "internal tranquillity" throughout the country. He minimized the importance of the extension of the emergency provisions, which would enable him to govern directly for the next three years, by saying,

> That is simply and solely an enabling bill, simply and solely a precautionary measure disguised to cover all eventualities. . . . I give you this assurance—*If we can repair the electoral machinery before 1948 and if conditions are such as to permit a fair election to be held then that election will be held and parliamentary government will be resumed, no matter how soon that may be after the return of civil government.*[21]

By the governor's liberal interpretation of the White Paper, it was apparent that much leeway existed on timing; no leeway seemed to exist on priorities—reconstruction before political restoration— and on who was to evaluate existing conditions and decide when the country was ready to move from one stage to the next. It must also be noted that the governor avoided all discussion of the Frontier Areas; it would seem from this omission that he intended to deal with Burma proper and the Frontier Areas separately and that his remarks were intended to apply only to Burma proper.

In addition to his formal remarks the governor held private discussions with a group of invited political and ethnic leaders.[22] From

20. Ibid.
21. Ibid., pp. 36–38; the underscoring is in the original. For a summary of the speech see Collis, op. cit., pp. 245–246.
22. Seventeen leaders attended according to Collis, op. cit., p. 246. According to U Ba U, twenty indigenous leaders attended the meeting; Ba U,

these discussions he learned that the spokesmen for the AFPFL did not accept his interpretation of the White Paper, did not believe it binding on the British government in London, and did not believe it met the demands of their organization.[23] The governor discounted their remarks because the presence of leaders representing organizations other than the AFPFL seemed to indicate that the new organization did not speak for all the peoples of Burma.[24]

---

*My Burma: The Autobiography of a President* (New York, 1958), p. 185. Thus far, although no formal list of participants has been published, it is known from the above sources that the following were in attendance: for the AFPFL, Aung San, Than Tun, and Ba Pe; U Aye and Henzada U Mya of the prewar *Myochit* Party; Ba U and Sir Mya Bu of the prewar High Court; Sir Maung Gyee, a former Burmese councillor; Sir Paw Tun, prewar prime minister of Burma; Tin Tut of the Indian civil service; and U Pu, prewar prime minister of Burma. In addition, according to Cady, op. cit., p. 513, there were exministers U Ba Than, Ba Yin, and U Soe Nyun and former mayor of Rangoon, U Set. Cady also writes that "it was primarily due to Lord Mountbatten's insistence that he [Dorman-Smith] gave a special private interview to Thakins Aung San and Than Tun . . ." (p. 513). According to Mountbatten, op. cit., pp. 204–205, "I therefore entirely favoured Sir Reginald's inviting as many delegates as he wished from the less active parties. At the same time, I considered that the only potential trouble-makers were the politically active elements (of whom only the AFPFL and the PBF had so far manifested themselves)"; Collis, op. cit., pp. 245–246, confirms this in his narrative.

23. Collis, op. cit., p. 247.

24. Mountbatten, op. cit., p. 202, notes that when Aung San first met with Gen. Slim on May 16, 1945, he informed the British general that he represented the Provisional Government of Burma. Mountbatten reports that he conveyed this to the British chiefs of staffs and asked for instructions before taking further action: "I felt that it would be unrealistic not to treat the AFPFL as what it was: a coalition of the political parties commanding the largest following in the territory where I was engaged in conducting operations." Mountbatten then notes that he suggested to Dorman-Smith "that Lieut.-General Slim might be allowed to tell Major-General Aung San that His Excellency would consider the eventual inclusion of members of the AFPFL in his Executive Council, when Civil Government was restored; but Sir Reginald telegraphed that he could not for a moment contemplate giving an undertaking to consider this." For an account of the first meeting between Slim and Aung San, see William Slim, *Defeat into Victory* (London, 1956), p. 517.

According to one of the non-AFPFL participants at that meeting—U Ba U, a future president of the Union of Burma after independence—this was a false conclusion. Ba U records in his biography that—at the request of Aung San and Than Tun, the recognized leaders of the AFPFL—most of the leaders invited to the *Cumberland* met together before seeing the governor, agreed on the demands that all would put forward, and named U Ba Pe, a non-AFPFL leader, as their spokesman.[25] According to Ba U, the leaders agreed to ask for self-government and the right of participation in the administration of the country during the period prior to the full transfer of power. Ba Pe is reported to have gone beyond their agreement when he spoke to the governor and asked for the right of self-determination. The governor's only response was to restate his interpretation of the White Paper.[26]

It was the impression of the correspondent for the *Times* that the Burmese response to the governor's visit had been favorable: "The White Paper had been received with cynicism and was regarded as a document giving unlimited scope to his Majesty's Government for procrastination and obstruction. The leaders are now coming to see that through it they can obtain everything they want."[27]

Nothing could be resolved until the governor returned to power. In the weeks prior to his return he began filling the vacancies in the courts and naming some of his advisors with total disregard for the resolutions and suggestions offered by the AFPFL.[28] It responded by calling a meeting of its Supreme Council on October 6–8, 1945, and passing a number of new resolutions that restated the league's objectives and expressed its disapproval of the appointments. The AFPFL argued that such action tied the hands of the future caretaker government and requested the governor to reconsider his actions.

On the day the governor resumed power in Burma—October 16, 1945—he took the occasion to make a public address in which he

25. Ba U, op. cit., p. 184.
26. Ibid., p. 186.
27. *Times* (London), June 23, 1945, p. 3.
28. See n. 11.

restated his ideas and intentions under his mandate in the White Paper of May 17, 1945. The AFPFL on the next day published its rebuttal. It began by approving the governor's spirit of cooperation and goodwill and then took a number of exceptions to things he had said. In particular it disagreed with the governor on minorities both in Burma proper and in the Frontier Areas. The league argued that all the people of Burma fought fascism and "we can claim today that the peoples of Burma are more united than ever."[29] It was the objective of the AFPFL to "set up a voluntary union of peoples of Burma, with the right of self-determination to national minorities." The separation of the Frontier Areas from Burma proper, therefore, would perpetuate the division between the areas. Under separate administrations, the hill peoples were denied fundamental political rights they enjoyed whenever they moved into Burma proper; the AFPFL called therefore for the immediate granting of political rights to the people in the frontiers. The league pictured itself as the "symbol of the unity of the Burmese peoples and all lovers of Burma should encourage this unity to grow." If the governor refused to accept the word of the AFPFL that it spoke for most of the people, it was ready to go to the polls in a free election to prove its claims. The AFPFL recommended that electoral freedom be guaranteed by an international commission appointed by the United Nations. The statement concluded by heartily approving the governor's statement that under his administration there was flexibility in the White Paper. The AFPFL's Supreme Council—the drafters of this statement—said that it would "henceforth concentrate all its efforts to get the program changed."[30]

From the published documents available to date, this statement appears to be the first in which the AFPFL raised the question of the Frontier Areas other than in general terms. The reason seems clear. The White Paper directed the governor to reestablish the prewar pattern of separate administration for the areas outside of

29. AFPFL, op. cit., p. 74.
30. "Statement of the Supreme Council of Anti-Fascist People's Freedom League on His Excellency the Governor's Speech on 17 October, 1945," in AFPFL, op. cit., pp. 73–76.

Burma proper. Without comment, the governor, as one of his first acts, appointed H. N. C. Steavenson director of the Frontier Areas Administration with headquarters in Rangoon. The Shan States were placed in the charge of two Residents, and the prewar commissioner of the Shan States was eliminated. The governor had reestablished the administrative pattern—with the names of the officers changed—that had been in effect before 1925.[31] Clearly the governor and the AFPFL were opposed to each other on the administration of the Frontier Areas.

Representatives of AFPFL and the governor met together on October 19 to discuss the composition of the Executive Council. The governor thought it should be composed of fifteen members, of which he already had four appointees in mind. The AFPFL interpreted his remarks to mean that it would receive the remaining eleven portfolios and thereupon responded by naming eleven, provided that the governor recognize that the AFPFL's representatives were bound by its own "Instrument of Instructions."[32] According to this document, the representatives were to work as a team under a leader and a whip of their own choice. The AFPFL would assign the portfolios "so as to be able to carry out the responsibilities assigned to them by the Supreme Council" [of the AFPFL] and to resign in a body whenever working in the Executive Council no longer served the League's ends. They were instructed "to work the said Executive Council so far as practicable as popular Government . . . to mobilize the mass opinion as national sanctions behind the said Executive Council and to make [it] responsive to public opinion. . . ." In carrying out these instructions they should work to release all political prisoners, restore civil rights, subordinate bureaucratic measures in all organs of government to

---

31. Burma, *The Report of the Frontier Areas Committee of Enquiry, 1947*, pt. 1, Report (Rangoon, 1947), p. 15. Under the post-1925 system, there was a central executive within the Federated Shan States who controlled the federal departments. The report notes, "the *Sawbwas* therefore formed their own Executive Council including the representatives of the people."

32. "Instrument of Instructions," in AFPFL, op. cit., pp. 78–79; *Times* (London), October 24, 1945, p. 4.

popular political control, and report periodically to the Supreme Council of the AFPFL.[33]

To demonstrate their claim to represent all the peoples of Burma and their willingness to share leadership with representatives of affiliated political and ethnic groups, the AFPFL slate of candidates for the Executive Council contained six representatives of political organizations and five of ethnic minorities.[34] The governor refused to accept the nominees and the AFPFL's preconditions for joining the Executive Council. According to Collis the "conditions if accepted would have placed the Council under the League. The Governor, despite his statutory powers under Section 139, could have got nothing done without the League's permission. The League would have become, what it claimed to be, the provisional Government of Burma."[35]

After his conversations of October 19, the governor decided to create a council of eleven in which the portfolios of defense and external affairs would be held by British civil servants who were members on his staff and those for home affairs and finance would be offered to prewar Burmese political leaders who had evacuated Burma during the war—Paw Tun and Htoon Aung Gyaw. He offered the remaining seven to the AFPFL on the condition that he, and not it, would choose the representatives and that the appointees would not be bound by any party instrument of instructions. The AFPFL rejected his offer and argued that the Home Ministry should go to a man familiar with internal conditions in Burma as they had developed during the war. Because law and order was crucial it was important that the home minister know where illegal weapons were stored and how to collect them.[36] The

---

33. AFPFL, op cit., pp. 78–79.
34. The eleven nominees were U Aung San (AFPFL), Thakin Thein Pe (Communist Party), Thakin Mya (People's Revolutionary Party), U Aye and U Ba On (Myochit Party), Pyawbwe U Mya (*Sinyetha Wunthanu* Party), U Nyo Tun (Arakanese), Mahn Ba Khaing and Saw Ba U Gyi (Karens), U Razak (Burma Muslims), and U Ba Pe (Burman-Independent). According to the AFPFL publication Mahn Ba Khaing is misspelled Mahn Ba Khin.
35. Collis, op. cit., p. 257.
36. "The League's Rejoinder," in AFPFL, op. cit., pp. 83–84.

AFPFL maintained that their instrument of instructions was advisory and not mandatory and in no way interfered with a councillor's oath of office or the question of secrecy in the council. The AFPFL requirement that its representatives report to the League periodically was intended only to keep the organization informed of the progress of its own program and no more.[37]

This marked the second disagreement between the governor and the AFPFL. By rejecting the contention of the AFPFL that it spoke for Burma proper and by refusing to accept its conditions for entering the Executive Council, the governor demonstrated to the satisfaction of the AFPFL that, if he had wide latitude of interpretation regarding the establishment of that body, he did not intend to use it. The governor, on the other hand, viewed the AFPFL demands as excessive and, if complied with, as a limitation on his own power.

Implicit in this issue is the larger question of whether or not the AFPFL spoke for all the peoples in Burma proper, some of them, or just a few. From the Mountbatten report and the Collis book, it is apparent that the governor went on the assumption that the AFPFL spoke for a large number, but not all, and therefore rejected its claims and its demands. Without an election, it was impossible to prove who was correct. On the basis of his own assumptions the governor sought to encourage all political parties, leaders, and ethnic groups to come forward and speak for themselves. He scored a mild success when he detached two members from the AFPFL Supreme Council and got them to enter his council contrary to the League's decision on nonparticipation.[38] They represented one of the strongest prewar parties, the *Myochit* Party, and were included in the AFPFL's slate of candidates. His victory was not clear-cut, however, because the *Myochit* Party did not follow the two out of the AFPFL; Henzada U Mya, the acting president of the *Myochit* Party, refused to support their actions and held his party loyal to the AFPFL.[39] The governor-general also

37. Ibid., pp. 84–85.
38. U Aye and U Ba On (*Myochit* Party).
39. "List of Members of the Governor's Executive Council," in AFPFL, op. cit., p. 89.

succeeded in getting another AFPFL nominee to break with the organization and join his council independently. Mahn Ba Khaing, a Karen leader and the organizer of the Karen Youth Organization, was one of the two AFPFL representatives for the Karens; and his break signaled the weakness of the AFPFL as the spokesman for this community. His action, however, was offset by the fact that a popular young Karen leader, Saw Ba U Gyi, remained firm in his support of the AFPFL.

The governor's council, as finally announced, gave the appearance of being representative. In addition to the two *Myochit* members and the Karen leader, it included two prewar political leaders, Paw Tun and Htoon Aung Gyaw; a third *Myochit* member, U Lun; a *Sinyetha* Party representative, U Tharrawaddy Maung Maung; a prewar minister, U Pu; an unknown *Thakin*, Yan Aung; and two British civil servants. Future president of the Union of Burma, Ba U, evaluated this council as follows:

> Most of the members of the Executive Council were members of the old gang, two of whom were the late Sir Paw Tun and Sir Htoon Aung Gyaw. Neither enjoyed the confidence of the Burmese people, as they had gone away to India with the British at the time of the general evacuation in 1942. . . . There were two young Burman members, Yan Aung and Maung Lun, evidently put on so that the Government could say that the Young Burmans were also represented. But these two were mere nobodies; they had no following and no social, political or professional standing.[40]

The governor did not succeed in detaching any other parties or ethnic groups from the AFPFL. During the early part of 1946, he attempted to encourage U Saw as a political rival to Aung San. According to Collis, the British Labour government rejected the idea of including U Saw in the Executive Council. The governor, however, supported U Saw's move to form a coalition with Aung San and Paw Tun as the nucleus of a reformed executive council. This idea collapsed when the AFPFL refused to participate in the

40. Ba U, op. cit., p. 188.

## The Struggle for Political Unity, 1945–1946

scheme.⁴¹ Throughout the first half of 1946, Dorman-Smith remained unsuccessful in his efforts to reform the Executive Council to attract popular support. Although his offer to the AFPFL was never withdrawn, the League remained adamant in its refusal to enter on any terms other than its own.

---

During the first year after the liberation of Rangoon, there was much speculation about the AFPFL both in Burma and abroad. In particular there were real questions in the minds of officials, correspondents, and other observers of the Burmese scene about the leadership of the organization, the program and goals, the tactics, and most of all, its actual strength among the peoples in Burma proper and in the Frontier Areas. A *Times* correspondent, visiting Rangoon in March 1946, made the following evaluation of the AFPFL, which is representative of the reports being filed in responsible Western newspapers:

> A liberal-minded visitor inquiring locally about the AFPFL finds himself attracted and repelled. His attraction lies primarily in its newness, for the old parties active before the catastrophe came in 1942 have a squalid record. Its leaders possess youth, idealism and hitherto a reputation for integrity. . . . In their eyes, politics is no game of chess, no mere enjoyable pasttime for elderly experts, but a deadly serious affair signifying everything for the common people's welfare. Only one politician of the old school [U Ba Pe] was in their councils during my stay. A few days afterwards the former Prime Minister U Saw reappeared . . . and many must have been pleased by the denial of the report that the young U Aung San would stand down for him. But the AFPFL is totalitarian in its purpose and reports suggest that it has been tyrannical in some of its ways. Its aim apparently at a one-party state and its arrogance of approach explains the failure last year of the government and the party to agree on terms for its inclusion in the Executive Council.⁴²

41. Collis, op. cit., p. 279.
42. *Times* (London), March 8, 1946, p. 5. A fuller and more detailed examination of the AFPFL during the period 1944–1948 is found in Chap. 7.

The AFPFL's hold on popular support came from its relationship with Burma's armed forces—both those men in the new postwar Burma army and those in its own paramilitary organization, the People's Volunteer Organization (PVO), formed out of the demobilized PBF—through such political action as staging rallies, issuing manifestos, holding special holidays, and by making special appeals to the peoples of the Frontier Areas.

The AFPFL gained its initial prestige from its action in the Resistance Movement. Aung San's national popularity stemmed from his leadership of Burma's first national army since the end of the old Burma kingdom. The Allied armies recognized the existence of this indigenous force and associated it with their own ranks during the fighting; afterward the British offered it a place in the new Burma army formed after Japanese expulsion from Lower Burma. On June 2, 1945, Louis Mountbatten, Supreme Allied Commander, issued a policy directive that recognized the contribution of the indigenous armed force and the Resistance Movement:

> As regards the B.N.A. and the A.F.O., they have risen before it was clear to them that the British forces would, or could come to their rescue. And it could be said that they are rising for their own ends, and not for the love of us. . . . It is important that the Burmese should not be made to feel that their interests and ours are mutually exclusive; and the surest way to avoid this, is to see to it that the conduct of our civil affairs contrasts favorably with the way in which the Japanese conducted theirs.[43]

Mountbatten began to implement this policy even before it was published. On May 30, he and Dorman-Smith met in Ceylon and agreed to rename the Burman National Army and call it the Patriotic Burmese Forces. They also agreed to enroll PBF members on an individual basis in the newly proposed Burma army. The Supreme Allied Commander carried his ideas a step further when, on June 16, he informed both Aung San and Thakin Than Tun of this decision and outlined his plans to create a new Burma army from both the forces he commanded and those in the PBF. Aung

---

43. "Policy towards the Burmans, 2nd June, 1945," in Mountbatten, op. cit., app. F, p. 230.

San and Than Tun are reported to have accepted this and added the suggestion that those men not accepted might be given a gratuity or back pay to help them make the transition from war to peacetime. Mountbatten reported that this "seemed to me a sound suggestion."[44]

Neither Aung San nor the other Burma nationalists had any real intention of surrendering complete control over the indigenous armed forces and destroying the mystique associated with the revival of the nation's pride. The integration of the PBF in the new army did not proceed swiftly or smoothly. By September 1945, Mountbatten summoned Aung San and Than Tun to Ceylon to discuss the delays, and there it was agreed in writing to implement the earlier integration decision. The supreme commander warned the Burmese that until the PBF was disbanded and all illegal arms collected he could not transfer power to the civil authorities.[45] Despite this agreement the members of the PBF not taken into the new army remained idle and in the uniform of their war days. It was not difficult, therefore, in the period following the breakdown of political negotiations with the governor, to reorganize this political military force as a paramilitary homeguard to maintain law and order in a period of social unrest.

The People's Volunteer Organization came into being in January 1946 and openly trained throughout Burma in uniform and with mock weapons.[46] Its numbers, never published, were estimated to be between eight and sixteen thousand.[47] This politically controlled military force combined with the fact that the official Burma army was recruited in part from the former brother-in-arms of the new PVO confronted the government of Burma with a political pressure that had a strong revolutionary potential. On January 19, 1946, Mountbatten is reported to have passed on to Dorman-Smith

44. Mountbatten, op. cit., p. 204.
45. Ibid., pp. 204–205. For a copy of Aung San's AFPFL proposal to Mountbatten at the Kandy Conference, see Josef Silverstein (ed.), *The Political Legacy of Aung San* (Ithaca, 1972), pp. 23–24.
46. Collis, op. cit., pp. 264–265. For Aung San's explanation of the PVO and why it was brought into existence, see Silverstein, op. cit., pp. 30–32.
47. F. C. Jones, H. Borton, and B. R. Pearn, *The Far East, 1942–1946* (London, 1955), p. 286.

the warning of Gens. Wavell and Auchinleck that Indian troops would be unreliable in a Burma uprising and that they had only a few British and Dominion regiments in the Southeast Asia Command. Mountbatten recommended that every effort be made to avoid a rebellion.[48] The AFPFL never completely surrendered or lost control of the men under arms who gave it their initial loyalty, and the League used them as a political weapon both in dealing with the governor and in maintaining its prestige with the people.

The AFPFL also held the people through mass action, meetings, conventions, and continuous publicity of its decisions, resolutions, and bargaining sessions. Borrowing a tactic from the prewar politicians, the AFPFL staged its largest demonstrations on the steps or at the foot of important Buddhist pagodas, Shwedagon in Rangoon being a particular favorite.[49] One of its most important mass rallies was held August 19, 1945, at the Nay-thu-yain theater, to rally public support for resolutions passed the day before at the leaders' conference at AFPFL headquarters.[50] Its failure to get the governor to accept the AFPFL candidates and terms for participation in the Executive Council led to a mass meeting at Shwedagon on November 18 at which the AFPFL won adoption of resolutions (1) protesting the governor's action on the Executive Council membership, (2) calling for immediate elections in anticipation of convening a constituent assembly, (3) protesting the governor's planning reconstruction without calling on the public either for suggestions or for approval of his action, and (4) demanding the issuance of "a general amnesty in respect to all the political or war offenses committed during those periods."[51]

Also at that meeting the League's secretary-general, Thakin Than Tun, reported that since November 1, 1945, twenty-seven mass meetings had been held in twenty-seven towns in Upper Burma.

48. Collis, op. cit., p. 271.
49. The London Times, January 22, 1946, p. 3, and March 8, 1946, p. 5, gives interesting accounts of such meetings in Rangoon. A survey of the Burma press notes the use of Shwedagon by all political parties from as early as July 1945; see Sun, July 3, 1945.
50. See n. 11.
51. "Swedagon Mass Meeting: Governor's Executive Council," in AFPFL, op. cit., pp. 91–94. This document contains the four resolutions.

Similar action was taken in Rangoon, where, he estimated, two to three thousand people attended and supported the resolutions adopted by the AFPFL.⁵² In addition he announced that

> to further national unity the AFPFL arranging [sic] to hold an all Burma Congress on December 10 to 22. At that Congress, thirty delegates, will be invited for each district. Also at this congress the future program and rules of the AFPFL will be confirmed.⁵³

He concluded by restating three main principles of the AFPFL: to eschew use of force; to struggle on a national, not an ethnic, basis; to act in the interest of the country on all questions.⁵⁴

The AFPFL demonstrated on numerous occasions that it was master, both of its armed units and its mass support. Probably the best example demonstrating both was the Tantabin Affair. On May 18, 1946, at a rally in Tantabin sponsored by the Communists (who, by this time, were attempting to capture the AFPFL for their own purposes), the participants were fired on by the police and three were killed. The AFPFL decided to hold a large public funeral with Aung San delivering the oration. The governor feared this action would spark a revolt and appealed to Aung San to desist. Aung San refused but promised to hold the crowd in check. This he did and the incident passed without further violence.⁵⁵

The League did not have this control or prestige with the peoples in the Frontier Areas. Prior to January 1946, the League reported little or no activity in the area. Only through resolutions of unity and the fact that Frontier Areas people were in the higher echelons of the AFPFL, was interest and contact maintained. After full civil authority was restored throughout British Burma on January

---

52. "The Report of Thakin Than Tun, General Secretary, AFPFL, Made at the Mass Meeting Held at the Shwedagon Pagoda on the 18th November 1945," in AFPFL, op. cit., p. 107.
53. Ibid., p. 109.
54. Ibid., p. 110.
55. Burma, *Report of the Tantabin Incident Enquiry Commission* (Rangoon, 1947); see also Collis, op. cit., pp. 268–269 for Dorman-Smith's account of the events and his talk with Aung San.

1, 1946, the governor and the AFPFL both moved to strengthen their contacts with the hill peoples to gain adherence to their policies. Early in January the governor made a personal visit to Myitkyina to participate in the Kachin victory *manao* ("celebration"). Aung San attended the same celebration. While Dorman-Smith thanked the Kachins for their steadfast loyalty to the British throughout the war and promised schools and hospitals in the future, Aung San appealed for their support in the struggle for independence.[56] Aung San's visit marked the first time a Burmese leader had been invited to participate in a Kachin *manao*.[57]

In March 1946, the first Panglong Conference of the *sawbwas* was held in the Laikha State. Thirty-four chiefs attended, and the meeting was addressed by the governor's representative, Stcavenson; three Burmans, Thakin Nu speaking for the AFPFL, U Saw speaking for himself, and U Lun speaking for the governor's Executive Council; and Dr. Gordon Seagrave, who spoke nonpolitically on the medical needs in the area. The Shan chiefs also invited representatives of the Karens, the Kachins, and the Chins to participate as observers. The purpose of the meeting was "to discuss the welfare, trade and cultural aspirations of the States."[58]

The governor's address outlined the government's policy toward the hill areas. It opened with a restatement of the White Paper policy "to keep the Administration of the Frontier Areas as it was in the past under direct control of the Governor."[59] It went on to say that the governor looked to the future when the states might be joined with Burma proper in a political union, but until that time they would be administered separately. In the meantime progress would be made and each state would create to assist the chief a state advisory council representing all its ethnic groups. The governor hoped that the councils would evolve into fully representative institutions.

The *Times* reported that U Saw made a strong plea for the

56. Collis, op. cit., p. 270.
57. *New Times of Burma*, May 8, 1946, p. 3, a report of a speech by Steavenson.
58. *Times* (London), March 28, 1946, p. 3; Gordon Seagrave, *My Hospital in the Hills* (New York, 1955), pp. 64–67.
59. *New Times of Burma*, March 27, 1946, p. 3.

frontier peoples to unite with Burma proper for defense and economic measures while retaining full autonomy in other spheres of activity. His speech was reported to have been well received.[60]

The only published views of the participants or their guests were contained in the statement of the Kachin elders outlining their views and impressions. It opened with a refutation of Thakin Nu's statement at the meeting that the British were instrumental in separating the Kachins and Burmans and making them hate each other: "This we deny emphatically." In rebuttal they asked, "What have the Burman people done toward the hill peoples to win their faith and love?" Did not "a section of the Burmese public, who while saying that we all belong to the same race, blood and home call in the Japanese and cause the hill peoples to suffer. If therefore the Burmese want unity with the hill peoples they must change." They must recognize that "the British are our friends and their friends; they have done more than the Burmese Governments of old, and now they promise self-government." The Kachins want to protect their heredity rights, customs and religion; they also want to be treated as equals. When this is done "we shall be ready to consider the question of our entry into close relations with Burma as a free dominion."[61]

The Shan chiefs made no decision other than to reassemble the next year. Their presiding officer, the *sawbwa* of Tawng Peng, said they just wanted to hear all sides and make their decisions at leisure.

If the Burmese nationalists did not score any striking success at either the Kachin *manao* or the first Panglong Conference, they did learn firsthand the fears, ideas, and aspirations of the hill peoples and discover, too, the issues and feelings in the way of uniting the two areas for common political action.

During the spring of 1946, rumors persisted in Rangoon that the governor and his aides were instrumental in keeping the peoples of Burma proper and the Frontier Areas separate. These rumors

60. *Times* (London), April 3, 1946, p. 3. Saimong Mangrai, *The Shan States and the British Annexation* (Ithaca, 1965), pp. 306–307.

61. *New Times of Burma*, April 23, 1946, p. 3. The authors of this statement were Zau La, Chairman, Kachin Committee, Bhamo; Zau Lawn, Bhamo; Kumreng Gam, Myitkyina; Zau Aung, Bhamo; Hkum Heng, Kutkai, No. Shan State; Naw Seng, No. Shan State.

became so current that the government, through Director for the Frontier Areas Steavenson, held a news conference in order to issue a reply. Steavenson argued that, contrary to rumors, the government was instrumental in bringing the Burmans and the minorities together. He gave examples of the Karens and the hill peoples holding conferences during the war and resolving "to keep aloof from the Burmese and establish their own independent states," whereas, "since their return, the British have sought to restore harmonious feelings and now the hill peoples had agreed to unite with the Burmese when the latter could guarantee their well-being."[62]

Paying no heed to government protests, the AFPFL held a meeting of its Supreme Council on May 26 and passed a resolution reflecting its determination to unite and speak for all the peoples of British Burma. In the light of reports that the government intended to implement the White Paper in such a way as to create a separate Karen state under the protection of the frontier administration; create a new federation of Shan states (like the prewar federation); and make similar arrangements for the Kachins, Chins, and Nagas and "federate all these states and subject them to continual British dominion," the AFPFL considered it necessary to "declare the independence of Burma and all these states" and to convene a conference "of their representatives and discuss the creation of a Union of Burma with a view to unite in the fight against British imperialism and establish a free federated state."[63]

The resolution reflected both the growing hostility of the AFPFL toward the government and the growing determination of its leaders to speak for the whole of Burma. Its suggestion of a federal union rather than a unitary state established the basis for future AFPFL proposals that offered to guarantee protection for the ethnic, cultural, and religious minorities within a self-governing Burma.

During this period the leaders of the Karenni States visited Rangoon and declared their desire to remain independent of everyone: British, Burmans, Shans, Kachins, Karens, and so on. Only

62. Ibid., May 8, 1946, p. 3.
63. Burman, May 26, 1946, p. 2.

when the peoples of Burma proper, the Shans, and the Karens achieved sovereign status were they interested in joining any federation.⁶⁴ In the opinion of a Burman who had been the first appointee from among his people in the India civil service and who was at the time a newspaper editor,

> The association which the Burmese seek with their kith and kin in the frontier areas is a voluntary association of free people. Though the object of the resolution is worthy, the practical difficulties must be accepted and nothing done by the Burmese to give the impression to the other races that we are trying to force the pace. . . . A start was made at the Panglong Conference which did not, however, come to concrete decision on so vital an issue.⁶⁵

By Dorman-Smith's departure from Burma in June 1946, the situation was clear to everyone. The government was unable to implement its official policy because the politically conscious people of Burma proper under the leadership of the AFPFL were unified in their opposition to cooperating with the governor's efforts to put the policy to work. His failure can be traced to two sources already examined: his inability to split the solidarity of the main AFPFL leadership by offering membership in his Executive Council to particular individuals and the absence of rival popular leaders capable of winning support at the same time they gave the governor their loyalty. Only in the Frontier Areas was the May 17, 1945, policy put into operation, and there it was under a frontal challenge from the AFPFL. The arrival of the new governor, Hubert Rance, in September signaled the beginning of change in official British thinking on Burma; it also marked the beginning of an eighteen-month period when the League truly spoke for a majority in Burma.

---

During the summer of 1946, two significant developments took place that were to shed light on future developments. The Karens of the delta area, aware of the growing strength of the AFPFL and

64. *Burmese Review*, May 27, 1946, p. 7.
65. Ibid., p. 8.

the possibility of its winning its battle with the British, decided to send a goodwill mission to London to plead their case for special protection or separate statehood. The mission was composed of Sydney Loo-Nee, an old-time Karen leader who was a member of the Legislative Council; Saw Po Chit, a prewar minister of education; Saw Tha Din, chairman of the Central Karen Organization; and Saw Ba U Gyi, a prominent Karen leader in the AFPFL. The official purpose of the mission was threefold: to thank Britains and Americans for helping Karens in the past, to establish trade connections for Karen commercial undertakings, and to discuss on an unofficial level the prospects of the establishment of a separate Karen state.[66] It was believed that the Karens would ask that their state be formed out of territory—the entire Tenasserim Division and the Naunglebin Subdivision of the Pegu District—in which the Karen peoples did not constitute a majority of residents.[67]

Recognizing the divisive possibilities of such a move, U Tin Tut wrote in his *Burmese Review*:

> The progress of Burma toward united nationhood depends on the winning by the Burmese of the confidence and trust of the other races to whom Burma is also a home. On the other hand, the best protection for the minorities lies not in paper safeguards but in the regard and affection of the majority community and the growth of a true sense of national unity transcending all racial and religious barriers. . . . Whatever the attitude of His Majesty's Government may be, the future of the Karens in Burma is one which in the end must be settled by agreement between the Burmans and the Karens.[68]

This view was reflected in the conservative *Times* during the visit of the Karen mission. In an editorial it reviewed the whole concept of separate administration for particular areas and special protections for minorities in Burma proper. It admitted that the idea of separate administered areas "has been soundly condemned by Burman nationalists of every shade of opinion and it is by no means certain that all the peoples of the 'scheduled areas' really

66. *Burmese Review*, July 29, 1946, p. 8.
67. Sharing this area with the Karens were the Mons and Burmans.
68. *Burmese Review*, July 29, 1946, p. 8.

desire it." The editorial went on to say that before Britain moved to establish separate regions it ought first to explore all means of bringing the ethnic groups together. "It may well be that discussions with the leaders [Karen] now in Britain will show that the autonomy the Karen people desire is more compatible with close association with genuine Burmese political developments than they realize at present."[69]

At the same time, a movement in the opposite direction was taking place in the Anglo-Burman community. In the middle of July it called a meeting of its members and organized to implement a resolution its constituents in Simla had passed during the war calling for Anglo-Burmans to regard themselves as a people of Burma and to waive their existing special privileges and depend on the good faith of the majority community in Burma.[70]

Concurrent with this minority activity in Burma proper, an economic-political problem erupted in Rangoon and provided the nationalists with a strong bargaining weapon for dealing with the government. On September 5, the Rangoon City Police went on strike and appealed to all, even criminals, to assist their efforts to win higher pay and better conditions.[71] The appeal was answered by supporting strikes among other civil servants and by leadership

69. *Times* (London), August 24, 1946, p. 5.

70. *Burmese Review*, July 15, 1946, p. 8. For Aung San's position on the future of the Anglo-Burmans in Burma, see Silverstein, op. cit., pp. 90–92.

71. According to the *New Times of Burma*, September 7, 1946, p. 2, the police issued the following statement at their meeting: "We the members of the Rangoon City Police make this strong appeal on behalf of Burma to all self-centered individual bad hats and members of dacoit gangs to consider the welfare of the country and by way of supporting our cause, to keep the peace and to refrain from committing crimes during the period in which we are engaged in a demonstration to secure a status equivalent to that enjoyed by police forces in all free countries. All are specially warned that if this appeal is disregarded, we will take the most severe and drastic action either when we resume our duties according to our rank and status or when we become ordinary citizens if the Government will not receive us back." There is a question in the minds of current historians whether, at the outset, this was an economic or a political strike. Cady, op cit., p. 537, and Hugh Tinker, *The Union of Burma* (London, 1956), p. 21, are not sure. The Burma government, in its account published after independence, argues that it was political and not economic; see Ministry of Information, *Burma's Fight for Freedom* (Rangoon, 1948), p. 41.

from the AFPFL. On September 23, the AFPFL called a general strike, which the local presses reported "was observed by almost all the workers concerned."[72] The *Times*, among other British dailies, saw the political implications of the strikes and suggested that the cause emanated from the fact that the existing executive and legislative councils were unrepresentative and that the policy of the Burma government was not parallel with British policy in India:

> It is understood that influential political associations like the AFPFL . . . and the Myochit Party . . . would be willing to serve on the Executive Council provided that there was an increase of its powers and functions to bring it roughly into line with the interim Government of India. Much will depend on whether the British are willing to transfer to a reconstituted Executive Council jurisdiction over defense, external affairs and monetary policy, as has been done in India.[73]

This was the situation when the new governor, Hubert Rance, arrived in Burma to take charge. His first remarks to the people a day after his arrival suggested that he intended to interpret official policy differently from his predecessor. In discussing the relations between the peoples of the Frontier Areas and those of Burma proper, he pointed out that all ethnic groups had indicated their desires to advance politically and economically; "it will be my duty to foster this end, to give all assistance in my power to the realization of the declared policy of His Majesty's Government." In carrying out this policy, "it will be my object to ensure that the relations between the peoples of the hills and the plains should be as close and as intimate as possible."[74]

Following his declaration of intention to work for and with the popular leaders of the country, the governor began a round of discussions on local grievances and solicited ideas for their solution from local leaders. After communicating his observations to London, he authorized his director of public information to hold a news conference on September 24 and report that, having found

---

72. *New Times of Burma*, September 24, 1946, p. 1.
73. *Times* (London), September 12, 1946, p. 3.
74. *New Times of Burma*, September 3, 1946, p. 3.

London sympathetic to the Burmese views, "he was now in a position to go forward with the formation of a new Executive Council on a broader basis." The governor would continue his talks with the Burmese and was hopeful that they would accept his proposals.[75]

In spite of the volatile situation caused by the growing strikes in Rangoon, the governor continued to search for a solution to Burma's real political problem: the participation of popular leaders in the government. On September 27, he was able to announce, even while the strikes were in progress, that he had formed a new executive council of eleven, six representing the AFPFL; one each from the *Myochit*, *Dobama*, and *Sinyetha* Parties; one Karen; and one independent. The governor made a radio broadcast announcing that the council would have all the authority and power its ministerial predecessor enjoyed under the 1935 Act. In addition the new council would be kept fully informed of developments and matters concerning the Frontier Areas even though responsibility would, for the time being, continue to reside with the governor. "The Council is as representative as I have been able to make it."[76] The portfolios were divided so that the major ministries were allotted to the AFPFL representatives. Aung San became responsible for defense and external affairs, Thakin Mya for home, Thein Pe for agriculture and rural economy, Aung Zan Wai for social services, and Ba Pe for commerce and supplies. The only other major portfolio, finance, was assigned to an independent, U Tin Tut, formerly of the Indian civil service. The *Sinyetha* nominee did not accept membership because his party would not participate in the government, and the Communist Party representative was forced to resign a few weeks after taking office because of a split between his party and the AFPFL.[77] The creation of this representative Executive Council with the participation of the AFPFL and with real power in the hands of the councillors marked the end

75. Ibid., September 21, 1946, p. 1.
76. *Times* (London), September 27, 1946, p. 4; *Burmese Review*, September 30, 1946, p. 8.
77. *Burmese Review*, September 30, 1946, p. 8; *Burman*, October 13, 1946, pp. 1–2.

of the initial phase of the nationalists' struggle for a part in determining the nature of the interim government. It also fulfilled the second and third resolutions of the AFPFL passed on August 18, 1945.[78] The new Executive Council demonstrated its ability to lead the people by negotiating a satisfactory end to the general strike.

78. See n. 11.

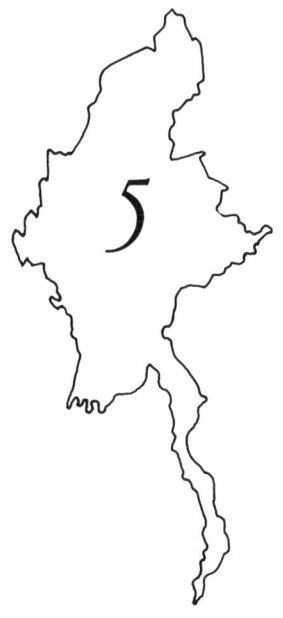

# 5

## The Struggle for Political Unity 1946-1948

The change in British colonial policy implemented by Governor Rance in September did not satisfy the demands of the Burmese nationalists. In their view, the change was extremely limited, for it gave neither definite answers nor specific promises for a national election, a constituent assembly, and a terminal date for colonial rule. Decisions on such matters could not, however, be made in Rangoon; they had to be made by the government in London. Late in December the Labour government of Prime Minister Attlee decided to act, and the Burmese were invited to send delegates to England to negotiate the future course of British–Burmese relations. The success of the London meeting was climaxed by the signing of an agreement by Aung San and Clement Attlee outlining the steps to independence.

The crucial issue left to be decided was not whether Burma would remain in the Commonwealth but whether the Frontier Areas would join in a political union with Burma proper and create one new nation. The decision rested with the people in Burma and was not to be known until the Constituent Assembly met and drew up a fundamental law that all the delegates approved. At that moment a national consensus was found, and political unity was established through the rights and obligations embodied in the constitution.

---

Between October and December 1946, the AFPFL concentrated its attention on assisting the governor to administer the country, finding ways to draw the Frontier Areas into closer association with Burma proper, and preparing an immediate program that looked to the formation of a constituent assembly as its objective. The last two concerns were partially addressed in a series of resolutions the AFPFL passed on November 4, 1946. The AFPFL demanded that the tribal areas under the direct jurisdiction of the governor be transferred immediately and incorporated in Burma proper.[1] This resolution also called for the orderly incorporation of the Frontier Areas into a future federation with Burma proper and for equal treatment of the peoples in both areas:

> Our policy in regard to the Frontier Areas of Burma will be to seek cordial relations with the peoples of these areas with a view to the formation of a union or a federation of Burma formed by the willing consent of all the races inhabiting the whole of Burma. Although we shall be willing at all times to assist by financial and other means in the welfare and development of the Frontier Areas, it is not our intention to impose on the races inhabiting these areas any form of union which they themselves do not desire and should such union or federation be formed, it will be our policy to leave to the States such autonomy as they may need for the control and management of their own internal affairs. At the time when the constituent assembly is to be elected for Burma it will be our policy to invite the people of the Frontier Areas to join in the work of such assembly under conditions as may mutually be agreed upon in order that should the races of the frontier areas so desire, these areas would be able to march with Burma proper to full autonomy.[2]

1. *Times* (London), November 4, 1946, p. 3.
2. *New Times of Burma*, November 8, 1946, p. 5; for comment and criticism of the resolution, see the *Burmese Review*, November 11, 1946, p. 8.

Using this policy as a basis, the Burmese negotiated afresh with the hill peoples and eventually won their support. Aung San personally visited the Frontier Areas in the weeks following the resolution to explain the ideas of the AFPFL and guarantee that his organization and the Executive Council would adhere to this commitment. He visited the Kachins, Chins, and Shans in late November and early December and the Karens in the Tenasserim District in late December. The press reported that Aung San received a warm welcome among the Kachins, who promised "to work in unity with the Burmans, who they hoped would regard them as brothers."[3] Discussions with the Kachin leaders at a meeting in Myitkyina produced three resolutions by the local leaders, which called for the immediate creation of a Kachin state out of the Bhamo and Myitkyina districts, the recognition of this state by the British government, and pending this development, maintenance of the status quo.[4]

Within Burma proper, the AFPFL continued to work among the minorities to win and hold their support. On November 18, 1946, at the celebration of National Day, a large parade and rally was staged in which all communities—Indian, Chinese, and Anglo-Burman—were reported to have participated.[5] One of the features of the rally was the speech given by the Anglo-Burman spokesman, E. Barnard, in which he called on all Anglo-Burmans to consider themselves Burmans. Speaking with the passion of a Burmese nationalist, he indicted the British "imperialist" for deceiving Anglo-Burmans with spurious safeguards "and in reality, using them for British and not Burmese interests." Now, he said, was the time for Anglo-Burmans to "shake-off the shackles of imperialism and stand alongside the Burmese solidly and completely in their fight for a free and independent Burma."[6] This signified an important

3. *New Times of Burma*, December 5, 1946, p. 5.
4. Ibid., December 19, 1946, p. 1. The signatories of the resolutions were Sinwa Nawng, Kareng La, Zau La, Zau Lawn, Hkun Hpung, and Naw Seng.
5. Ibid., November 19, 1946, p. 1.
6. Ibid., p. 2. Aung San made a specific response to the Anglo-Burmans a few weeks later. See Josef Silverstein (ed.), *The Political Legacy of Aung San* (Ithaca, 1972), p. 90–91.

shift among the leaders of the Anglo-Burman community and a narrowing of the gap between the Anglo-Burmans and the Burman majority.

On the issue of an immediate program, the AFPFL resolutions of November 4 called for (1) steps to be taken to send Burmese envoys abroad and to obtain a seat in the United Nations; (2) all foreign troops to be withdrawn immediately; (3) all foreign firms to cease exploiting Burma's resources; (4) government projects controlling the production and distribution of rice, timber, and oil to be transferred to Burman concerns; and (5) the franchise act passed by Parliament to be amended to limit to Burmese citizens only the right to vote in Burma.[7] The last two resolutions were incorporated in an AFPFL ultimatum issued on November 12 that also declared that the British must accept these terms or else the AFPFL would resign from the Executive Council.[8]

The AFPFL did not have long to wait for its reply. On December 20, 1946, Prime Minister Attlee spoke in Parliament and outlined his government's new policy for Burma. A Burmese delegate representing the Executive Council would be invited immediately to visit England and consult with the British on the last stages of the country's transition to independent status. He reasoned that, on the

---

7. *Times* (London) November 4, 1946, p. 3. The franchise bill was passed in Parliament in June 1946 as an act to amend the law relating to the Burma legislature. During the second reading, it was amended from the floor by D. R. Rees-Williams (Labour) to permit the Buddhist monks and nuns to vote; see ibid., June 29, 1946, p. 2. In an editorial, the *Times* saw this amendment as a regressive step and one that was out of harmony with Burmese wishes. It argued further that it would probably benefit the old discredited politicians at the expense of the new young leaders; see ibid., September 24, 1946, p. 5.

8. The ultimatum was published in *New Times of Burma*, November 13, 1946, p. 1, and read: "(1) On January 31, 1947, the British Government shall declare that within one year from that date Burma will have her freedom; further, that the forthcoming elections should be held independent of foreign participation with a view to setting up a Constituent Assembly as denied by the Supreme Council. (2) The Burma Governor shall guarantee the setting up of the present Government Executive Council as a National Government by January 31, 1947. (3) Between the present time and January 31, 1947 all decisions reached by the Supreme Council in connection with the project schemes should be carried out."

basis of developments in India, a new policy ought to be inaugurated in Burma: "His Majesty's Government do not regard the White Papers as unchangeable in the light of developing circumstances." Britain, he said, now wants to see the Burmese "attain their self-government by the quickest and most convenient path possible. They will have the right to decide whether or not to remain in the Commonwealth and the right to draw up their own new constitution. In order to speed the process, the Burmese, like the Indians, can make their forthcoming election an election of the Constituent Assembly rather than of a Parliament as provided under the existing 1935 Constitution." Finally, "His Majesty's Government are of the opinion that the Burmese Government which has now been formed should, within the existing Constitution, exercise a full measure of authority in Burma." The British government, he promised, will not interfere in the day to day affairs in Burma and, once the delegates arrive, will make every effort to remove any restrictions the Burmese "may feel still exists in this regard."[9]

Speaking for the Opposition, Winston Churchill responded to the statement of the prime minister by deploring the government's haste in granting independence. Referring to the existing state of unrest in Burma, he said "it would have been reasonable to allow law and order to be established and the people to settle down on their farms and in their habitations. Then we could have resumed the question of self-government, to which we had definitely pledged ourselves—but all in due course and due time."[10] The "due course" would have been to grant self-government within the Commonwealth; and then, as members of that mystical body, the Burmese could have exercised what Churchill called "the escalator clause" to leave or remain in the Commonwealth. Throughout his speech he referred to the parallel in India and deplored the haste there as much as in Burma:

9. Great Britain, *Parliamentary Debates* (Commons), 5th series, 431 (December 20, 1946): 2341–2343; *Times* (London), December 21, 1946, p. 4.
10. Great Britain, op. cit., pp. 2343–2346, 2348–2350; *Times* (London), December 21, 1946, p. 4.

What spread over a number of years would be a healthy and constitutional process and might easily have given the Burmese people an opportunity of continuing their association with our congregation of nations, has been cast aside—just as we are seeing in home affairs the unseemly haste of legislation—disorganizing our national life and impeding our recovery.[11]

If Churchill and those who shared his views were disappointed over the haste suggested in Attlee's statement, the AFPFL also was disappointed that no time limit was established for transferring power and no reference was made to the future of the Frontier Areas.[12] The AFPFL response was slow in coming because at the time of the statement U Aung San was away in Moulmein and not easily reached. On his return to Rangoon, the Supreme Council of the AFPFL met and decided that the statement was a satisfactory basis for further discussions. The *Times* correspondent writing from Burma at the time said that, although extremist elements in Burma might reject the British offer, it "has given much satisfaction to the more moderate Burmese who accept Mr. Attlee's statement as a gesture indicating a change in the British outlook on Burma and as proof of the sincerity of British intentions toward Burma."[13]

A warning for the future was sounded in Rangoon on December 20. Thakin Ba Sein, a member of the Executive Council and leader of the *Dobama* Party, announced the formation of a new coalition, which he called the Democratic National United Front, in which all political parties except the AFPFL were joined. The new front called for complete independence, national unity, and democratic freedom. Among the cofounders were U Saw and Dr. Ba Maw. The *Times* reported that

> Although the present Executive Council has not been put into office by democratic elections, there can be little doubt that as a whole, it represents the views of most Burmese and though a group of older politicians are attempting to create a counter-coalition as a possible alternative Government, it is unlikely that the Governor

11. See n. 10.
12. *Times* (London), December 27, 1946, p. 3.
13. Ibid.

would be able to form a new Council commanding popular support if the present one resigned.[14]

The Ba Sein–U Saw–Ba Maw coalition never materialized because the Attlee statement altered the political situation in Burma. The people of Burma interpreted it as meeting most of the AFPFL demands that had been published in its November ultimatum; the British willingness to negotiate raised the prestige of the AFPFL; and rival political movements found little support in the Burmese papers. The political competition between the AFPFL and the older politicians was suspended temporarily when the government announced that the delegates would include three AFPFL members, U Aung San, Thakin Mya, and U Ba Pe; one representative from the *Myochit* Party, U Saw; one from the *Dobama Asiayone*, U Ba Sein; and one independent, U Tin Tut. As a broadly representative delegation it could rally united popular support for the mission. The delegation did not include any spokesmen for the Frontier Areas because they were outside the jurisdiction of the Executive Council.

If the members of the AFPFL were elated over the change in British attitude, it was not discernible from the remarks of their leader, U Aung San, at a New Year's Day demonstration or at a press interview in New Delhi five days later. To his own people Aung San said he was not able to predict the outcome of the future negotiations:

> Perhaps we may secure our demands, but if we do not we must be prepared for the next move. We do not want to stage a rebellion or anything like that; we wish to gain our freedom as peacefully as possible. Nevertheless, we must be prepared for the final struggle to achieve our goal. I therefore appeal to you to remain united, patient and vigilant.[15]

On the same day, the AFPFL released a new Frontier Areas policy statement calling for simultaneous freedom for Burma proper and the Frontier Areas; the immediate appointment of a representa-

14. *Times* (London), December 23, 1946, p. 4.
15. Ibid., January 2, 1947, p. 4.

tive from the Frontier Areas to the Executive Council to advise on local problems; and the inclusion of the Frontier Areas and the Karenni States at the Constituent Assembly, where they could decide whether to join a Burma federation.[16]

At his press interview in New Delhi, Aung San announced that Burma's goal was complete independence; "there is no question of dominion status for Burma." He also set a time limit on his period of negotiation: "I must get a settlement before January 31, 1947, otherwise there will be a deadlock. We must be back in Burma before January 31." Replying to a question on the withdrawal of British troops, an old AFPFL demand, he said he did not think he would make such a demand because "most of the British troops in Burma happen to be Indian troops"; but, he added, pending their withdrawal he would demand "that the Government of Burma assume complete control of these troops while on Burmese soil."[17]

The traces of belligerency conveyed in some of Aung San's remarks were gone when he and the delegates met Prime Minister Attlee. In response to the warmth and friendliness of Attlee's opening remarks, Aung San spoke quietly and to the point, taking up the major issue left unmentioned in the British pronouncement of December 20, political unity between Burma proper and the Frontier Areas:

> We can confidently assert here that so far as our knowledge of our country goes, there should be no insuperable difficulties in the way of a unified Burma provided all races are given full freedom and the opportunity to meet together and to work without the interference of outside interests. So far as we are concerned, we stand for full freedom of all the races of our country, including those in the so-called Karenni States, and we hold strongly the view that no such race and no regime in our country should be denied now the fruits of the freedom that must shortly be achieved by our country and our people.[18]

16. *New Times of Burma*, January 1, 1947, p. 1.
17. *Times* (London), January 6, 1947, p. 3.
18. Ibid., January 14, 1947, p. 3.

He closed with an expression of appreciation that Burma was to be allowed to choose its future form of relations with Britian and observed that all should be complete within a year.

Not to be outdone by his political rival, Aung San, Thakin Ba Sein also responded to the British prime minister's opening speech. He demanded independence for Burma: "Nothing short of complete independence will satisfy our aspiration." All Burma's present unrest and chaos stemmed, he said, from the absence of a definite British statement to this effect. Inasmuch as, in his words, Burma had no social or communal problems, "hers is a homogenous nation," the British must accept the principle of independence as the basis of future discussion.[19] No rebuttal was offered and the delegates began their serious negotiations.

On January 27, the discussions ended successfully with the signing of an agreement embodying their decisions. Without altering the 1935 constitution the agreement provided that the Executive Council would enjoy the same powers as the interim government in India. More specifically it said that the council would "be treated with the same close consultations and considerations as a Dominion Government and will have the greatest possible freedom in the exercise of the day to day administration of the country."[20] On matters of defense and external affairs the council was to be consulted fully and associated with all decisions; the Burmese forces would be placed under the government of Burma and a high commissioner for Burma would be appointed. In place of the legislative council, it was agreed to elect a constituent assembly in April 1947. The right to vote or be elected was restricted to Burma nationals, who were defined in the agreement "as a British subject or subject of an Indian State who was born in Burma and resided there for not less than eight years or ten years immediately preceding either January 1, 1942 or January 1, 1947."[21]

19. Ibid.
20. Great Britain, *Conclusions Reached in the Conversations between His Majesty's Government and the Delegation from the Executive Council of the Governor of Burma*, Cmd. 7029, 1947, p. 2, hereafter the Aung San–Clement Attlee Agreement.
21. Ibid., annex A, p. 5.

On the all-important issue of the Frontier Areas, it was agreed that, although both the Burmese and the British wanted to achieve early unification of the two areas with the consent of their inhabitants, for the present the two should "be closely associated with the Government of Burma in a manner acceptable to both parties." The agreement called for free access to both areas by all inhabitants of Burma, and it looked ahead to the next Panglong Conference as a time when consultation could be held and a decision made. The agreement also provided for a committee of inquiry to investigate the sentiments of the peoples in the Frontier Areas and make recommendations on the future association of the two.[22] In the struggle for national unity the Aung San–Clement Attlee Agreement marks a turning point in the legal and formal relations between Burma proper and the Frontier Areas. Specifically, it established the steps to be taken for the areas to be united and provided guarantees of respect for the rights and opinions of the peoples involved.

In his parliamentary defense of the agreement, Attlee repeated that "ultimate unification has always been our policy" and added that the agreement gave protection to all concerned.[23] In the short and spirited debate that followed, the prime minister's statement was challenged in several ways, particularly by Mr. R. Butler and Mr. G. Nicholson, both of the Conservative Party. When Butler asked whether the Karens were consulted on the agreement, Attlee replied, "There was no specific Karen delegation because this was a Delegation of members of the Executive Council."[24] To a question by Nicholson about the mission of the under-secretary of state to Burma, the Prime Minister said,

> We want to see that the people of Ministerial Burma and the people of the plains have a full opportunity of discussing the matter with one another, and we want to assure ourselves as to what are the views of the people of the frontier areas.[25]

22. Ibid., p. 4.
23. Great Britain, *Parliamentary Debates*, op. cit., 432 (January 28, 1947): 778.
24. Ibid., p. 782.
25. Ibid.

The agreement also provoked dissent within the Burmese delegation. U Saw and Thakin Ba Sein rejected it and refused to affix their signatures. They justified their action by the fact that the agreement included no terminal date for Burma's colonial status. On their return to Burma they resigned from the Executive Council and joined Ba Maw in a movement to wreck the agreement, but their efforts found little support among the people.

While the London episode reveals a great deal about the legal and formal relations between Great Britian and Burma and between Burma proper and the Frontier Areas, it also leaves many questions unanswered. For one thing it seems clear that the British government assumed that the frontier peoples would accept some sort of immediate union with Burma proper because the agreement included no alternatives should the two areas fail to unite. Moreover the whole episode has an air of urgency about it, suggesting that the leaders in Britain were determined to come to some sort of settlement even if it were necessary to work out the details later. This seems clear from Attlee's answer to Nicholson. To those in Parliament who believed that the government owed some sort of debt to the loyal minorities in Burma, this seemed an irresponsible way of fulfilling an obligation. At the same time, there were those in the House of Commons, such as Mr. T. Driberg (Labour), who were just as adamant that nothing delay the realization of Burma's independence. The debate was too short to air fully all opinions and questions. Churchill asked whether or not the government intended in the future to "afford us an opportunity of debating this dismal transaction."[26] The prime minister's affirmative reply carried the limitation that the debate must wait until the Burmese delegation return "to Burma and discuss the matter."[27] The Burmese leaders, however, did not wait for a new debate in the Commons; instead they immediately plunged into the next problem, how to translate the mandate they won in Britain into political reality in Burma.

26. Ibid., p. 779.
27. Ibid.

The first opportunity to test the sentiment of the frontier peoples after the London meeting was the second Panglong Conference held in February 1947. The conditions this time were radically different from those prevailing when the earlier conference was held. British policy had changed and now favored immediate unification of the Frontier Areas and Burma proper. The Aung San–Clement Attlee Agreement suggested three alternate ways to unite the areas provisionally without delay: A small group of representatives could be appointed from the Frontier Areas to advise the governor and work with the Executive Council; a single representative of the Frontier Areas could be appointed as an Executive Councillor in charge of Frontier Areas affairs; or the frontier leaders could devise an original third method.[28] Thus the conference participants from the Frontier Areas were under pressure from both the Burmese and the British government to make an important political decision about their future; the Shans no longer had the leisure to listen to all sides and linger over their decision.[29]

Representing the British government as an observer at the deliberations at Panglong was Undersecretary of State for Dominion Affairs A. G. Bottomley, who came from England to attend. As he explained his mission on the eve of the meeting, he was

> to find out whether the peoples of the Frontier Areas wished to be associated with Ministerial Burma during the interim period before the new Constitution was drafted.[30]

He reported also that his government would accept any spokesman freely appointed by the frontier people to speak for the area in the Executive Council; thus it became possible for a citizen of nonchief status to be appointed.[31]

The Panglong Conference began on February 7, 1947; among the delegates were the *sawbwas* of Yawnghwe, North Hsenwi, Laikha, Mongpawn, and Hsamongkam, members of the Shan States' Peo-

28. Aung San–Clement Attlee Agreement, op. cit., p. 4.
29. See chap. 4.
30. *New Times of Burma*, February 6, 1947, p. 1.
31. Ibid.

ple's Freedom League representing the Shans; Duwa Sinwa Nawng and other chiefs representing the Kachins; Hlin Maung, leading the Chins; U Aung San and U Tin Tut representing the Executive Council; and Bottomley and the new director of the Frontier Areas, John Leyden, representing the British government.[32]

The first participants to arrive on February 6 were the Shans and the Kachins. They drew up a five-point resolution outlining their own demands, which included the same political rights and privileges granted the Burmese; in addition, if the frontier people joined the Executive Council, they wanted political autonomy in their states; they did not want to be bound automatically by the terms of the Aung San–Clement Attlee Agreement; and they wanted to be guaranteed the right of secession from the proposed federation after Burma received its independence.[33] The Chins met with the Shans and Kachins on February 7 and gave their approval to the above resolutions. In addition they added three more stipulations, which were approved by the other two groups. Their proposals were that the Kachin and Chin states have the same privileges to draw on the central revenues as the Shan States already enjoyed,[34] that the Burmese agree to supplement any local financial deficit, and that the frontier peoples form a supreme executive council of the united hill peoples to decide on future policies between Burma proper and their areas.[35]

Following these informal preliminary sessions were official meet-

32. *Times* (London), February 10, 1947, p. 4.
33. *New Times of Burma*, February 11, 1947, p. 1.
34. Although all the Frontier Areas were dependent on the Burma government for some financial aid, they had little to say about its amount and little to do with its expenditure, but the situation in the Shan States was different. In 1922, a federal fund was created and maintained by contributions from the states and the Burma government and by receipts from minerals and forests. After 1937, the contributions from the Burma government were not considered a gift but a carefully calculated allotment due the States in consideration of revenue accruing to the central government from taxation of commercial activity in their territories. According to Burma, *The Report of the Frontier Areas Committee of Enquiry, 1947 pt. 1, Report* (Rangoon, 1947), p. 14n., this arrangement was being sought by the other Frontier Areas.
35. *New Times of Burma*, February 11, 1947, p. 1.

ings in which all interested parties were represented. Here Aung San, speaking for the peoples of Burma proper, welcomed the peoples of the Frontier Areas to join with Burma proper in self-government and independence. He allayed their fears of potential Burmese dominance by promising that the Executive Council had no intention of interfering in local administration or usurping local autonomy. He promised that decisions on political institutions for the states and tribal areas would be left to the people and chiefs concerned. His major thesis was that

> it is now for you to decide your future and to decide whether you will share our freedom as equal partners or whether you will continue in your present position of dependence.[36]

Sao Saimong Mangrai, writing some years later, recalled that Aung San won the support of the Shans with straightforward talk and specific promises. He quotes Aung San as having promised that the first president of independent Burma would be a Shan, that three councillors representing the Frontier Areas would be added immediately to the Executive Council, and that there would be equal financial treatment for Ministerial Burma and the Frontier Areas. On the latter point Aung San is quoted as having said, "If Burma receives a kyat, you will also get one kyat."[37] Sao Saimong Mangrai summed up the conference and the position of the Burmans:

> Here at Panglong the Burmese *bilu* unmasked himself, and the Shans, Kachins and Chins found him to be not the *bilu* they were wont to regard him but an ordinary human being as themselves, who regarded them as equals and colleagues."[38]

On February 12, the Kachin, Chin, and Shan leaders came to an understanding on their future relations with Burma proper according to the following terms:

---

36. *Times* (London), February 10, 1947, p. 4.
37. Saimong Mangrai, *The Shan States and the British Annexation* (Ithaca, 1965), pp. 308–309.
38. Ibid., p. 309.

1. A representative of the Hill peoples, selected by the Governor on the recommendation of representatives of the Supreme Council of the United Hill Peoples shall be appointed a Counsellor to the Governor to deal with the Frontier Areas.

2. The said Counsellor shall also be appointed a Member of the Governor's Executive Council, without portfolio, and the subject of Frontier Areas brought within the purview of the Executive Council by Constitutional Convention as in the case of Defense and External Affairs. The Counsellor for Frontier Areas shall be given executive authority by similar means.

3. The said Counsellor shall be assisted by two Deputy Counsellors representing races of which he is not a member. While the two Deputy Counsellors should deal in the first instance with the affairs of their respective areas and the Counsellor with all the remaining parts of the Frontier Areas, they should by Constitutional Convention act on the principle of joint responsibility.

4. While the Counsellor, in his capacity of Member of the Executive Council, will be the only representative of the Frontier Areas on the Council, the Deputy Counsellors shall be entitled to attend meetings of the Council when subjects pertaining to the Frontier Areas are discussed.

5. Though the Governor's Executive Council will be augmented as agreed above, it will not operate in respect of the Frontier Areas in any manner which would deprive any portion of these areas of the autonomy which it now enjoys in internal administration. Full autonomy in internal administration for the Frontier Areas is accepted in principle.

6. Though the question of demarcating and establishing a separate Kachin State within a Unified Burma is one which must be relegated for decision by the Constituent Assembly, it is agreed that such a State is desirable. . . .

7. Citizens of the Frontier Areas shall enjoy rights and privileges which are regarded as fundamental in democratic countries.

8. The arrangements accepted in this Agreement are without prejudice to the financial autonomy now vested in the Federated Shan States.

9. The arrangements accepted in this Agreement are without prejudice to the financial assistance which the Kachin Hills and the Chin Hills are entitled to receive from the revenues of Burma, and the Executive Council will examine with the Frontier Areas Counsellor and Deputy Counsellors the feasibility of adopting for

the Kachin Hills and the Chin Hills financial arrangements similar to those between Burma and the Federated Shan States.[39]

The Panglong Agreement is a major landmark in the struggle for national unity because it established the basis on which the future union would be built. Its significance was twofold: It marked the first agreement between the peoples of the Frontier Areas to act in concert with each other as well as with the leaders from Burma proper, and it established the principle of equality between the peoples of the two areas. The agreement incorporated not only the three major participating ethnic groups' specific earlier demands (except for the right of secession) but the suggestion in the Aung San–Clement Attlee Agreement that a single councillor for the Frontier Areas be added to the Executive Council to join the two areas provisionally. The fact that the Burmese leaders accepted the principle of equality for the two areas and recognized the right of the peoples in the Frontier Areas to retain their internal political autonomy suggests their maturity and realism. They were able to win a complete victory with their gesture of magnanimity and goodwill.

The British representative, Bottomley, was impressed by the proceedings at the conference and said in an interview after his return to Rangoon, "My inquiries have shown that complete understanding exists between the Frontier Areas and Burma . . . and I believe there is genuine sincerity on the part of those people to merge with the Burmese."[40] With the appointment of Sao Samhtun, sawbwa of Mongpawn, as the Frontier Area councillor, Sima Duwa Sinwa Nawng of the Kachin area as one deputy councillor, and Vum Ko Hau of the Chin Hills as the other, the first step toward uniting the Frontier Areas and Burma proper was completed.[41]

39. Burma, op. cit., pp. 16–17; hereafter *FACOE*.
40. *New Times of Burma*, February 18, 1947, p. 1.
41. On his appointment as a deputy councillor, Sima Duwa Sinwa Nawng said, "We the people of the hills now declare our intention of entering the fight for freedom with the Burmese . . . we have complete faith in the Burmese people" *New Times of Burma*, March 12, 1947, p. 2. After the Panglong meeting, the Chins held a unity conference, attended by three thousand,

Despite its importance the Panglong Agreement did not settle all ethnic problems in Burma; for the Karens, the largest minority in the territory, neither participated in the conference nor approved the agreement. Many of the numerically smaller minority groups of the Frontier Areas likewise did not participate or accept the agreement. It fell, therefore, to the Frontier Areas Committee of Enquiry to provide the patient ear and listen to all the fears and aspirations of the many peoples in Burma.

The committee, composed of Burmans, minority representatives, and Europeans, was provided for in the Aung San–Clement Attlee Agreement. The British government chose D. R. Rees-Williams to act as committee chairman and W. B. J. Ledwidge (who originally came from England as Bottomley's associate during the Panglong Conference) to act as secretary. The Burma Executive Council designated U Tin Tut, Thakin Nu, U Khin Maung Gale, and U Kyaw Nyein, the latter three representing the AFPFL. U Kyaw Nyein later was replaced by Saw Myint Thein of the Karen Youth Organization, an AFPFL affiliate organization. Representing the Frontier Areas and the minorities were the Frontier Area Councillor, his two deputies, and Saw Sawkey of the Karen National Union.[42]

As it was the agreed objective of both the British government and the Burmese who attended the London conference "to achieve the early unification of the Frontier Areas and Ministerial Burma with the free consent of the inhabitants of those areas," the mandate of the Committee of Enquiry was to find and recommend "the best method of associating the Frontier peoples with the working out of the new constitution for Burma."[43] The committee considered that its duty was to take testimony from representatives of the scheduled areas as defined in the 1935 constitution. This territory composed 47 percent of the total area of Burma and was inhabited by an estimated 2,400,000 people, 16 percent of the total

---

at which they resolved to accept the agreement and to work with the AFPFL for national unity; see New Times of Burma, March 9, 1947, p. 1. The agreement was approved by the British Parliament on April 2, 1947.

42. FACOE, 1: 18.

43. Ibid., p. 1; Aung San–Clement Attlee Agreement, op cit., p. 4.

Burmese population.⁴⁴ The major administrative units in this territory were the Federated Shan States; the Bhamo, Myitkyina, and Katha districts; the Chin and Arakan hill areas; the Salween District; and the Karenni area; the Naga Hills District; and those fringe areas of Burma proper where a large concentration of Karens lived. At the time the committee was planning its work, the Panglong Conference was held. The committee fully approved the Panglong Agreement and thought it in no way superseded its own mandate and activity.⁴⁵

After holding twenty-four public meetings in March and April, the Committee of Enquiry unanimously agreed to make certain recommendations. It based its findings on the testimony it received, although its work was hurried and its witnesses were often uncertain of their own position, mandate, and support. First, its major recommendation was that the Frontier Areas be given representation in the Constituent Assembly. In the committee's view, the Frontier Areas ought to receive forty-five delegates to the constitutional drafting assembly, not because the size of the population warranted that many, but because the areas were fragmented administratively and divided ethnically. It recommended against using normal election procedures (compiling electoral rolls, campaigning, and voting) because of the limited time before the convening of the Constituent Assembly in June, the difficulties of travel, and the general lack of familiarity of many frontier peoples with the electoral process. Second it recommended that the delegates from the hill areas have equal status with the delegates from Burma proper in the deliberations and committee assignments. Third it recommended that participation in the Constituent Assembly did not automatically commit the frontier peoples to federation with Burma proper. Fourth it recommended that no Constituent Assembly decisions regarding state governments be considered passed unless a majority of the frontier delegates joined in support.⁴⁶

44. *FACOE* 1: 2.
45. Ibid., pp. 17–18.
46. Ibid., pp. 22–26: The division of the forty-five seats: Federated Shan States (including Kokang and Mongpai), 26; Kachin Hills, 7; Chin Hills with the Arakan Hill Tracts, 6; Karenni, 2; Salween District, 2; Somra Tract, 1; and Homalin Subdivision, 1.

Testimony reflecting fears, aspirations, and crosscurrents of opinion moved the committee to make some suggestions (rather than binding recommendations) that shed light on the problems of uniting the two areas. These were intended primarily to guide the delegates to the Constituent Assembly in understanding their fellow members from the hill areas. The committee began by suggesting the creation of a federation in which the Federated Shan States and the Kachin Hills should become constituent states. It was unclear from the testimony whether the Chins wanted statehood in the proposed federation or amalgamation of their area with Burma proper.[47] Much of the confusion turned on the terminology, which was never precise and at times misleading. The word *union*, for instance, was used to mean amalgamation most of the time, and *federation* to mean the creation of a federal state; but the two were also used interchangeably, which led to some of the misunderstanding.[48]

The Karens of the Salween area also presented a confused case on this question. Their initial spokesman, Saw T. Po Ku, said that, in theory, it was possible for the Salween area peoples to form a state in a federation with Burma proper.[49] A cospokesman, Saw Chittee, said, "Constitutional questions like these are beyond our understanding. Our view, in brief, is that, if Burma gets one rupee, we want one rupee. The Karens must have equality with the Burmans. Detailed discussions are beyond us."[50] Two days later a Karen leader from Shwegyin, an area adjoining the Salween area, offered the opinion that the Karens could federate only if Burma remained in the British Commonwealth; otherwise the Karens would seek some other way of maintaining British protection.[51] A few weeks later a new delegation of Salween Karens appeared before the committee, repudiated the stàtements of Saw T. Po Ku,

47. Ibid., 2: 71–98.
48. See the exchanges between the committee and Chief Thang Tin Lien, ibid., pp. 74–75, and the Chin representatives' corrective statement of April 20, 1947, ibid., p. 85.
49. Ibid., p. 123.
50. Ibid., p. 124.
51. Ibid., pp. 126–134, the testimony of Saw Marshall Shwin.

and said the Salween Karens would be satisfied to see their area remain as a district in Burma proper.[52] The change reflected a disagreement among the Karens; the latter statement was made by the local leaders without consulting the Karen National Union (KNU), in which the educated plains Karens were the dominant group. The KNU spokesman, Thra Tha Htoo, argued before the committee that the Burma Executive Council had influenced the less sophisticated hill Karens with certain political favors in order to win their adherence to union with Burma proper, but he did not deny that his own organization had sought to influence the Salween Karens.[53]

A slightly different situation was revealed in the Kachin area. There the Burmans in the lowlands argued against the creation of the Kachin State because their territory was earmarked for inclusion in the new state. Their argument turned on the issue of losing their status as part of Burma proper. The Burman spokesman, U Saw Yi, argued that "for a very long time history relates that the Kachins have been in the Burmese nation on a friendly basis and now that Burma is to be liberated I do not see any reason why they cannot behave in the same way and come into Burma again. Since they want to be a separate state, for the same reason we want to be outside their state."[54] He called for the creation of a unitary state in preference to the proposed federal union.

This sort of testimony reflecting both absence of political sophistication and diversity of thinking in the Frontier Areas led the Committee of Enquiry to observe that

> the picture that emerged from this welter of evidence is that of a federated Burma with the federated Shan States and the Kachin Hills as two constituent States and with the Karenni States possibly another, but with Burma proper enlarged by the possible incorporation of the Chin Hills . . . the Salween District . . . should reduce the craziness of the patchwork quilt which the present administration of the Frontier Area resembles.[55]

52. Ibid., pp. 147–152, the testimony of Saw Lu Lu.
53. Ibid., pp. 152–164, the testimony of Thra Tha Htoo.
54. Ibid., p. 70, the testimony of U Saw Yi.
55. Ibid., 1: 27.

The committee went on to observe that because of the different stages of political development of the peoples of Burma it might be advisable to postpone the creation of a full-fledged federation and create instead an interim arrangement with a federal council to handle relations between Burma proper and the Frontier Areas. The council could eventually grow into a genuine federal body. The committee saw the Supreme Council of the United Hill Peoples, an institution created by the Panglong Agreement as an advisory body, as an excellent institution that could "play a part of considerable importance in advising Frontier Area States in the proposed Burma federation on subjects which are within State jurisdiction and upon which joint action on a common doctrine is desirable."[56] From the committee report it appears that it visualized the gradual drawing together of frontier states into a single body in order to deal with Burma proper as an equal, the two areas to unite in a federation after the frontier states had matured.

Throughout its period of hearings the committee heard a uniform demand for internal autonomy. There was division, however, over which subjects must be preserved for state administration and which might be transferred to the central government. The committee warned of the danger of reserving too much for the states and leaving the central government weak in dealing with the world. While it recognized a certain impropriety in determining federal and state subjects, it warned that the failure to grant power to the central government on foreign trade, interstate commerce, and federal finance would be a serious oversight.[57]

Throughout the testimony the issue of a state's right to withdraw from the proposed federal union came up repeatedly. The Chins, Kachins, Karenni, and others all demanded this protection. The Burmans from Bhamo, who were to be included in the Kachin State, were the only group to raise their voice against this right.[58] The advice of the Committee of Enquiry was "that if such right is contained in the federal constitution for Burma, it will have to be carefully limited and regulated."[59]

56. Ibid., p. 28.
57. Ibid., p. 28.
58. Ibid., 2: 67.
59. Ibid., 1: 29.

A close reading of the testimony reveals a good many other aspects of the problem of ethnic and political unity. For one thing it confirmed the continued existence of fear harbored by the Karens and Burmans over the excesses of violence each committed against the other during the war. In a memorial to the governor, Saw Marshall Shwin, president of the Shwegyin Karen Association, bluntly stated,

> The Karens of this area do not want to live among their neighbors who are by nature turbulent and rebellious who never hesitate to commit robbery and dacoity, to carry on strikes and sedition and who are prone to resort to rowdyism and hooliganism. . . . The Karens of this area went through a series of bitter experiences during the war attributable to the treachery of some of their crafty neighbors. They shall not forgive and forget the atrocities and rape committed at Papun in April and May, 1942, they shall not forget hateful measures of religious intolerance, highhandedness and barbarism committed in certain parts of the area during the Japanese occupation.[60]

Orally, a Karen representative of the KNU carried on a bitter exchange with U Tin Tut and Thakin Nu. The Karen argued that the Burmese have no goodwill toward the Karens; the Burmans responded by contending that bad elements exist among all ethnic groups and the outrages of a few should not blacken the rest. The Karen, Thra Tha Htoo, remained unconvinced and said that Burmese excesses in the past were the stumbling blocks to future unity and mutual trust:

> And this is the thing which has always been the stumbling block for the Karens in the way of accepting the will of the Burmese Government readily. They feel that this history might repeat itself, and that they might be treated badly again. Such a state of things is in the minds of the Karens. Therefore it is advisable that some definite steps should be taken to display good will toward the Karens, because we see only from our Karen point of view. The Burmese may have their own say, but according to Karens, they are very aggressive.[61]

60. Ibid., 2: 175–176.
61. Ibid., p. 168.

During the period of the hearings, the KNU presented its demands for an autonomous state in the southeast area bordering the sea and for the inclusion of Karens, equal to one-fourth the total membership, in the Executive and Legislative Councils.[62] About the same time a more moderate proposal was put forth by a delta Karen leader, Saw Johnson D. Po Min, asking for a smaller state created out of the territories of Toungoo, Salween, and the Pyinmana Hill Tract.[63] The public expressions of the Karens made it clear that they were united in their distrust of the Burmans and that this would be a barrier to their future relations. They were less united in their demands for an autonomous state, being divided on its size, location, and relationship with Burma proper.

Probably the most overt expression of faith and goodwill by a minority group toward the Burmese leaders came from the Nepali Association and the All-Burma Gurkha League. The spokesman for the Gurkhas came before the committee and requested Burma citizenship for the members of his community. They wanted not only to continue to make their home in Burma but to serve in its army and, if need be, recruit other Gurkhas in Nepal to swell the ranks of the nascent Burma armed forces.[64]

The hearings also revealed an interesting insight into the language problem. Spokesmen for Falam and Siyin Chins made a strong request that instruction in their schools be carried on in Burmese. This had been the practice prior to 1924; against their will, the colonial administration changed the language of instruction to English and the vernacular. In the new Burma, the Chins wanted Burmese restored.[65] On the other hand the Karen spokesman argued before the committee that the hill Karens did not understand any language except their own and they wanted no English or Burmese speakers as administrators; this was the practice in the past, and the people were too backward to learn other languages and unable to communicate with foreign officials who spoke the Karen dialects haltingly.

The committee served two valuable purposes: It carried out its

62. Ibid., p. 179.
63. *New Times of Burma*, March 1, 1947, p. 1.
64. FACOE, 2: 62–64.
65. Ibid., pp. 75, 80.

mandate with dispatch and it provided a forum in which all the major ethnic groups could exchange ideas, express fears and confidences, and reveal the true nature of unity in Burma. The British government approved the report of the Committee of Enquiry and accepted its recommendations "subject to such elaboration as may be found necessary to give full effect to the recommendation . . . for protecting the position of Frontier peoples in the Constituent Assembly in regard to matters of direct interest to them."[66]

---

At the time the Frontier Areas Committee of Enquiry was holding its hearings, a political struggle was taking shape in Burma proper over which group would lead Burma in fashioning its constitution. According to the Aung San–Clement Attlee Agreement the body of representatives to the Constituent Assembly would be larger than the previous legislatures under the 1935 Act. It was agreed that the Constituent Assembly would have twice as many representatives elected from the noncommunal, Karen, and Anglo-Burman constituencies. Each voter in the noncommunal and Karen constituencies would have two votes, and each voter in the Anglo-Burman constituency would have four votes.[67] Under this system it was envisaged that there would be 182 representatives elected from noncommunal, 24 from Karen, and 4 from Anglo-Burman constituencies. This, together with 45 representatives chosen from the Frontier Areas, would create a Constituent Assembly of 255 members.

The AFPFL had a clear advantage over all other groups entered in the contests. It had a national organization with well-known leaders and enjoyed the prestige of having been instrumental in winning the concessions from the British earlier in the year. In eighty-two contests for seats in the noncommunal constituencies, the AFPFL candidates stood unopposed.[68] Despite this commanding lead in automatically elected delegates, the AFPFL campaigned hard and acted as though it were faced with a real challenge.

66. New Times of Burma, May 20, 1947, p. 2.
67. Ibid., March 5, 1947.
68. Times (London), March 29, 1947, p. 3; April 9, 1947, p. 15; of the eighty-two, seventy were returned from rural constituencies and twelve from urban.

The Communist Party originally decided not to participate in the election because it opposed the Aung San–Clement Attlee Agreement. By February 27, 1947, its leaders realized that the public generally approved the agreement, so the Communists made a partial effort to reenter the AFPFL and capture its leadership. The Communist Party announced its desire to work with the AFPFL to make the election a success and prevent the Democratic National United Front of the Myochit, Mahabama, and Thakins from wrecking the agreement. On Resistance Day, March 27, the Communists joined the mammoth AFPFL rally held at the steps of Shwedagon Pagoda in an effort to revive their public image of participation in the anti-Japanese movement as a constituent member of the AFPFL.[69] The Communist Party proclaimed publicly:

> We desire to avoid all conflicts with the AFPFL in spite of disagreements over many issues and we desire to put an end to civil strifes which are likely to help the imperialists.[70]

The statement concluded by promising not to oppose the AFPFL and to contest only in those places where the Communist Party had a large majority. By election time the Communists had twenty-nine candidates in the running.[71]

Although the AFPFL did not readmit the Communist Party to its organization, it accepted as fact, without written confirmation, that a truce existed between the two organizations for the duration of the election campaign. A large part of Thakin Nu's AFPFL keynote address on Resistance Day was devoted to the roads to socialism. In Nu's view, there were two, the peaceful British way and the violent Russian one. He concluded by saying that Burma must take the road that fits existing conditions: peace rather than violence. With the Communists sharing his platform it was clear to all for whom his remarks were intended.[72]

The largest opposition groups in Burma, the Democratic National United Front and the Karen National Union, decided to boycott

69. Ibid., March 29, 1947, p. 3.
70. Burman, February 27, 1947, p. 1; Burmese Review, March 3, 1947, p. 7.
71. Times (London), March 24, 1947, p. 3.
72. Ibid., March 29, 1947, p. 3.

the election and sponsored no candidates. Although some candidates who stood as independents were affiliated with these opposition parties, they campaigned without open party support. Dr. Ba Maw, the leader of the *Mahabama*, explained his reason for keeping his party out of the election: that his organization had no power, or as he put it, "no guns":

> The people have now come to have a great belief in force. The Japanese came into Burma with the gun. The British drove them out with the gun. It is not elections which are going to decide the future of Burma, but the gun. You drove the Japanese out of Burma but you left Japanese militarism and power worship . . . we have learned that there is one freedom which counts for more, the freedom of the gun. . . . All you want in Burmese politics is to start on the winning side and to have plenty of guns.[73]

Because the Democratic National United Front had no large-scale national organization, private paramilitary force, or positions of authority, it justified its withdrawal from the election on the premise that the voting would not be honest and its supporters would be intimidated.

The Karen situation was slightly different. They were disappointed over Britain's refusal to support their demand for a separate Karen state; they also thought they would be underrepresented with 24 delegates in a body of 255 at the proposed constituent assembly. The Karen National Union, the oldest and most articulate organization among the delta Karens, refused outright to participate in the election. Rees-Williams, the chairman of the Frontier Areas Committee of Enquiry, wrote some months after his departure from Burma that Aung San had promised the KNU that the AFPFL would sponsor six Karens in the general noncommunal constituencies in order to give them thirty actual delegates. "By a foolish decision, the Karens in Ministerial Burma refused to take part in the working of the Constituent Assembly and boycotted the election."[74] Once the KNU decision was clear,

---

73. Ibid., April 12, 1947, p. 3.
74. *New Times of Burma*, September 14, 1947, p. 2 (reprinted from *Eastern World*, July 1947).

their representative in the Executive Council was forced to resign his post, and his place was taken by U San Po Thin, a Karen leader representing the Karen Youth League (KYL), an affiliate organization of the AFPFL. Eighteen KYL candidates for the Karen constituency seats were unopposed, and all were seated in the Constituent Assembly.[75] Although these delegates were young and without high standing among the Karens, they represented a new trend in Burma: the attempt to bridge communal antagonism and work cooperatively for national objectives.

The AFPFL won an overwhelming victory at the polls. Because it was unopposed in many areas and opposed by individuals rather than parties in others, it is impossible to evaluate the real strength of the AFPFL among the people. In Rangoon no more than 60 percent of the voters cast ballots, and in some city constituencies as few as 20 percent did. Heavier voting took place elsewhere, notably in Toungoo. The *Times* observer in Burma reported that the election was orderly and the election officials discharged their duties with dispatch and efficiency.[76] The final results were 173 representatives from the AFPFL, 7 from the Communist Party, 2 independents, 4 Anglo-Burmans, and 24 Karens.[77] In the light of this success Aung San's victory pronouncement was something of an understatement:

> I think the AFPFL should get a clear majority and it should not be difficult for us to come to a decision on the Constitution of Burma within a few months.[78]

The election legitimated the AFPFL claim to political leadership in Burma. Further, it demonstrated a veneer of unity among the ethnic groups in Burma by filling all the seats in the Constituent Assembly with delegates who agreed on the broad political objectives and, more important, accepted the leadership and initiative of the AFPFL. The real opposition to the AFPFL, both as leaders of the country and as the source of political ideas, forfeited their right to

75. *Times* (London), April 9, 1947, p. 5; April 14, 1947, p. 3.
76. Ibid., April 10, 1947, p. 3.
77. Ibid., June 11, 1947, p. 4.
78. Ibid., April 11, 1947, p. 3.

air their views in the coming constitutional convention by boycotting the election and leaving their followers without representation at that meeting. Although the absence of a genuine contest made it impossible to measure the relative strength of the parties, the election had the effect of confirming the AFPFL claim to national leadership. The *Times* correspondent expressed this point as follows:

> It is not easy to estimate the AFPFL's backing in this country, nor is this likely to be accurately reflected in the election results. . . . But there can be no doubt that the AFPFL is by far the strongest and most important organization in Burma today deriving its main strength from the youth of the country.[79]

With the election completed and the AFPFL's mandate confirmed, the party moved rapidly to capitalize on the sentiment for national unity that had been growing since the signing of the Aung San–Clement Attlee Agreement. Its first move was to publicize and mobilize support for its constitutional ideas. For three days, May 20–23, it held a convention attended by seven hundred delegates from the country at large. Among the participants were the members of the Supreme Council of the AFPFL, the elected AFPFL delegates to the coming constituent assembly, and representatives from the AFPFL membership at large. The convention proceedings were directed by the national leaders, Aung San, Thakin Mya, Kyaw Nyein, and others. Its major purpose was to draft a resolution embodying the fundamental constitutional principles the AFPFL delegation to the Constituent Assembly would support.[80]

A draft of the resolution was prepared prior to the convention; after its formal introduction at the party convention, it was sent to a special committee of one hundred, who were to consider and make recommendations. On May 23, the revised draft was returned

79. Ibid., April 9, 1947, p. 5.
80. Ibid., May 20, 1947, p. 3.

to the assembled delegates and unanimously approved.[81] In addition the special committee drafted a model constitution, which was also passed by the party conventions.[82]

Aung San's speech at the opening of the convention is significant because in it he argued that "it was impractical to proceed at once to a Socialist State and under present conditions, a capitalist economy could not be avoided as an intermediate stage."[83] He also is reported to have said that capitalism must be controlled and "as a preparation for State Socialism, the constitution should provide that all mineral and other wealth underground, the forests, sources of natural power, railways, ports and telecommunications were national property." The goal of the new state was to reserve the means of production either "as the property of the entire people or of the people's cooperative organization."[84] His remarks provided a limitation on the area of the economy to be socialized and a timetable for its realization. His statement was intended to dampen enthusiasm of the extremists within his organization and to divide them further from the rival Communists.

Thakin Mya devoted his remarks to a commentary on the AFPFL proposals for the new constitution and gave special attention to ethnic problems. He emphasized the fact that the decisions on the future organization of the State rested not with the AFPFL alone but with the nation as a whole:

> It is obvious also that the constitution as finally adopted, must be acceptable not only to the Burmese and Karens, but also to a substantial majority of all the races inhabiting Burma.[85]

81. Ibid., Burma, Ministry of Information, *Burma's Fight for Freedom* (Rangoon, 1948), pp. 48–49.
82. Burma, Ministry of Information, op. cit., p. 49; Maung Maung, *Burma's Constitution* (The Hague, 1959), pp. 231–250, which contains a reprint of the AFPFL draft constitution originally published in the *Burmese Review*, May 26, 1947.
83. *Times* (London), May 21, 1947, p. 3. Aung San restated some of these propositions in the closing address and expanded on others; see Silverstein, op. cit., pp. 92–100.
84. *Times* (London), May 21, 1947, p. 3.
85. Ibid.

To realize this objective, the working committee of the AFPFL made specific recommendations in the form of separate resolutions. The territories of the Federated Shan States including Kokang and Mongpai, the Karenni Hills, the Kachin Hills, and the Chin Hills excluding Kampetlet Subdivision would enter the proposed union as union states, autonomous states, or national areas, depending on whether they met the qualifications for each category.

To enter as a union state, a territory and its population must exhibit a defined geographic area with a character of its own, unity in language different from the Burmese, unity in culture, community of historical traditions, community of economic interests and a measure of economic self-sufficiency, a fairly large population, and the desire to maintain its distinct identity as a separate unit.[86] To protect large ethnic minorities living in these and other territories, the resolution proposed that

> whereas such rights of national minorities as i) human rights, ii) national and cultural, iii) freedom of association with cultural autonomy, iv) due representation in the legislature, shall be guaranteed to a group of citizens who differ from the majority in race, language, culture and historical traditions and form at least one-tenth of the population of the unit concerned.[87]

To knit the union together the committee proposed the creation of a bicameral legislature at the national level. In the Chamber of Nationalities, members representing "Burma, union states, autonomous states, national areas and national minorities" would be united.[88]

This was the first time the AFPFL made a specific federal proposal. Previously it had talked of a federal union in which the states would enjoy certain rights and privileges, but it never expressed its ideas in detail. These resolutions embodied most of the suggestions made by the Frontier Areas Committee of Enquiry and the Panglong Agreement, and they were intentionally designed to allay minority fears or misgivings about their future in an independent

---

86. New Times of Burma, May, 21, 1947, p. 1.
87. Ibid., p. 5.
88. Ibid.

state. The guarantee to national minorities, which formed one-tenth of the area's population, was intended to meet the demands of the Karens in Burma proper and to assure them that the majority ethnic group, the Burmans, had no intention of "Burmanizing" or mistreating them. This federal scheme was the AFPFL's solution to the problem of guaranteeing ethnic and cultural diversity while at the same time uniting the people in a workable political organization.

The resolutions of the working committee were considered by a special committee of about one hundred.[89] It reported to the convention at large on May 23, 1947. Thakin Mya again acted as rapporteur; in the course of his remarks he gave the assembled delegates further information on the proposed federal institutions. He announced that there would be a cabinet seat created for a minister of nationalities, chosen from the members of the Chamber of Nationalities, who would represent a union or autonomous state, a national area, or a national minority. The proposed Chamber of Nationalities "shall consist of 160 members comprising 32 from the Shan States, 13 from the Kachins, 9 from the Chin States, 4 from the Karenni, 32 Karen representatives and 70 from the remaining territories including Burma."[90] Thus it was the intent of the AFPFL to give recognition to the minorities in both the national government and the legislature. The cabinet ministership provided them with a voice in the national executive; the permanent majority of one in the legislature assured them collectively of the means to protect their interests against the majority ethnic group.

As a further concession the special committee eliminated an indirect reference to Burma as a Buddhist nation by substituting "Our beloved land" for the working committee's "Land of Pagodas."[91] This was in deference to the Christian and Muslim communities, which composed important minorities in Burma. Also as a concession to the Karens, the new resolution provided for the

89. This special committee was reported to number 91 in ibid., p. 6; 101 in the *Burman*, May 21, 1947, p. 1; and 111 in Maung Maung, op. cit., pp. 83, 231.
90. *New Times of Burma*, May 24, 1947, p. 6.
91. In the original resolution, Section 12 read "This Land of Pagodas attains its rightful and honorable place in the world. . . ."

creation of a Karen affairs council to "aid and advise the Union Government on matters relating to the Karens."[92] This was the only such council proposed and was offered in view of the fact that Karens in the delta would not be able to form their own state because of their permanent position as a minority there. The resolution made no distinction among peoples in granting basic civil, political, and religious rights. The model draft constitution drawn up after the resolution was unanimously approved by the assembled delegates included a right of secession.[93]

In three days the AFPFL succeeded in focusing the nation's attention on the deliberations of the convention, broadcasting its ideas on the proposed constitution, and providing the people of Burma with a model constitution. While it united public opinion behind its determined leadership, it gave its critics and opponents a target to attack. Criticism was raised by Ba Maw, who called a press conference after the convention closed and sought to muster the dissident elements behind his leadership. He said the AFPFL constitutional proposals sought to institutionalize national disunity. Opening his argument with a broad statement that "Burma's chief strength has always been her remarkable unity," he proceeded to the main point of his attack by saying,

> Present day realities have only increased the impulse and the need for still more unity. Under the British, the communal question appeared as the first crack in the unity of the country. That this crack . . . could disappear by itself was proved during the war. But now the British are leaving it seems that in place of a communal question, there is to be a multi-national one. Burma will be not one but many nations, kept balanced and apart by the Constitution itself.[94]

Ba Maw's criticism was quickly answered in the press. The *New Times of Burma* said in an editorial,

---

92. *New Times of Burma*, May 24, 1947, p. 1; Burma, Ministry of Information, op. cit., pp. 49–57.
93. Maung Maung, op. cit., p. 245.
94. *Burman*, May 27, 1947, p. 1.

We do not quite fathom the motive or reason for Dr. Ba Maw's statement . . . unless [he] would wish to convince us that the "one blood, one voice, and one command" shibboleth of the occupation days has not done much to create a multi-national question to which he has referred.

We need not rip up old wounds to recall the harm done by this essentially fascist slogan to alienate the sympathy and love of the Shans and the other people of the Frontier Areas during the Japanese occupation. But now when this unity among the peoples of Burma has been achieved by the free will, mutual understanding and cooperation of all the peoples of Burma there is no reason to be unduly apprehensive about the appearance of a multi-national problem. The Chamber of Nationalities is an effective guarantee against such eventualities.[95]

In many ways the debate between Ba Maw and the *New Times of Burma* is an extension of the differences of opinion entertained by him and the AFPFL during the war. From the beginning the AFPFL sought to build ethnic and political unity by giving recognition and protection to ethnic, cultural, and political differences. Ba Maw, on the other hand, rejected both the initial premise of ethnic diversity and the tactic of institutionalizing apparent differences. Arguing that the peoples of Burma were fundamentally one, Ba Maw worked during the war toward the removal of barriers separating peoples rather than the strengthening of them. Although Ba Maw's present argument found little support, the question of what constituted the basis of national unity in Burma was settled neither by the AFPFL convention resolutions nor in the Constituent Assembly that followed.

---

The final stage in the struggle for independence and political unity that began in June was realized three months later. On June 9, the members of the Constituent Assembly gathered in Rangoon to hear the inaugural address of Thakin Mya, and they began their deliberations on June 16. For the next three months the delegates made steady progress, and on September 24, 1947, they ap-

95. *New Times of Burma*, May 28, 1947, p. 2.

proved unanimously the new constitution for an independent Burma. The only shadow over this historic meeting was the assassination of Aung San, Thakin Mya, and five other key leaders on July 19, 1947. It occurred while the assembly was in recess and robbed the nation of its leaders at a crucial point in the nation's march to independence. Only the quick actions of the governor in appointing a new council and of the police in apprehending the assassins prevented further tragic consequences in the wake of the political murders. Although Aung San, Thakin Mya, and the others died before independence was realized, the course they plotted was adhered to by their successors and their goals were achieved on schedule.

On June 9, 1947, all the delegates to the Constituent Assembly except those from the Karenni area gathered in formal session.[96] The highlight of the first day's meeting was Thakin Mya's address. Although brief, it dealt in large part with the issue of national unity. Unlike the official AFPFL pronouncements advocating unity in diversity, Thakin Mya's argument was much closer to Ba Maw's statement criticizing the AFPFL constitutional resolution. He said it augured well that at this historic convention representatives from all parts of the land were participating, "picking up again the thread of our rightful destiny sharing in the shaping of the common future of our country and associating with each other in laying down the foundation of a new and re-united Burma." He stressed the points that differences between the peoples of Burma were "superficial," that "hardly any nation was more homogenous" than Burma, that "economically and geographically our country is an indivisible unit," and that the ethnic and political differences were the product of "a century of foreign rule." From this he concluded that if the peoples of Burma could "rise above the narrow sectarian spirit of mutual suspicion and distrust" their delegates could write a constitution acceptable to all and the people could build a "great and united nation."[97]

96. The Karenni area delegates were still undecided on the question of joining the future union of Burma.
97. *Burman*, June 11, 1947, p. 2; Burma, Ministry of Information, op. cit., pp. 91–92.

Thakin Mya's speech made clear that even within the highest ranks of the AFPFL there were those who believed it better to emphasize the unities among the peoples, to give an idealized version of what everyone in the League wanted Burma to be, than to stress the diversity and disunity of a great deal of Burma's history.

On June 16, the delegates settled down to the important task of drafting the constitution. They elected the permanent officers and formal committees, and appointed the special advisors who were coopted by the membership in the preceding week. To open the formal session Aung San moved a 7-point resolution embodying the constitutional principles in the AFPFL resolution. The first point dealt with the issue of Burma's political future: It was resolved that the new constitution proclaim the country an independent sovereign republic to be known as the Union of Burma.[98] In his commentary on the resolution, Aung San said that "if the transfer is not effected peacefully and through negotiation we shall then resort to other means."[99] To the representatives of the Frontier Areas he offered the alternatives of joining the new union or aligning themselves with British imperialism.[100] Despite Aung San's defiant words there was no disagreement among the delegates on this issue, nor was there any real surprise among the British in Burma or England. The AFPFL had supported this position throughout the postwar period and was taking this opportunity to state it officially.

The other six points were also significant. It was resolved that the "Union shall comprise such units as shall be specified by the Constitution" and the extent of their autonomy "shall be defined in the Constitution." Further it was resolved "that the Constitution shall provide adequate safeguards for minorities."[101] These two provisions signified an important shift in AFPFL thinking on the minority and federal question. In the 14-point AFPFL convention resolution the authors defined three categories of constituent polit-

98. Burma, Ministry of Information, op. cit., p. 93; *Times* (London), June 17, 1947, p. 3; *New Times of Burma*, June 16, 1947, p. 1.
99. *Times* (London), June 17, 1947, p. 3.
100. Ibid.
101. Burma, Ministry of Information, op. cit., p. 93.

ical units, laid down seven qualifications for statehood, and specified the rights to be guaranteed to the minorities. The absence of these specific qualifications and guarantees suggests that the thinking of the AFPFL leaders had undergone important changes that corresponded with the views put forward by Thakin Mya in his opening address, although the available public record provides no explanation.

The remaining provisions of the Aung San resolution were as follows: All power originates from the people; all peoples of Burma are guaranteed justice, equality, and freedom of speech, religion, assembly, and action; Burma's territorial integrity shall be maintained according to justice and international law; Burma accepts its responsibility to work for peace and friendship with the other sectors of the world.

On June 17, the members of the assembly debated and voted on the Aung San resolution. Prior to the vote, spokesmen for the Frontier Areas expressed their satisfaction with the ideas incorporated in the proposal. The sawbwa of Yaunghwe, speaking for the Shan chiefs, said that it "brought equality to all indigenous races of Burma without discrimination." He assured Aung San that the peoples of the frontier "had no intention of returning to the darkness." Mahn Ba Khaing, a Karen member of the governor's Executive Council, supported it in behalf of his people. Sima Duwa Sinwa Nawng, speaking for the Kachins, approved the resolution and added that "if after freedom is obtained and then the freedom of the Kachins were impaired, then we Kachins will fight the Burmese and appoint our own King if necessary."[102] With one voice the delegates adopted the resolution and moved to the next order of business: drafting the constitution on the basis of the resolution. A constitutional committee of seventy-five was appointed to draft the document and present it at the next session of the assembly. The committee divided itself into numerous subgroups, and the main Constituent Assembly adjourned until July 29, 1947.

Between the adjournment and the final approval of the constitution on September 24, the leaders of Burma proper, the Frontier

---

102. New Times of Burma, June 17, 1947, p. 1.

Areas, and the other minorities negotiated on the extent of state powers, the nature of Union–state relations, and the physical area of the separate states. The first to agree on their future status were the Chins. Their delegation of seven approved the inclusion of the Chin Hills as a special district of Burma proper and not as a separate state. They announced that they looked to the Burmans for assistance in the development of their area and they wanted new schools in their district in which Burmese would be the language of instruction.[103]

The Shans and Kachins did not want to submerge themselves and demanded the status of semiautonomous states. After extended negotiation, it was agreed to create one Shan state out of several states existent under British rule. In the new state, no separate elected legislature was provided for; instead it was agreed that the elected members to the Union legislature would form a state council with legislative powers and that the head of the new state would have a second role as minister for the state in the Union cabinet.[104]

The Kachins also gained the status of a state. Their territory was created by joining the Myitkyina and Bhamo districts. Their political organization was similar to that created for the Shan State except that in order to protect the large non-Kachin minority in their area it was agreed that, although the head of the state would be a Kachin, not less than one-half of the state ministers will be non-Kachins.[105] It was also provided that one-half of the Kachin seats in the Chamber of Nationalities be reserved for non-Kachins. A local paper commenting on this solution said,

> The net result of these safeguards is that the successful government of the Kachin State can be the result only of good will and cooperation between the Kachins and non-Kachins of the State.[106]

Negotiations with the Karens were more difficult, and no real agreement on a specific state emerged. The Burmese leaders were

103. Ibid., June 27, 1947, p. 1.
104. Times (London), August 16, 1947, p. 3.
105. Ibid., August 18, 1947, p. 3.
106. New Times of Burma, January 16, 1948, p. 2.

willing to have a Karen state created out of the Salween District, the Karenni States, and the Toungoo hill area. The Karen delegates objected on two counts: It did not include the larger population of Karens living intermingled with other ethnic groups in the delta, and it was not viable economically.[107] Further, without the participation of delegates from the Karenni area, it was impossible to get their views on and their approval of any settlement of the future of their territories. The deadlock was resolved temporarily when Thakin Nu suggested that the Constituent Assembly leave the Karen State undefined and insert a provision in the constitution that would permit such a state to be created "as soon as agreement can be reached between the Karen territories and the Karens of Burma generally."[108]

The long-awaited Karenni delegation took its seats at the final meeting of the assembly. It was empowered to unite their territory with the new Union of Burma if they were granted the status of a constituent state.[109] This was agreed and the areas of Kantarawaddy, Bawlake, and Kyebogyi were joined to form the Karenni State with the same rights and privileges as the Shan State. Although the *Times* called the federal solution ingenious,[110] there were many in Burma who showed far less enthusiasm. The assembly decision to accord the Karens special representation in the Union legislature and to create a special adminstrative unit to handle Karen affairs until a final Karen settlement was obtained found little enthusiasm among the Karen leaders outside the AFPFL.

One other minority was not satisfied with the federal solution and the specific guarantees provided in the constitution. The In-

107. *Times* (London), August 16, 1947, p. 3.
108. Ibid.
109. The Karenni delegates, originally chosen to represent their area, never participated in the Constituent Assembly. According to the *Times* (London), September 24, 1947, p. 3, the delegation was recalled after the Constituent Assembly voted unanimously to prohibit their attendance. In response to this, a mass meeting was held in the Karenni area [place and time unspecified] and new delegates were named. They were sent to Rangoon with instructions to join the Karenni territory with the new Union. See also *New Times of Burma*, September 24, 1947, p. 1.
110. *Times* (London), September 25, 1947, p. 5.

dians were not represented at the Constituent Assembly. Neither the Aung San–Clement Attlee Agreement nor the Frontier Areas Committee of Enquiry made provision for them or recommended their inclusion in the assembly as a separate ethnic unit. Just prior to the historic meeting, the All-Burma India Youth League held a conference and called on the leaders of the AFPFL "to put right the patent injustice in restricting the political and cultural rights of the Indians resident in Burma, who take Burma as their home."[111] They demanded all fundamental rights granted to other citizens of Burma "including the right to have cultural autonomy in respect to expression, association and education." If these were granted the Indians pledged "to be the first to fight attempts at separation and disruption of Indo-Burmese unity."[112] Because the constitution as drafted made no special provision for the Indian minority in Burma, the governor of Burma thought it necessary to issue a statement on the future of the Indian in Burma. In addition to affirming that the Indian was welcome as a citizen of Burma and was protected by the fundamental rights guaranteed to all classes and individuals, it added that

> It will also be the especial care of the Government to look after the interests of the minority communities and though no seats have been reserved for the Burmese Indian community in either House of the Legislature the Government has no doubt that the political parties will take particular care to afford members of the community with equal opportunity of other races in securing representation in Parliament and in securing political office. The Government takes this opportunity of recording their appreciation of the decision of the Burma Indian community not to seek any particular constitutional privilege or protection.[113]

In their treatment of the various minorities both within and without Burma proper, the Burmese political leaders sought to gain political unity in two ways. With particular indigenous minorities such as the Chins, the new constitution erased the rigid political

111. *New Times of Burma*, May 28, 1947, p. 6.
112. Ibid.
113. *Times* (London), September 26, 1947, p. 3.

and ethnic boundaries and sought to provide the institutions whereby it would be possible to assimilate and integrate them with the majority Burmans. With other indigenous minorities such as the Shans, Kachins, and Karens, the new constitution provided various degrees of political and cultural autonomy and special status and sought to provide unity by guaranteeing diversity. If this dual and contradictory solution did not prove perfect, it did satisfy a majority of the people concerned and made it appear that national unity had been achieved.

As a symbol of the new Union, the Constituent Assembly chose a new flag. Composed of a red field and blue canton with six white stars, the flag represented both the struggle for independence and the unity of the five largest ethnic groups—Burmans, Chins, Kachins, Karens, and Shans—symbolized by the five stars clustered around a larger sixth star representing the Union.[114]

The tragic assassination of the key political leaders and architects of Burma's independence provided the opportunity to demonstrate the new unity. While the governor raised a Burman, Thakin Nu, to the office of chief councillor, the Constituent Assembly elevated a Shan chief to its presidency and made it possible for him to serve as the first president of the independent Union of Burma. Thakin Nu took the occasion of the election of the *sawbwa* of Mongpai as the president of the Constituent Assembly to point out that this act of the assembly was proof of the mutual respect and understanding among the ethnic groups. He was reported to have said that it marked the end of the old divide-and-rule policy of the British that had kept the peoples of Burma apart and that it answered the insinuation from abroad that the Burmese were oppressors of the frontier peoples.[115]

The constitution that welded Burma into a political union was adopted unanimously on September 24, 1947. Even the Communist members of the assembly voted for the draft, although they went on record as not in full accord with all of its provisions.[116] But the unity symbolized by the constitution was untested, and its political

114. Ibid., August 2, 1947, p. 3.
115. New Times of Burma, July 31, 1947, p. 1.
116. Times (London), September 25, 1947, p. 3.

THE STRUGGLE FOR POLITICAL UNITY, 1946–1948          133

solutions were unacceptable to many of the leaders and groups that had not participated in the assembly. A large portion of the delta Karens refused to accept its provisions for their future status. Some Arakanese and Mon political leaders expressed their dissatisfaction that their areas were not given statehood. By November 1947, the Communist Party of Than Tun found reason to disagree with the final treaty settlement between Burma and Great Britain, and negotiations between the Communists and the AFPFL to reunite were broken off.[117]

None of these developments dampened the ardor and enthusiasm of the AFPFL and the people who gave it their support. The Union of Burma as an independent federal state became a reality on January 4, 1948. The optimism and hope of the moment was best expressed in the Independence Day message of Sao Shwe Thaike, the president of the Union:

> Today is for us not only a day of freedom but also a day of reunion. For a long time, the principal races of Burma, the Mon-Arakanese, Burmese, the Karens, the Shan and the Kachins and the Chins have tended to look upon themselves as separate national units. Of late, a nobler vision, the vision of a Union of Burma, has moved our hearts, and we stand united today as one nation determined to work in unity and concord for the advancement of Burma's interests and for the speedy attainment of her due position as one of the great nations of the world. It is unity which has brought our struggle for independence to this early fruition and may unity continue to be the watchword for every member of the Sovereign Independent Republic to be henceforth known as the Union of Burma.[118]

117. Ibid., November 19, 1947, p. 3.
118. Burma, Ministry of Information, op. cit., p. 5.

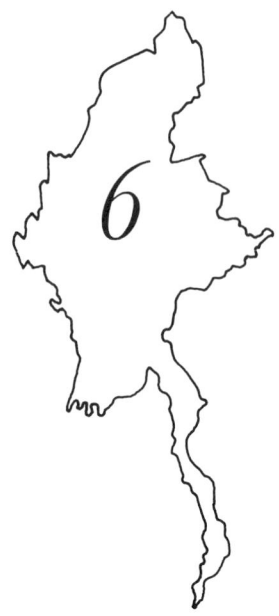

# 6

# Aung San and U Nu

Between 1945 and 1948, two men, Aung San and U Nu, guided the destiny of the nationalist movement and the peaceful struggle for independence. In so doing, each contributed to the nation's thought and helped shape the nation's institutions. Up to a point their careers and goals were very similar. Both fought to establish an independent Burma and to include all the ethnic minorities in the new state; both differed, however, on the meaning of the term *national unity* and on methods for realizing it. The differences between them are in part explained by the different historical situations each found. While Aung San's life was cut short at the moment when Burma was about to achieve peaceful independence, U Nu continued to lead Burma until 1962—with two brief periods out of office—and therefore had the greater impact upon transforming promises and theory into practice.

U Aung San and U Nu were neither political philosophers nor original thinkers in the sense of having constructed new theoretical political systems. Instead they were very practical individuals whose immediate concern was to find a workable mold into which the diverse desires and goals of the nationalist groups could be channeled and blended. The product of their thought indicates an eclectic approach to ideas and a pragmatic approach to politics. With the exception of their shared adherence to the twin ideas of independence and national unity, no idea or goal was beyond revision or replacement. By cooperating and not competing with each other, they guided the nationalist struggle; at the death of Aung San, Nu succeeded to the leadership, providing a smooth transition that gave the appearance of an unbroken continuation of all the policies and ideas of the movement. Yet Nu then brought his own ideas to the fore and poured a new content into many he had inherited from Aung San. Thus, while the phrases and slogans remained the same, their meanings did not. This is one of the causes of the confusion and misunderstanding that later undermined national unity in Burma.

---

Although Aung San has been dead since 1947, his name and influence still remain extremely important in contemporary Burma. During the 1956 election his picture was used as a political symbol by rival groups; his name was constantly invoked by all parties and candidates to buttress their appeals. Since independence his picture has been displayed alongside that of the current Union president in every government office and in most places of business throughout the nation. With a main thoroughfare and a public park in Rangoon named for him and with a national holiday to commemorate his assassination and that of his colleagues, Aung San is a living symbol in contemporary life. Yet despite his importance no official or authoritative biography exists and no collection of his speeches, writings, and public papers has been compiled.[1] Thus

1. The material on Aung San in this chapter is drawn largely from his collection of speeches and from an autobiographical essay published in mimeograph form while he was still alive. Although the volume was unedited and uncorrected, it is the only available public record of this man. According to Kyaw Sein, a former comrade-in-arms during the war and until nationalization the proprietor of the People's Literature House in Rangoon, the AFPFL planned, in 1956, to publish a complete volume of Aung San's papers and speeches but, to date, it has not appeared. Aung San's volume is entitled *Burma's Challenge 1946* (n.p., n.d.); it has been reprinted in Josef Silverstein (ed.), *The Political Legacy of Aung San* (Ithaca, 1972), pp. 40–

it is difficult to separate the man from the growing body of myths.

From his autobiographical essay it is clear that Aung San thought of himself as middle class and modern. He described himself as "a son of well-to-do gentry and a distinguished line of patriotic ancestors."[2] His education began in vernacular schools and ended in the University of Rangoon. He considered himself a student "with promise of a brilliant academic career" who allowed student and national politics to interfere and finally displace his scholarly interests and pursuits.[3] His major studies at the university included English literature, modern history, and political science. After earning a bachelor's degree, he studied law for a short while.[4] It is clear that this background in the Western liberal tradition was a major source of his ideas; its influence can be detected in his later proposals for the constitution of independent Burma.

His political activity put him in contact with the nationalist movements of two countries, Burma and India. Here he came in contact with Marxist thinkers and some of the Marxist literature. His political career at the university included participation and leadership in the 1936 students strike and in the formation of the All-Burma Students' Union. This activity projected him into national prominence and brought him an appointment by the government to a committee created to consider amendments to the University Act.

Nineteen thirty-eight marked his final transition from student to political life. In that year he joined the *Dobama Asiayone* ("We Burmans Society") and became its secretary-general. In the following two years he served on the Working Committee of the All-Burma Peasants' League and helped organize the Freedom Bloc, an organization that combined a wing of *Dobama Asiayone* with

---

100. Other sources are extremely meager. The best two are W. D. Sutton, Jr., "U Aung San of Burma," *South Atlantic Quarterly* 47 (1948): 1–16; and Maurice Collis, *Last and First in Burma* (London, 1956), pp. 133–135, 232 and passim. Neither of these attempt to examine the ideas of Aung San. For a series of appreciative essays by Aung San's former comrades in arms, see Maung Maung, *Aung San of Burma* (The Hague, 1962).

2. Aung San, op. cit., p. 1.
3. Ibid.
4. Ibid.

Ba Maw's *Sinyetha* ("Poor Man's") Party. In 1939 he was arrested for "conspiring to overthrow the Government by force" but was released without prosecution. In the next year the British authorities sought to arrest him again, this time for being a subversive, but they failed to find him.[5]

Aung San escaped arrest the second time by going to India and participating as an official delegate in the Ramgarh meeting of the Indian National Congress; later he traveled about the country and returned secretly to Burma where he helped to organize the Rangoon University Students' Union campaign against the war and imperialism. His friends prevailed on him to leave the country in order to avoid certain arrest; he went to China to seek foreign aid for his anti-imperialist activities. At the International Settlement at Amoy he was intercepted by Japanese agents and taken to their country, where he was drawn into the planning for invasion and subversion of the colonial government in Burma.

Through his work in the *Dobama Asiayone* he became closely associated with such Marxists as Thakin Soe, Ba Hein, and Than Tun and began his informal study of Marxism; through his work in the Freedom Bloc he became thoroughly acquainted with the peasant socialism of Ba Maw. During the Japanese occupation he joined with Thakin Soe, Than Tun, and other Communists and with Thakin Mya, Kyaw Nyein, and other socialists of the secret People's Revolutionary Party and organized the Resistance Movement against the Japanese.[6] During this latter period he temporarily joined the Communist Party but later withdrew. He described the interlude as follows:

> When I met Thakin Soe secretly in August 1944 to hammer out the anti-Japanese movement and organization, he urged me to join the Communist Party with him. I agreed to join it finally but left it afterwards as I disagreed with some of his views and with his sectarianism and other incidents relating to him. I have still a genuine interest in Communism and the Communist Party.[7]

5. Ibid., p. 2.
6. Ibid., pp. 2, 8; "Resistance Movement," in Aung San, op cit., p. 9.
7. *Burman*, March 9, 1946, p. 1.

From those who knew him during the last two years of his life, more details can be added to this picture of Aung San. Gen. Slim, the commander of the British Fourteenth Army, met Aung San in the field in 1945 and appraised him as follows:

> I was impressed by Aung San . . . I judged him to be a genuine patriot and a well balanced realist. . . . The greatest impression he made on me was his honesty. He was not free with glib assurances and he hesitated to commit himself, but I had the idea that if he agreed to do something he would keep his word.[8]

Maurice Collis, a former British civil servant in Burma and a noted writer, met Aung San in 1947. He had previously drawn an impression of the man from his examination of Governor Dorman-Smith's papers, which he was using in the preparation of a study on wartime Burma. Collis writes that from Dorman-Smith's papers Aung San emerges as a shy and quiet person who was terribly lonely; he accepted the informal friendship and warmth extended to him by the governor, even though they were political rivals.[9] Collis himself met and observed Aung San at a moment when the Burmese leader was celebrating the signing of the Aung San–Clement Attlee Agreement. He noted Aung San's poise and assurance and remarked that his reserve had thawed; "he was genial and gay."[10]

The change in Aung San's personality and the growth of his self-confidence as the nation's leader can be detected from his speeches. Speaking on the role of leadership in general and his own contribution to the Burmese nationalist movement in particular, Aung San said in 1946, "No man, however great, can alone set the wheels of history in motion."[11] He went on to say that, with the backing of the people, leaders can do remarkable things including the alteration of the general course of history. Considering his own role in Burma at that moment, he said, "We have an arduous way to traverse before we reach our goal. And you want me to pilot you safely to that journey's end. I cannot thank you easily for that

---

8. William Slim, *Defeat into Victory* (London, 1956), p. 519.
9. Collis, op. cit., p. 270.
10. Collis, op. cit., p. 287.
11. "Problems for Burma's Freedom," in Aung San, op. cit., pp. 6–7.

gesture of trust and confidence . . . I cannot dangle any promise of speedy results or sudden windfalls of millenium before you."[12]

When he returned triumphantly from England in February 1947 and demanded public support for the agreement he had worked out with the British, he suggested the power one man had had in altering history's course:

> And was it not I who pulled Burma out of the stage in which she was neither held in regard by men nor respected by dogs, to the level of a nation whose affairs have attracted the attention of the world? . . . From the day we took office in the Government you must have seen that I have, as is well-known to the country, worked in the interests of the country. And now I have made a success of the job, securing the establishment of a Constituent Assembly, the investment of powers to the Interim Government and the principle of granting to the Frontier Areas the same rights and privileges that we enjoy. . . . I will assure freedom for Burma within a year.[13]

This is the man who led Burma to the threshold of self-government and who put his stamp on the nation's thought about the character of Burmese nationalism and the idea of national unity.

---

Aung San's conception of national unity follows from his ideas on nationalism. When asked to define nationalism he said,

> In my view . . . every nation in the world must be free not only externally but internally. That is to say . . . every nation in the world being a conglomeration of races and religions should develop such a nationalism as is compatible with the welfare of one and all, irrespective of race or religion or class or sex. That's my nationalism.[14]

By this he did not mean a strictly plural society with groups living in a common territory yet in little or no contact. Rather, as he saw it, nationalism meant sharing a common life, the development of

12. Ibid., p. 2.
13. *Burman*, February 6, 1947, p. 1.
14. *New Times of Burma*, December 10, 1946, p. 4.

common interests, the use of a common language, and the growth of a feeling of community "which gives us a consciousness of oneness and the necessity of oneness."[15]

Further, he held that nationalism was a dynamic concept, "ever changing in form and content."[16] Thus he argued that the goals and meaning of nationalism in the prewar period were no longer valid in the postwar period. The need for social harmony between ethnic groups had been one of his chief concerns during the war, and that experience conditioned his thoughts about the new Burma he and others hoped to create after independence. Throughout the postwar period Aung San pleaded with his followers not to interpret Burmese nationalism narrowly; it could only result in ugly consequences.[17]

From this view of nationalism it is clear that national unity was a vital problem for the peoples of Burma. On more than one occasion he said that national unity meant "unity of the entire people, irrespective of race, religion, sex and sectarian and party interests, in action and not in words for national tasks and objectives."[18] While each group would retain the basic elements of its historical identity and some of its interests, "on national questions, they should and must come together and work together without sectarianism in the affair."[19]

Aung San's idea of unity in diversity was the basis for the answers he gave to many of the problems that came to him. In a report to the Executive Committee of the AFPFL in November 1946, he criticized the feudal administration in the Shan States as being "out of date";[20] yet he qualified his remark as a personal opinion and said "it was a matter really for the Shans themselves and others in like manner to decide for themselves."[21] In a report to the nation delivered just prior to his departure for the second Panglong Conference, he stated that "the affairs of the Frontier

15. "Problems for Burma's Freedom," op cit., p. 13.
16. Ibid., p. 12.
17. Ibid., p. 13.
18. Ibid., p. 21.
19. Ibid.
20. *New Times of Burma*, November 2, 1946, p. 2.
21. Ibid.

Areas are the concern of the peoples of those areas. If they declare they want the same rights and privileges as ourselves, they will get them."[22] He restated this position at the conference by saying, "The Hill People would be allowed to administer their own areas in any way they pleased and the Burmese would not interfere in their internal administration."[23] Thus, in practice as well as in theory, Aung San stood for local autonomy and diversity for groups that wanted to retain their difference.

Aung San looked upon the Anglo-Burmans as different from the other minorities in Burma, and for them he had a slightly different prescription. He called on them to submerge their separateness from the majority ethnic group and identify themselves with the people and the coming new state. In an address to the Anglo-Burmans he said,

> Let me be perfectly frank with you, your community in the past did not happen to identify yourselves with national activities; on the other hand, you were frequently on the other side. Now you have to prove that you want to live and be with this country by words and deeds. So far as I am concerned, I am perfectly willing to embrace you as my own sisters and brothers.[24]

To the Chinese and Indians who made Burma their home, he offered a place in the new society. In his address, "Problems for Burma's Freedom," he said that he harbored no ill will or bitterness toward either group. He said it was up to them to choose whether or not to join the indigenous peoples in creating a new state, but choose they must "and choose once and for all whether they want to be our friends or foes."[25] To the Indians in particular he said, "We have no axe to grind, we nature [sic] no feeling of racial bitterness and ill-will."[26]

22. *Burman*, February 6, 1947, p. 1.
23. *New Times of Burma*, February 11, 1947, p. 1.
24. "An Address to the Anglo-Burmans," in Aung San, op. cit., p. 3; *New Times of Burma*, December 10, 1946, p. 4.
25. "Problems for Burma's Freedom," op. cit., p. 11; see also *Burman*, January 26, 1946, p. 2.
26. "Welcome India," in Aung San, op. cit., p. 3.

In Aung San's view there was even a place for Europeans in the new Burma. Should they wish to remain in Burma after independence, "we will offer our hand in friendship but relations cannot definitely be on the present basis of master and servant. It must be only on terms of equality."[27]

By the time the AFPFL congress met in May 1947, before the Constituent Assembly, Aung San had worked out his ideas on how the minorities and the majority should be combined in the new state. He opened his address to the delegates by suggesting a set of principles as a basis for the new constitution, among them the principle that "various national minorities must be able to enjoy proper rights due to them."[28] He then turned to Josef Stalin's *Marxism and the National and Colonial Question* for a precise definition of a nation and for the criteria for determining a nation and a national minority.[29] He suggested that the constitution establish areas with varying degrees of political autonomy depending on how close they came to meeting Stalin's criteria for nationhood.[30] From his own study of the minorities he concluded that, in addition to the majority group, only the Shans could be classified as a nation, for they had a territory; were a race; had a language; were sustained by a separate economic base; and had common interests, culture, and traditions.[31] The remaining identifiable groups he classified as national minorities that had racial differences from each other and from the Burman majority; had separate languages, culture, and traditions; and formed at least 10 percent of the total population. They lacked a separate economic base. To unite these separate ethnic groups and the Burman majority, he called for the establishment of a union "with properly regulated provisions as

27. "Problems for Burma's Freedom," op cit., p. 11.
28. "Address at the Convention Held at Jubilee Hall, Rangoon, the 23rd May 1947," in Aung San, op cit., pp. 3–4; hereafter "Address at the Convention."
29. Ibid., pp. 6–8.
30. Josef Stalin, *Marxism and the National and Colonial Question* (London, 1942), p. 8: "A Nation is a historically evolved, stable community of language, territory, economic life, and psychological make-up manifested in a community or culture."
31. "Address at the Convention," op cit., p. 6.

should be made to safeguard the rights of the National Minorities."[32] He went on to explain,

> We must take care that "united we stand" and not united we fall. The sort of union which Lenin deprecates with its parts contradictory to the whole—would be quite impossible. It must be a union which can develop its economy unitedly.[33]

He explained to his listeners what he meant by the idea of economic unity. The central government must control, through nationalization, the major means of production, transport, natural resources, and communications. His goal was to prohibit the establishment of capitalism under which private owners manipulated "business as they please and [reestablish] the old evils of monopoly and exploitation." This, he said, would not be socialism because Burma's economic position was then such that socialism would be by no means possible. Burma, he said, was in a precapitalist stage; therefore more private enterprise had to develop—but its development would have to be controlled. Land, he argued, must be given to the people in order to end landlordism. Ultimately the state must nationalize it, but until that was possible it was necessary to "strive to enable every tiller to have his own land."[34]

> The economic plan which I've outlined although not entirely free of capitalism is not capitalist, neither does it attain socialization. It is somewhere betwixt and between. I call it New Democracy.[35]

On religious freedom and the separation of church and state, Aung San held a consistent view drawn from the Western liberal tradition. At the AFPFL congress before the Constituent Assembly, he stated categorically that "in politics there is no room for religion in as much as there should be no insistence that the President of the Republic should be a Buddhist or that a Minister of Religion

32. Ibid., p. 8.
33. Ibid.
34. Ibid., p. 4.
35. Ibid., p. 5.

should be appointed to the Cabinet."[36] Those, he said, who made "a fine point of these issues are saboteurs; against them we must fight if the unity is not to be doomed."[37]

His ideas on the separation of church and state had been expressed before. In his address, "Problems for Burma's Freedom," Aung San declared that religion was a matter of individual conscience. Politics, he said, "must see that the individual also has his rights including the right to the freedom of religious worship. But here we must stop and draw the line definitely between politics and religion."[38] Clearly he sought to avoid the unnecessary creation of tensions in a society in which a large Karen Christian minority and a smaller Burmese–Indian Muslim minority shared common territory with the Burmese Buddhist majority.

Aung San did not go beyond these limited suggestions in answering the question of how national unity, predicated on preserving ethnic, cultural, and religious pluralism, could be established. The 7-point resolution he offered was broad and vague, leaving it to the members of the Constituent Assembly to work out the details of the exact nature of the federal union. Assassination prevented Aung San from translating his ideas into practical programs and policies. The responsibility for leading the people through the final stages of separation from Great Britain and into self-government fell to U Nu, a man of different temperament and outlook.

---

U Nu, the man who pledged himself and the nationalist movement "not to veer by one jot or tittle from *Bogyoke's* wishes," made his own contribution to the idea of national unity and the politics of Burma.[39] Although U Nu and Aung San shared many common experiences, their backgrounds and personalities differed widely and were reflected in their thought. Nu was older than Aung San and, unlike him, born in the South. He attended Myoma National

36. *New Times of Burma*, May 24, 1947, p. 6; in "Address at the Convention," op. cit., there is no reference to this statement.
37. *New Times of Burma*, May 24, 1947, p. 6.
38. "Problems for Burma's Freedom," op. cit., p. 4.
39. Nu, "If We Are Faithful to Bogyoke," in *Towards Peace and Democracy* (Rangoon, 1949), p. 1.

High School in Rangoon during the nineteen-twenties and there was exposed to the nascent nationalist movement and the special activity of student leadership. He attended the University of Rangoon for the first time that same decade and graduated with a bachelor's degree in 1929. Following a brief career as superintendent of the National High School in Pantanaw, he returned to the university in 1934 to study law. It was then that he and Aung San met and began a friendship that lasted until the assassination.[40]

Following the 1936 student strike, which Nu helped to lead, he abandoned his law studies and entered politics as a full-time activist in the *Dobama Asiayone*. The threat of war in 1939 brought strong restrictive measures against indigenous political activity; Nu and some of his colleagues in the party found their way into jail about the same time that Aung San was making his escape from Burma. The war and the creation of a Japanese-sponsored indigenous government under Ba Maw provided the conditions that reunited Nu and Aung San; both were drawn into the puppet government. Despite Nu's knowledge of the resistance activities of Aung San and others, he did not actively participate in planning and executing the revolt of 1945.[41]

After the war and the return of the British, Nu temporarily retired from politics, but at the urging of Aung San he returned in 1946 as the vice-president of the AFPFL. The post was newly created with the intention that the holder should direct the party organizational work.[42] An evaluation of Nu from that time provides an interesting commentary on his ideas and personality:

> Thakin Nu is neither a Communist nor a Socialist. He is an independent political thinker with views somewhat inclined to the

---

40. Richard Butwell, *U Nu of Burma* (Stanford, 1963). Two short studies that attempt to do more than outline Nu's life and career are Hugh Tinker, "Nu, the Serene Statesman," *Pacific Affairs* 30(2) (1957): 120–137; and E. Hunter, "Introduction," in Nu, *The People Win Through* (New York, 1957), pp. 1–50. Shorter accounts are available in the *Guardian* 2(7) (1955) and in the Burmese press. *U Nu: Saturday's Son*, trans. Law Yone, ed. Kyaw Win (New Haven, 1975) is Nu's autobiography.
41. Nu, *Burma under the Japanese* (New York, 1954), pp. 98–110.
42. *Burman*, October 3, 1946, p. 2.

philosophical and spiritual side. He is no fanatic. In fact, there is nothing narrow or parochial about his outlook. . . . He is a man, who with his vision and idealism, can lead the AFPFL to greater glory.[43]

Although he did not seek membership in the Constituent Assembly by participating in the regular election, he permitted his colleagues to nominate him as a candidate for a seat that had become vacant. Victory in the special election brought him to the assembly, where he was chosen to be president.[44] Following Aung San's assassination he succeeded to the presidency of the AFPFL and, upon selection by the governor, to the office of chief councillor in the Executive Council.

Though it seems that Nu's primary interest, like Aung San's, was politics, other activities and interests helped form his ideas and competed for his attention. Nu's proclaimed life-long interest and ambition has been to become a successful creative writer. In a long autobiographical sketch written in 1943, Nu said,

> Political work is ceaseless and true politicians have to work like beavers. The present writer pays due homage to the determination, zeal, industry and tenacity of these admirable workers for the country. In the ever changing pattern of politics, however, he sees them in all their vicissitudes, now combining, now falling apart, now proponents and now opponents, now friends, now enemies, veritable playthings of change. He feels sorry for them. But the rough and tumble of their life is not for him. He prefers to lead the life of imagination. He must have privacy for his thoughts.[45]

In his efforts to develop his writing talent, Nu came under several influences, of which he acknowledged Shakespeare, Shaw, Conrad, and Dale Carnegie as the most important. An examination of his writings suggests that to the list should be added Freud, Marx, Stalin, Mao Tse-tung, and the teachings of the Buddha. His reach-

43. Ibid.
44. Burma, Ministry of Information, *Burma's Fight for Freedom* (Rangoon, 1948), p. 63.
45. Nu, "Man, the Wolf of Man," *Guardian* 1(8) (1954): 11–12.

ing for a philosophy is reflected in his early novella *Man, the Wolf of Man* (1943), in which he sought to unite Marxist and Buddhist ideas, and also in a novel on sex and human behavior in which he made an effort to unite Freudian ideas with Buddhism.[46] During the prewar years Nu organized a literary study group that concentrated on European left-wing writings. John Furnivall notes in an article on the early *Thakin* movement that many of the young nationalists such as Nu and Aung San were attracted to the doctrines of Marx and Lenin, only to reject them later because they could "not reconcile Marxist materialism with Buddhism and [could not accept] the Communist doctrine of the inevitability of violence."[47] This point is confirmed in Nu's study of the war period; speaking of the reason he did not particpate in the actual uprising, he said, "There was of course no idea that when I went into hiding I would handle a gun. Every one who knew me was well aware that in this kind of thing I should be less than useless."[48]

Although Nu struggled hard to adopt a Western approach to society and morality, he never was able to go too far because of his deep-rooted faith in Buddhism. Unlike Aung San, who accepted the Burmese religion as part of tradition but neither demonstrated religious piety nor made public use of his faith for political ends, Nu was and continues to be a genuinely religious man, and he has mixed politics with religion. Early in his political career, when he found campaigning too taxing, he renounced the world and was ordained a monk.[49] Since that time he has returned frequently to the monastery for short periods to renourish his faith and engage in public religious activity as part of his daily routine. Nu has worked constantly since independence to revive public interest in religious activity in the hope of strengthening the social bonds and reducing the crime and rebellious activity that had plagued Burma since the end of the Burman monarchy.

Through his religion, writing, and public life, Nu developed a

46. Nu, *All Men Are Fools* (Rangoon, 1943), in Burmese.
47. John S. Furnivall, "Twilight in Burma," *Pacific Affairs* 22(1) (1949): 16.
48. Nu, *Burma under the Japanese*, op. cit., p. 106.
49. Nu, "Man, the Wolf of Man," op. cit., p. 10.

talent for communicating with the people. Through his use of fables, myths, religious sayings, and the language of the street, Nu identified with the masses. Unlike Aung San, he usually adopted an indirect approach to convey his ideas, although he has on occasion reacted in an abrupt, hasty, and direct fashion to unexpected events or activity. For example, the death of a youthful bystander during a student riot over the government's cancellation of a national examination prompted Nu to act without prior discussion and pass all candidates regardless of their preparation and ability.[50]

Nu presents a more complex, less predictable personality whose approach and ideas depart widely from those of his predecessor.

---

U Nu's ideas on national unity result from his assumptions about the nature of man and the history of Burma. From his religious background, Nu accepted the premise that man's nature was imperfect but improvable. Man's tendency to do evil was a human weakness that could be overcome only through conscious effort. Man must learn that his worst enemies are greed, hatred, and ignorance; that human senses reveal only fleeting phenomena; that his destiny is old age and death and his wordly possessions are a temporary thing.[51]

Living in society men develop their propensity to do evil by oppressing other men whether or not they are members of their own ethnic group. Nu expressed this idea very well when he said,

> Life in this depraved world may be likened to a journey in a leaky boat. As the men in a leaky boat are required to be constantly throwing away the rushing water just to keep the boat afloat, the people of this world, ridden with greed and anger, must always be alert to the dangers of communal conflicts, dangers of class exploitation and danger of one section of the community seizing political power and oppressing the people.[52]

50. *Nation*, March 24, 1956, p. 1.
51. Nu, "Burma's Goal," in *Forward with the People* (Rangoon, 1955), pp. 46–47.
52. Nu, "Our Policy and Programme," in *From Peace to Stability* (Rangoon, 1951), p. 83.

Nu argued that the problem of national disunity was as old as Burma's history. It had three sources: misunderstandings "caused by the natural barriers of water, dense forests and mountains; dissension and discord which naturally arise in the course of centuries"; and colonial rule, which encourages mutual distrust and antagonism between peoples. An examination of Burma's history reveals that in precolonial times there were only three short periods when the country was united and these came as a result of force and violence under strong Burman kings; following the death of these men, "their kingdoms, instead of being firmly established, crumbled like a house of cards."[53]

Although Nu never accused the British of creating disunity, he held them responsible for perpetuating and using it to strengthen their own power, seeking to make themselves a necessary force in the maintenance of law and order among antagonistic ethnic groups. Because the British institutionalized the separation between the peoples of the frontier and those of the plains, "there was no spontaneous spirit of intimate relationship" whenever peoples from either group met. Under British rule, "it was as though someone was forever watching in the background to detect and deal drastically with such expressions of love and good will."[54] Nu compared the development of the peoples of Burma under British rule to the "undergrowths beneath big trees" and said "full physical, intellectual, mental and economic development had not been possible."[55]

For Nu, national unity implied three relationships: unity among ethnic groups, unity among political groups, and unity between the people and the government.[56] He never tired of arguing that unity was natural among ethnic groups in Burma because all their members were "sons and daughters of this land."[57] All the original in-

53. Nu, "Democracy versus the Gun," in *Towards Peace and Democracy,* op. cit., p. 205.
54. Nu, "Towards a Welfare State," in *Burma Looks Ahead* (Rangoon, 1953), p. 69.
55. Nu, "Not Yet Out of the Woods," in *Towards Peace and Democracy,* op. cit., p. 149.
56. Nu, "The Road to Unity," in ibid., p. 10.
57. *New Times of Burma,* May 21, 1948, p. 1.

habitants of Burma, the Shans, Karens, Kachins, Chins, Kayahs, Mons, Arakanese, "are sharers of the same earth and the same water from the same cradle to the same grave . . . we are all kinsmen living in the same house in the same homeland."[58] The act of political union, he argued, was a voluntary one; therefore each must accept an equal responsibility to protect its creation.[59] Further, as coequals, all must progress together in matters of politics, economic growth, and social development; "if any portion of the Frontier Areas continues to be backward, the Burma Union would be weakened in the same way a weak limb weakens the whole person."[60]

Whereas these assumptions were not too different from those held by Aung San, the conclusions Nu drew were very different. Unlike Aung San, whose solution was unity in diversity, U Nu was fundamentally opposed to the idea of separate states and the many implications of the principle of unity in diversity. Instead he favored a unitary state in which ability would determine who would be the administrators: "My idea is that Burma should have a unitary constitution, and I want leaders with the required qualifications, whether they are Karens, Shans, Chins, Kachins, Karennis, Mons, or Burmans, to administer it."[61] He argued that "the solution of the minority problem lies in the cementing of racial bonds between all communities rather than in the dismembering of the Union and the creation of separate states." He cautioned his listeners to remember that, because "every one was delirious for freedom" after the war, the nationalist leaders were compelled by circumstances to accept separate states in order to avoid delay in realizing the goal."[62]

Even though Nu agreed to the establishment of a Karen state and in 1958, for political reasons, was ready to accept the idea of states for the Mons and Arakanese, he still maintained his original view on ethnic-based states: "To tell my personal opinions frankly,

58. Ibid., October 7, 1947, p. 1.
59. Nu, "Road to Unity," op. cit., p. 11.
60. Nu, "The Nature of Leftist Unity," in *Towards Peace and Democracy*, op. cit., pp. 134–135.
61. Nu, "Review of the General Situation," in ibid., p. 174.
62. Nu, "Not Yet Out of the Woods," in ibid., p. 152.

States are not desirable. That is why I have repeatedly urged minorities not to ask for separate States."[63]

Nu also differed with his predecessor on minority rights for ethnic groups, such as the Karens, who were permanent minorities within the established states; but as Aung San's faithful successor he argued before the Constituent Assembly that it should adopt his predecessor's idea of special privileges and rights for the Karens pending the establishment of their own state.[64] In 1951, during the debate in the Provisional Parliament on the constitutional amendment to establish a Karen state, Nu took the position that the Karens must surrender their special privileges in exchange for the new state. He rested his argument on two points: (1) The continuation of Karen minority rights after statehood would stimulate comparable demands from all other minorities and destroy the unity and cohesiveness of the Union, and (2) the concept of minority rights was not consistent with the idea of national unity; rather, it was "a clever invention of the Imperialists to enable them to divide and rule for as long as they please." He concluded his argument by saying that "as long as we allow this spectre of minority rights to continue in our midst, so long shall our efforts to achieve unity and solidarity be of no avail."[65]

Nu's twin ideas—a unitary state and equal political rights for all— were the basis of his concept of national unity. It implied the submersion of local identities and mutual mistrust in favor of creating a new identity equally shared by all and based on new community values and ideals. It accepted the democratic method as the basis of political action. Nu sought to realize his concept in many indirect ways. For example, when the country was faced with a serious rebellion by a large segment of the Karen population, he took the position that it was not an ethnic problem but a citizenship problem:

> As Prime Minister, I see only two problems in the Union; the problem of bad citizens and the problem of good citizens. Bad

---

63. *Burma Weekly Bulletin*, n.s., 7(12) (July 3, 1958): 88.
64. Maung Maung, *Burma's Constitution* (The Hague, 1957), p. 181.
65. Nu, "The Karen State," in *Burma Looks Ahead*, op. cit., p. 15.

citizens are those who infringe the tenets of our Constitution and whether they are Shans, Kachins, Chins, Karens, Karennis, Mons, or Burmans, they must be treated as such. Similarly, anybody from any community who upholds the Constitution must be treated as good citizens.[66]

From this view Nu never departed despite the long and bitter military struggle between the rebellious sector of the Karens and the government or those between the Mons or other ethnic groups and the government. Nu stood ready to embrace all as Burmese if they chose to uphold the constitution and support the State. Throughout his administration he sought to heal communal antagonisms by nominating qualified Karens and other minority members to high posts in the AFPFL, the government, and the military.

Nu saw religion as a valuable social cohesive. Unlike Aung San, who urged a rigid separation between church and state, Nu saw the state's role in religion as twofold: first to ensure religious freedom for adherents of all faiths to practice their particular religions and second to encourage a revival of religious interest to help instill moral and social values that would in turn lead to an end to insurgent activity, a reduction in criminality, and a reintegration of the society.

Nu argued that "the Government should not employ religion as a cloak, for politics; but . . . should encourage all religious activities in the same manner as it does all other branches of activity, in order to give the nation maximum physical and mental happiness."[67] Faced with the political problem of a large element of Karens in revolt and the religious problem that the majority of these Karens were non-Buddhists, Nu refused to comfort those who argued that national disunity was fostered by religious diversity. His position was that among the rebels were members of all religious faiths, and he reminded all who would listen that the government opposed the insurgents, "not on account of the religion they profess,

66. Nu, "Review of the General Situation," op. cit., p. 167.
67. Nu, "Towards a Welfare State," op. cit., p. 92.

but for the obvious fact that they are taking up arms against the lawfully constituted Government."⁶⁸

On the role of religion in the society, Nu often argued that the state needed more than capable men and women or technicians—it needed moral men and women: "Even if the majority of us are not skillful and capable, we must strive for a society where we set high moral values and fear to plot, discuss and commit evil." To raise the moral standards of the community, he said, "we find religion of the greatest value"; therefore "we have encouraged all religions of our nationals to the best of our ability."⁶⁹

Though encouraging religious freedom and the growth of all faiths, Nu is not a religious neutral. He is a Buddhist who believes that, as approximately 85 percent of the population share his faith, Buddhism ought to be encouraged and assisted so that its impact can be felt both by the faithful and by those outside the fold who might adopt it if they understood it. Nu strongly believes that "all Buddhists in any part of this country must be made to live and act according to the teachings of the Lord Buddha." His government urged the passage of a number of bills designed to encourage the faith, expand religious higher education, and reform the sangha. He urged the support of these measures by arguing that "we have been prompted by the sole consideration to combat effectively antireligious forces which are rearing their ugly heads everywhere."⁷⁰

The apparent inconsistency between religious freedom and the encouragement of all religions on the one hand and on the other hand the use of state funds to expand the religious activity of only one faith did not bother Nu. Both goals were socially and politically significant; moreover, he had no clear philosophy of government that necessitated constancy of thought. For him, religion was a necessary social cohesive, and he stood ready to encourage all religious or pseudoreligious activity, from Buddhism to Moral Re-Armament, so that the people "will be good citizens

---

68. Nu, "Religion, Hope of the World," in *From Peace to Stability*, op. cit., p. 73.

69. Nu, "Towards a Welfare State," op. cit., p. 91.

70. Nu, "Propagation of the Dhamma," in *From Peace to Stability*, op. cit., pp. 107, 109.

of the Union in accordance with their religious teachings." The ultimate goal of good citizenship was his recurring theme, and he believed that it was realizable "if we have the wholehearted cooperation of the leaders, representatives and members of every religion in the country."[71]

Nu demonstrated his attachment to the goal of national unity through national identification in other ways. He sponsored and supported a program of Burmese literature. Through the Burma Translation Society he urged local writers to encourage "our own indigenous literature in order to foster a Burmese outlook" and to contribute toward the "cultural renaissance of the country." As a guide to what the Burmese outlook might be, he called on the writers to deal "with Burmese thought, Burmese character, Burmese shortcomings and the real state of Burmese society. Such works give true Burmese outlook."[72]

> The real Burmese background I have in mind is no other than the fact that the Union of Burma is now a sovereign Independent State with its indigenous people . . . working hand in hand for a new era. They are building a new world of their own in a democratic way and they are marching towards the goal of common prosperity. In other words, our Union is building a new pattern of culture.[73]

The new pattern of culture Nu envisioned included a program of mass education that would provide rudimentary public health, first aid, reading, and writing for the illiterate masses living in the remote areas of the several states. He sponsored the Mass Education Movement, which trained recruits as field teams to carry the national language and modern social ideas to remote areas in Burma proper and also to places that constitutionally fell under the jurisdiction of the several states. Through education Nu hoped the

---

71. *Burma Weekly Bulletin*, n.s., 7(12) (July 3, 1958): 86.
72. Nu, "Cultural Renaissance," in *From Peace to Stability*, op. cit., p. 215.
73. Nu, "Intellectual Development," in *Forward with the People*, op. cit., pp. 105–106.

people would develop and extend the common culture and broaden their horizons beyond local limits.[74]

Throughout his administration as prime minister and as president of the AFPFL, Nu labored to build national unity through a variety of programs aimed at transcending ethnic diversity and antagonism, or as Nu once expressed it, "to convert their clanism to patriotic nationalism so that any insult or threat to the Union becomes as unbearable as an insult or threat to one's own family."[75]

Nu's ideas and tactics are in sharp contrast to those of Aung San; they also indicate the different problems each man faced. Nu, as successor to Aung San, felt obligated to follow the path marked out by his predecessor; but as times and circumstances changed, he gradually developed his own approach, not bothering to worry any longer whether he was acting consistently with the ideas of Aung San. As a result, there occurred between Nu and the minorities many misunderstandings that reflected the dichotomy between Aung San's promises and Nu's practices.

The second element in Nu's concept of national unity was political unity. Faced with the reality of trying to administer a nation torn by revolution almost from the day of its establishment, Nu's most immediate problem was to reweld the diverse forces that had combined in the preindependence period to win Burma's freedom. Originally Nu thought the cohesive that could unite the major antagonistic forces—the Communists, the People's Volunteer Organization, and the Socialists—was their common desire to transform Burma into a socialist state. Unfortunately the three disagreed on the meaning of the concept. Early in 1948, Nu sponsored the Leftist Unity Plan, which promised to reconstruct Burma in the image of the then-new but undefined and undeveloped people's democracies of Eastern Europe.[76] The rejection of his plan by the

---

74. Nu, "New Responsibilities," in *From Peace to Stability*, op. cit., pp. 184–185.

75. *Burma Weekly Bulletin*, n.s., 7(15) (July 24, 1958): 109.

76. Nu, "The Program," in *Towards Peace and Democracy*, op. cit., pp. 92–97; idem., "The Nature of Leftist Unity," in ibid., pp. 106–138. Compare his program and conception of socialism as expressed therein with A. C. Sobolev, *People's Democracy, A New Form of Political Organization of Society* (Moscow, 1954), pp. 5–114. Nu had the Russian and not the

Communists and a large sector of the PVO left him free to abandon it in favor of a more humanitarian socialism that sought to eliminate man's three relentless enemies: bloody conflict, famine, and epidemics. Their cause, according to Nu, was "the exploitation of man by man born of this system of private ownership."[77]

To create a socialist state, Nu said, the people must work along two lines. Their economic task is production and distribution of commodities necessary for human life and the material improvement of each other. Their moral task is to reexamine their values and attitudes and adopt a more cooperative approach to each other. For Nu, the methods and goals of socialism must be blended with the teachings of Buddhism. It mattered not to him that Buddhism as a religion looked to the salvation of man through escape from samsara; he saw its lessons as a guide for social harmony and peace in this world. It mattered not that socialism looked to man's material improvement in this world; he saw it as a social system that eliminated the extremes of poverty and wealth and competition between individuals. For Nu, Buddhism and socialism could be united, with the resulting synthesis, an improved social order.[78]

To attain these socialist goals Nu advocated a democratic form of government. He rejected one-party dictatorship like Russia's because it implied rule by force:

> It seems to me that there is only one way by which a one party dictatorship can be set up in Burma. This is no other than the ruthless suppression of people and keeping them under tether and rein like cattle.[79]

Acquiring power by force breeds fear, and fear leads to suppression and elimination of the basic human freedoms mankind has striven to attain. One-party dictatorship, Nu said, inevitably suppresses

---

Chinese model of New Democracy in mind; compare his program with Mao Tse-tung, "On New Democracy," in *Selected Works of Mao Tse Tung*, vol. 3 (Bombay, 1954), pp. 106–156.

77. Nu, "Our Policy and Programme," in *From Peace to Stability*, op. cit., p. 86.
78. Ibid., p. 87.
79. Ibid., p. 88.

organized religion; any system that so renders man to the will of other men and denies him the opportunity to live as a whole man has no place in Burma. The only system that allows the individual the freedom and the opportunity to develop himself to the fullest is the democratic system.[80] Under democracy men choose their leaders and approve or reject their programs by a process that allows for peaceful change. To hold power, the government must constantly strive to hold the people's support. This does not mean that government must pander to a fleeting whim or sudden impulse of the community but that it must exercise power in conformity with the law. Thus, for Nu, democracy is constitutional democracy.[81] From these propositions he drew the conclusion that,

> if the Government becomes vicious and you want to remove it, go to the people and ask for power by means of the democratic method. . . . This is how power can be wrested without bloodshed. To ignore the existence of this method and to follow blindly the method of bloodshed betokens an entire absence of discrimination.[82]

Nu failed to reconcile the various political malcontents who chose rebellion, despite the fact that his government offered amnesties and tried to satisfy their demands by constructing a socialist state before establishing peace and order.[83] During his second administration (1957–1958) he admitted that his earlier tactics had been unsuccessful; he proclaimed his new goal was to establish law and order first and socialism second.[84] Though the priorities were reversed, the ultimate goal of socialism remained. Speaking before the Third Congress of the AFPFL in January 1958, Nu declared, "Our policy and program cannot be anything else but

80. Nu, "Burma's Goal," in *Forward with the People,* op. cit., p. 51.
81. Ibid., pp. 52–55.
82. Nu, "I Choose Democracy," in *Towards Peace and Democracy,* op. cit., pp. 61–62.
83. *Nation,* September 24, 1946, p. 2; Nu, *Premier's Report to the People: Law and Order, National Solidarity, Social Welfare, National Economy, Foreign Affairs* (Rangoon, 1957), pp. 47–57.
84. Ibid., p. 56.

to seek for a mandate from the people through democratic means and to build a Socialist State according to that mandate."[85]

In April 1958, Nu provoked an open split in the AFPFL that resulted in nearly seven months of political crisis and threatened to rekindle civil war throughout the country.[86] He defused the situation by stepping out of office in favor of Gen. Ne Win and a caretaker government. Nearly four years later, after he had resumed office following a national election in 1960, the issues of ethnic and political unity combined to threaten the nation's stability. Nu, true to his beliefs, called a federal seminar and invited the leaders of all ethnic groups to participate and "speak their hearts" in an effort to save the Union and avoid bloodshed. The federal seminar was Nu's way of employing a democratic solution to solve the crisis. Unfortunately he failed because the military seized power by coup d'etat, imprisoned Nu and nearly all the minority leaders, and replaced constitutional democracy with dictatorship. Nu's actions in these two historic events confirm his deep commitment to peaceful and democratic principles. His failure in 1962 was not due to his loss of faith in the system he helped to erect; it was rooted instead in a society and a segment of the leadership that neither trusted nor really understood what he had tried to do.

The third element in Nu's concept of national unity was unity between the government and the people.[87] The government, he argued, was not the agent of an alien power but the servant of the people; "all Government servants should realize that they are both wielders of power in their own capacity and representatives of the people who collectively delegate certain powers to them."[88] Their

85. Burma Weekly Bulletin, n.s., 6(43) (February 6, 1958): 376.
86. See Nation, Burman, or New Times of Burma from April 24 through October 29, 1958, for a daily account of the accusations and rebuttal of the major participants. See also Burma Weekly Bulletin for the same period for the official version of some of the major events and speeches. For a firsthand account and description of the period, see John Badgley, "Burma's Political Crisis," Pacific Affairs 31(4) (1958). U Nu's assessment of events leading up to the split are included in his U Nu: Saturday's Son, op. cit., pp. 323–325.
87. Nu, "The Road to Unity," op. cit., pp. 14–15.
88. Nu, From Peace to Stability, op. cit., p. 114.

duty was not to consider Burma proper alone, as in the British period, but to consider the Union as a whole. Their guiding principle must be that "no act which would be prejudicial to the integrity and stability of the Union of Burma may be committed," for to do so "will be the most serious offense which a civil servant can commit by official conduct against the people and against the Government which employs him."[89]

The civil servant must learn to live and work with the political leaders and the people. Prior to independence the civil servant sought promotion and distinction by protecting the interests of his employer, the alien government; the politician, however, was his enemy, for the political leaders were in the forefront of the struggle for independence from alien rule. "The circumstances therefore placed the Government servants and the politicians in opposite camps and their interests could never be reconciled."[90] After independence the two, having the same goal—furthering the interests of the Union of Burma—must work together to realize it. "Under these conditions . . . a large part of the initiative that used to come from the Secretaries to Government has been taken over by the Ministries."[91] The people's elected representatives make policy, and the civil servants carry it out. Through this kind of cooperation the people and the government can be united in purpose and action:

> Some of us have a very superficial view of this aspect of unity. To them unity means the existence of cordial relations between the indigenous races of the Union. . . . In fact unity goes deeper than this. Real unity signifies more than the existence of cordial relations between these people; it signifies cordial relations amongst the various groups of these people too. In fact, unity has a deeper significance still. Cordial relations must exist between the Government servants and the people, and still more, between the peoples themselves and the Government servants themselves.[92]

89. Nu, "The Role of Government Servants," in ibid., p. 29.
90. Nu, *From Peace to Stability*, op. cit., p. 111.
91. Nu, "The Role of Government Servants," in ibid., p. 33.
92. Nu, "The Moral Battle," in *Towards Peace and Democracy*, op. cit., p. 233.

A defensive arm of the government—the military—also had a significant role to play in building national unity. Nu argued that the army and its auxiliary forces have the duties of creating "firm national solidarity" and of "instilling the citizens of the Union with an overwhelming sense of respect for the Constitution of the Union."[93] The military must be opened to all indigenous ethnic groups; it must protect all the people, regardless of their ethnic origins, who live in the Union; and it must remain loyal to the State.

U Nu called on the armed forces to look upon the civil servant with a feeling of equality rather than superiority. Both branches of government service are vital and necessary to the people and the State; both have a responsibility to maintain high moral standards if they are to hold the people's support.[94]

In calling for a higher sense of moral and civic responsibility among the military, Nu was aware that in its ranks were men and women who represented the best and worst in Burmese society. As late as 1958, in the face of a political crisis that forced him to call on the military to maintain law and order and form a caretaker government until new elections were held, Nu thought it necessary to remind his successor that there were still numerous complaints from the people about individual "acts of oppression, atrocious cruelty and murder" by members of the armed forces.[95] This must be corrected if the public were to respect and not fear the military.

---

Although both men were faced with fundamentally different political problems—Aung San had to create the Union and U Nu had to hold it together—it was their different views of what national unity meant that created problems for the future of national unity. The minorities both in and out of Burma proper looked to Aung San's promises and ideas of unity in diversity to justify maintaining their political, ethnic, and cultural differences. At the same time the majority of people in Burma proper and many among the

93. Nu, "Soldier's Other Duties," in ibid., p. 153.
94. Nu, "The Moral Battle," op. cit., pp. 234–237.
95. *Burma Weekly Bulletin*, n.s., 7(25) (October 2, 1958): 192.

minorities took as their goal U Nu's ideas on the creation of a national identification and the submersion of local differences. Aung San's death at the height of his career and his position as the hero of the independence struggle have meant that his legacy could not be repudiated openly. Therefore his successors have paid lip service to his ideas and promises while moving ahead on their own course. The national political party, the AFPFL, which both headed, reflected their different views as each became its leader.

# The Anti-Fascist People's Freedom League 1945-1948

The organization that led the postwar nationalist movement and at the same time acted as the linchpin holding the varied ethnic and political forces together in the struggle for independence was the Anti-Fascist People's Freedom League. Its loosely structured organization with affiliated parties in various states served as a conveyor of ideas and policies between Rangoon and the countryside, as the recruiting ground for leaders, and as the means for drawing together the nation's ethnic and political groups and social classes for common ends. In its multiple tasks the AFPFL was never wholly successful. Having neither a consistent set of principles and goals nor strong central control, it could not transcend all the ideological differences and personal rivalries among its leaders and between leaders and followers. As a result the organization was never able to capitalize fully on its prestige and goodwill as the party of liberation and national unity and as the personal organization of Aung San. Because its shadow fell so completely across the nation, influencing all social and political developments during this period, it is necessary to look closely at the organization and see how it performed its tasks as agent and catalyst for unification.

## The Anti-Fascist People's Freedom League

To understand how the AFPFL was able to affect many of the events of this period, one must first understand its formal structure and its more important operating rules. The original pattern of organization developed pragmatically during World War II, when the AFPFL was a secret revolutionary movement. To carry out its conspiratorial tasks it was led by a small group united by close personal bonds developed out of long years of prewar association. The men and women recruited to the ranks of this anti-Japanese movement were organized in one of several groups that combined to form the League. The line of authority passed from the top down; the affiliate groups were united only through their leaders. This wartime pattern persisted for a short time after the Japanese were expelled from Burma.

After the war the AFPFL was described to representatives of the world press as a "combination of various political groups and organizations and communities" and not "as a party." Within the confederation there were two types of members: those recruited individually and directly into an AFPFL subunit and those who entered indirectly and automatically as members of an affiliate organization.[1] To give the league cohesion, all members and affiliate groups accepted the Leninist principle of democratic centralism and looked to the Supreme Council as the highest authority.[2]

The only formal rules guiding the AFPFL until 1946 were incorporated in the "Provisional Rules of the Supreme Council of

1. "Queries and Replies at the Press Interview Given by Anti-Fascist People's Freedom League on 14th May, 1945," in AFPFL, *From Fascist Bondage to New Democracy: The New Burma in the New World* (Rangoon, 1945?), p. 39. In addition to the political groups (Communist Party of Burma, People's Revolutionary Party) and the Burma National Army, the AFPFL included the Women's Freedom League; the Youth League; the Karen Central Organization; the Arakanese National Congress; and the Shan Association including the Shan Youth and some *sawbwas, sanghas,* authors, and others. Of these, only the political groups and the Women's Freedom League played significant political roles in the future activities of the AFPFL.

2. Ibid., p. 40: "Although the organization was based on democratic centralization, we stress more on centralization than a democratic basis as that was inevitable under the Japanese."

the Anti-Fascist People's Freedom League."[3] These remained in effect until superseded by a formal constitution.[4] Under the provisional rules the Supreme Council was the highest organ in the AFPFL; during the war it was limited to nine members, who were said to have equal status in its deliberations.[5] After the war it was enlarged to include three representatives from each affiliate party, mass organization, and ethnic group plus ten nationally known political leaders.[6] Chief among the latter group was U Ba Pe, a leading figure in the nationalist movement since the nineteen-twenties. The provisional rules directed the Supreme Council to accept as its guides the following principles: collective leadership under democratic control; nationalism; civil control of the military; democratic rights for the people; and democratic procedure in government.[7]

Because the affiliate groups were strong in their own right and had leaders and programs not always compatible, the provisional rules provided that: (1) All member parties represented in the Supreme Council must pledge to abide by the decisions of that body. (2) The Supreme Council would arbitrate disputes between parties or organizations, and its rulings were final. (3) All political activity authorized by the Supreme Council must be conducted in its name. (4) Members of the Supreme Council must not engage in personal attacks on each other.[8]

To create direct AFPFL subunits under the control of the Supreme Council, the provisional rules authorized recruiting members in village and town units; these units were then combined into township organizations and these in turn into district groups. Leaders at all these levels were chosen by their superiors in the next higher branch; the Supreme Council chose the district leaders.[9]

---

3. "Provisional Rules of the Supreme Council of the Anti-Fascist People's Freedom League," in AFPFL, op. cit., pp. 54–56.
4. AFPFL, *The Constitution of the Anti-Fascist People's Freedom League* (Rangoon, 1949), p. 1, hereafter AFPFL, *Constitution*.
5. "Queries and Replies," op. cit., p. 40.
6. "Provisional Rules," op. cit., p. 54.
7. Ibid., p. 55.
8. Ibid., pp. 55–56.
9. "Queries and Replies," op. cit., p. 40; "Provisional Rules," op. cit., p. 56.

Although the provisional rules made no mention of a national conference as the unifying element of the affiliates and subgroups, a spokesman for the AFPFL said that eventually a national conference would be called. In January 1946, the first All-Burma National Conference was held in Rangoon, and one of its chief functions was to consider the draft constitution that would replace the provisional rules.

The goals contained in the provisional rules were four: to fight fascism; to win the right of self-determination; to reconstruct Burma by democratic means; and "to create a new Burma based on voluntary union recognizing the right of self-determination for all national minorities, including the right of secession."[10]

The provisional rules did not go into greater detail; it remained for the AFPFL constitution to fill in the details and close the gaps in the loose federation. The new constitution made a number of significant changes in the institutions and rules. It established the National Conference as the highest body in the league.[11] Although it authorized an annual meeting of the National Conference, it also provided that such national meetings could be postponed with the approval of the Executive Committee or the Supreme Council.[12] The National Conference's duties were to approve all past activity of the League, elect the president, and consider any resolutions the delegates or leaders introduced. Its delegates were to be drawn from the AFPFL subunits, affiliate groups, members of the last Supreme Council, and all secretaries of the Executive Committee.[13] Each district was entitled to send a minimum of thirty members, and the Supreme Council or its Executive Committee was empowered to allot seats to representatives from the states.[14]

Under the constitution executive power between sessions of the National Conference was lodged with the Supreme Council and its Executive Committee. The Supreme Council was greatly enlarged to include a minimum of two delegates from each district AFPFL and affiliate organization; further, the states were authorized

10. "Provisional Rules," op. cit., pp. 54–55.
11. AFPFL, *Constitution*, Art. 13.
12. Ibid., Art. 29.
13. Ibid., Art. 31.
14. Ibid., Art. 33.

to have representation in this body as well. In addition the elected Supreme Council was empowered to coopt fifteen extra members.[15] The Supreme Council was empowered to make decisions between sessions of the National Conference—a power it passed on to the Executive Committee—to amend the constitution, to prescribe the method of electing the president of the AFPFL, and to convene special conferences when necessary.[16]

Having enlarged the Supreme Council so that it was no longer capable of taking continuous action in daily affairs, the constitution provided a new executive body, the Executive Committee, whose only elected member was the president; he chose fourteen comembers and they coopted five others. The constitution provided that the Executive Committee should share many of the duties entrusted to the Supreme Council, such as settling disputes arising from ambiguity in the constitution and establishing the rules and regulations for the subunits of the AFPFL. It also gave the Executive Committee sole power to disband, expel, or reinstate and administer directly any AFPFL organization should the need arise.[17] Beyond this the constitution was silent; the Supreme Council was authorized to give additional powers to the committee if needed.[18] In practice the Executive Committee was the most powerful organ of the League. It included the major political figures who held power both in the government and in the mass organization. Being small and located in Rangoon, it met weekly, made all the fundamental decisions, and established the policies that guided the activity of the AFPFL.

Two major changes were made at the district level and below. First, member units were permitted to elect a panel of nominees for their own executive committees. In theory this reversed the former practice and appeared to reduce the control of the higher units over the lower ones;[19] in practice the subunits submitted the names of their nominees to the higher body for approval, thus

15. Ibid., Art. 34.
16. Ibid., Arts. 30, 37.
17. Ibid., Arts. 24, 25, 27.
18. Ibid., Art. 38.
19. "Supplement to the Rules," in ibid., Sec. 1.

keeping control in the hands of the leaders. Second, the members of affiliate groups could join subunits of the AFPFL. The constitution also provided that an annual conference would be held at each of the three sublevels and attended by delegates representing direct and indirect members.[20]

Unlike the provisional rules, the constitution defined the qualifications of membership.[21] Individual membership in an AFPFL subgroup was open to anyone eighteen years or older who was a member of one of the indigenous ethnic groups or who was a naturalized Burmese citizen. Anyone desiring to join had to pledge to abide by the rules and decisions of the AFPFL, to help in the struggle to attain the goals of the organization, and to work for the implementation of its policies.

To finance the AFPFL the constitution authorized the organizations to collect dues from both individual and affiliate members, the exact amount to be determined by the Supreme Council.[22] Initially dues were fixed at one *kyat* (21 cents) per member and there was no entry fee. The moneys collected were to be divided between the local unit, the township unit, the district, and the national headquarters.[23] Affiliate groups were instructed to transfer 5 percent of their annual collected subscription to the national headquarters of the AFPFL.

On the question of affiliate groups the constitution had a great deal more to say than the provisional rules. It permitted the admission of all racial and mass organizations after approval by the Supreme Council or the Executive Committee; all members entering via an affiliate group were pledged to abide by the rules of the AFPFL and accept its decisions and policies.[24] Affiliate organizations were prohibited from taking decisions on racial questions without first obtaining the consent of the ethnic group concerned.[25]

20. AFPFL, *Constitution*, Arts. 14–16.
21. Ibid., Arts. 4–7.
22. "The Annual Subscription," in ibid., Sec. 1.
23. Ibid., Secs. 5, 6; the monies were divided as follows: local unit 10 percent; township 50 percent; district 20 percent; national headquarters 20 percent.
24. AFPFL, *Constitution*, Art. 6.
25. Ibid., Art. 26(A).

The constitution, unlike the provisional rules, sought to weld together the affiliates and the AFPFL organization at levels beneath the top and so create a truly united party. As already noted, members who originated from affiliate groups were permitted to join local subunits and participate as individuals in the annual conferences of the AFPFL. The indirect member, attending the local and township conference, was permitted to cast an equal ballot with the direct member.[26] These provisions not only insured the linkage of the indirect members with the AFPFL leadership but made it possible for the leadership to influence the programs, ideals, and tactics of the affiliates. Clearly it was Aung San's desire that the AFPFL widen its authority and become the party of national unity:

> We feel that the AFPFL should be on the definite basis of mass membership, individual as well as collective, a basis which is firmer and clearer than the nebulous form of a multi-party national front. As such, we feel that the existence of political parties, which have, one and all, no mass membership, within its fold is incompatible with its development into a definite, mass national organization which we consider to be the only practicable and historically prescribed form of national front in Burma at this moment.[27]

The affiliate was to be neither coequal nor potential competitor; thus there was no longer room for political parties in the league. Individuals belonging to political parties could join the AFPFL directly, as members of a subunit, or indirectly, as members of a mass or racial group affiliated with the AFPFL.[28] Under this change, the new list of subordinate groups included many that did not appear in earlier announcements and omitted others that had dominated the League.[29] Two of the omitted parties were the

26. Ibid., Arts. 14–16.
27. Aung San, *Presidential Address Delivered by Major-General Aung San at the Second Session of the Supreme Council, AFPFL, Held on the 16th May, 1946* (Rangoon, 1946), p. 35.
28. Ibid., pp. 35–36.
29. AFPFL, *Constitution*, p. 20, lists the following as affiliates: All-Burma Youth Organization, Burma Teachers Council, Burma Trade Union Congress, Burma Women's Freedom League, Burma Federation of Trade Organizations, People's Volunteer Organization, All-Burma Fire Brigade

Communist and the People's Revolutionary, which by this time was called the Burma Socialist Party (BSP). Without them, the dominant affiliated organization was the People's Volunteer Organization (PVO), the successor to the disbanded Burma National Army and the personal organization of Aung San.

As a result of its reorganization, the AFPFL took the form of a strong, centrally controlled political organization with nonrival mass ethnic and social groups as its auxiliaries. Read in this light, its pronounced major objectives reflect its national character and its apparent nonideological orientation. The four major objectives were: to organize all the indigenous peoples of Burma, their descendants, and those people who accept Burmese citizenship for the purpose of winning freedom in keeping with the principle of self-determination; to build Burma into an independent state with the general consent of the various indigenous peoples of Burma; to win the right of self-determination for the peoples of Burma; and to rebuild Burma in accordance with the general consent of the peoples.[30]

As will be seen later, the formal constitution disguised the real power structure of the AFPFL and the actual relationships between it and other political parties. At the time Aung San was advocating the adoption of the constitution by the Supreme Council in May 1946, the AFPFL secretary-general was Than Tun, the head of the Burma Communist Party; and one of the leading members of the Supreme Council and a close advisor to Aung San was Thakin Mya, the president of the Burma Socialist Party. After the constitution was adopted and the former confederate parties were dropped in theory, they actually remained until they were expelled in the case of the Communists or voluntarily withdrew in the case of the Socialists. In the case of the Socialists even formal withdrawal did not break the ties between the two organizations because the Socialist leaders remained active in the mass organizations. Despite Aung San's announcement of the end of the AFPFL as a

---

Organization, All-Burma Karen Youth League, Burma Muslim Congress, and Mon National Association.

30. Ibid., Art. 3.

national confederation or front, that very image remained and became a source of popular unrest and party tension after his death.

---

The history of the AFPFL as the party of national unity only began in January 1946, for prior to that time it was active mainly in Burma proper and drew its strength from political, social, and ethnic groups of that area. Although it advertised itself as a national front with supporting units in the Frontier Areas, this support was more nominal than real. It was not until January 1946 that Aung San and other AFPFL leaders traveled to the Frontier Areas and gained support for the nationalist struggle for independence.

During this initial phase, the Communist and Socialist Parties provided the leadership, ideas, and main support of the AFPFL. In their efforts to influence the nonideologically oriented leaders and mass membership, they rivaled with each other. Initially the Communist Party sought to win control of the AFPFL by direct recruiting to its own ranks, by making it appear as though all AFPFL decisions were its own, and by capturing the leadership of the AFPFL. According to Socialist Party versions of the period, the Communists refused to pursue a revolutionary line. In 1945, after the expulsion of the Japanese from Burma, the Communists tried to win favor with the British by reporting where the Socialists had hidden their arms and with the peasants by fostering "no rent, no revenue" campaigns and encouraging farmers to hold the land they were cultivating regardless of legal ownership.[31] To counter these tactics the People's Revolutionary Party reformed itself as the Burma Socialist Party in August 1945 and embarked on a campaign to recruit supporters among the peasants and workers; the BSP created the All-Burma Peasants' Organization and the Burma Trade Union Organization. Under the leadership of Thakin Mya, whose association with peasant organizations dated from 1938,

31. Hla Aung, "A Short History of the Burma Socialist Party" (unpublished article in typescript given to the writer by its author during an interview in March 1956), p. 3; "Report of the Secretary General of the People's Revolutionary (Socialist) Party, December 1946," in Ba Swe, *Guide to Socialism in Burma* (Rangoon, 1955), in Burmese, pp. 9–21 (translated for the writer in Burma by U Aung Chan Tha).

the BSP was more successful than the Communist Party in recruiting large mass followings.[32] The tactics of the Socialists were to work within the AFPFL and to strengthen it. Thus both of these mass organizations were affiliated with the AFPFL.

To counter the strength of these two active political parties, Aung San organized and controlled the People's Volunteer Organization. Because the PVO lacked ideology or political objectives beyond winning the nation's independence, its ranks were open to the rival appeals and ideas of the Communists and the Socialists, resulting in a leftist orientation to the organization. While Aung San lived, it was his organization and he could count on its discipline, loyalty, and support. It provided him with a power base that was augmented by the popular support he drew as the nation's leader and hero, and these together with the rivalry between the Communists and Socialists made it possible for Aung San to lead the AFPFL.

The four most important mass organizations affiliated with the AFPFL at this time were the Women's Freedom League, the All-Burma Youth League, the Karen Youth League, and the All-Burma Muslim Congress. These were more than nominal groups; each had a social basis, leaders, and a set of nonpolitical goals. The All-Burma Youth League, under the leadership of U Ba Gyan, was the successor to the East Asiatic Youth League; by the end of 1945, it was reported to have six hundred branch organizations and seventy thousand members. Its major purpose was to do social reconstruction work; its secondary and political role was to give support to the AFPFL.[33] The Women's Freedom League, formed before the war, had as its primary aim the improvement of the condition of women throughout Burma; its secondary and political role was to draw female support to the AFPFL.[34] By mid-1946, it was reported to have fifty thousand members and 123 branches.[35] The Karen Youth League was composed of Karens who

32. *Burman*, January 12, 1946, p. 1; this was a short biographical sketch of Thakin Mya; it revealed that, among other things, he organized the All-Burma Cultivator's Association in 1938.
33. Ibid., December 29, 1945, p. 2.
34. *New Times of Burma*, July 12, 1946, p. 3.
35. Ibid.

broke away from the Karen National Union and supported the idea of an independent Burma shared by Karens, Burmans, and the other indigenous ethnic groups. Its leader, Mahn Win Maung, was an early supporter of Aung San and trusted the latter in his relations with the Karens.[36] The All-Burma Muslim Congress was a small but articulate group that sought to be accepted as Burmans. As expressed by its vice-president, U Aung Sein, in January 1946, Burman Muslims wanted "to play their part and to pull their own weight in the reconstruction and rehabilitation of their mother country." They gave their whole support to the AFPFL and were proud of their recognition as a constituent group.[37]

According to the report of the AFPFL secretary-general of November 18, 1945, the League also included the prewar parties *Sinyetha*, *Dobama Asiayone*, and *Myochit*, either as affiliate groups or on an unofficial cooperating basis.[38]

The first All-Burma National Conference of the AFPFL, scheduled for Rangoon in December 1945 and postponed until January 1946, drew a vast attendance from all areas of Burma that attested to the popular support of the AFPFL. The resolutions received strong vocal approval, and their anticolonial and anti-British themes were reported to have found great favor with the delegates.[39]

The most significant aspect of the conference was the public demonstration of conflicts and tensions within the AFPFL leadership over personality and ideology.[40] U Ba Pe, an independent, was publicly criticized by Thakin Soe, a Communist Party leader, for

36. *New Times of Burma*, September 14, 1947, p. 2; November 29, 1947, p. 2 (editorial).
37. *Burman*, January 27, 1946, p. 1.
38. "The Report of Thakin Than Tun, General Secretary, AFPFL Made at the Mass Meeting Held at the Shwedagon Pagoda on the 18th November 1945," in AFPFL, *From Fascist Bondage to New Democracy*, op. cit., pp. 108–109. There is no evidence that the three prewar parties were represented officially at the first All-Burma National Conference.
39. *Times* (London), January 22, 1946, p. 3; January 25, 1946, p. 3; Aung San, *Presidential Address*, op. cit., pp. 5, 32.
40. Interview with Thein Pe Myint (formerly Thein Pe) in April 1956 in Rangoon; Burma, Ministry of Information, *Burma and the Insurrections* (Rangoon, 1949), p. 2; Virginia Thompson, "Burma's Communists," *Far Eastern Survey* 17(9) (1948): 103–105.

his anti-Russian address. To maintain unity in the AFPFL leadership, Soe's fellow-Communist leaders demanded that he substantiate the charges or withdraw them. The issue went unresolved at the conference but was continued later within the Communist Party itself. The Soe attack on U Ba Pe revealed the diversity of opinion within the AFPFL on matters other than independence and foreshadowed the long history of personal rivalry and party splits that took place over the next twelve years.

---

Between the first National Conference and the second held in December 1947, a number of significant changes took place within the AFPFL. From the point of view of political unity, there were the break between the Communists and the AFPFL, the ascendancy of the Socialists in the league's leadership, and the transfer of power from Aung San to U Nu. From the point of view of national unity, the Frontier Areas' people associated themselves with the nationalist independence movement under AFPFL leadership.

The break between the AFPFL and the Communist Party followed a split that took place in March 1946 within the party itself as a result of the Thakin Soe episode at the National Conference and the disagreement it engendered among the party leaders. At the plenum session of the Burma Communist Party in February, Soe accused Than Tun, the chief of the party Politburo, and Thein Pe, the party secretary, of "Browderism"—compromising with imperialism—and not being revolutionary. The accused admitted the charge and temporarily stepped down. In March 1946, Thakin Soe attempted to fill the party's Central Committee with his followers, and this brought him into conflict again with Than Tun and Thein Pe. In a test of strength, Soe lost and withdrew from the party. He formed his own Communist Party of Burma, eventually referred to as the Red Flags, and withdrew as well from the AFPFL.[41] The Soe faction then embarked on a direct-action revolutionary program and was outlawed by the government on

41. Burmese Review, May 20, 1946, p. 8; Burma, loc. cit.; interview with Thein Pe Myint, op. cit.

July 10, 1946.[42] The remainder of the original Communist Party stayed in the AFPFL until it was expelled on October 10, 1946. The episodes leading to this action reflect the power struggle between Than Tun and Aung San for leadership of the nationalist movement.

Beginning in May, about the time that the AFPFL Supreme Council was planning to meet and consider the proposed constitution and the resolutions passed at the earlier National Conference, the Communist Party, under Than Tun and Thein Pe, stepped up its direct-action campaigns among the peasants to pay no rents and no taxes.[43] As the result of one of their mass demonstrations in Tantabin, a shooting incident occurred that threatened to initiate a wave of violence and direct action. Aung San refused to support the Communists and reduced the mounting tensions by cooperating with the governor, Dorman-Smith. No immediate action was taken against the Communists by the AFPFL.

After the Supreme Council adopted the new constitution, it was agreed that the political parties would withdraw from the AFPFL and their members would reenter the league as individuals, either directly or indirectly; but the decision was not enforced until October 1946.[44]

In July the Burma Communist Party tried to use the government's action in outlawing the Thakin Soe faction as an issue to win national support for itself and force the AFPFL to adopt its tactics and goals. Protest meetings were held in Rangoon in defiance of a police ban against unlicensed public meetings in order to demonstrate the strength of the Burma Communist Party and to take advantage of the temporary absence of a permanent governor. The AFPFL refused to lend support because it was not consulted before the Communist Party began its campaign; it also did not believe that such protests were the proper tactics at that

---

42. New Times of Burma, July 16, 1946, p. 1; the Communist Party of Burma (Soe faction) together with the Red Flag Cultivators were charged with violation of the Unlawful Associations Act (India Act XIV, 1908).

43. For Aung San's position on the "no rents, no taxes" campaign of the Communists, see Josef Silverstein, *The Political Legacy of Aung San* (Ithaca, 1972), pp. 33–34.

44. Burmese Review, October 14, 1946, p. 8.

moment. In protest Than Tun resigned as the AFPFL secretary-general and was replaced by U Kyaw Nyein, a founder of both the Socialist Party and the AFPFL.[45] To test its strength, the Burma Communist Party called on its subgroups, the All-Burma Trade Union Congress, the Burma Trade Federation, and the Women's Congress, and also the AFPFL mass organizations to attend its main rally. Less than one thousand attended its meeting, and neither the shopkeepers nor the local transportation workers gave it their support.[46]

In September the AFPFL's Supreme Council met to elect a permanent secretary-general. Aung San proposed Kyaw Nyein, the acting secretary-general, and the Communist Party countered by proposing Thein Pe. Aung San requested that the Communists withdraw their candidate; when they refused, a vote was taken and Kyaw Nyein won, 52 to 33.[47]

During this period the Communists opened a full attack on Aung San; he, meanwhile, was in the process of negotiating with the new governor, Hubert Rance, regarding AFPFL participation in the Executive Council. From September 28 through October 10, the Communists, through their daily, the *Forum*, maintained a steady attack against the AFPFL decision to participate in the Executive Council and against Aung San personally for betraying the nationalist cause, despite the fact that one of their leaders, Thein Pe, held a seat in the new Executive Council.[48] As a result, the AFPFL Executive Council met on October 12 (three were absent, Than Tun and Thakin Chit from the Communist Party and Pyawbwe U Mya) and voted to expel the Communist Party; its decision was referred to the Supreme Council for confirmation.[49] By the end of the month Thein Pe was dropped from the

45. Ibid., July 29, 1946, p. 8.
46. Ibid.
47. *Burmese Review*, September 2, 1946; Nu, *Premier Reports to the People on Law and Order, National Solidarity, Social Welfare, National Economy, Foreign Affairs* (Rangoon, 1958), app. 1(a), p. 47.
48. Ibid., p. 48.
49. *Burman*, October 13, 1946, p. 1; the official reason given for the Executive Committee's action was that the Communist Party refused to accept discipline and give their loyalty to the AFPFL; ibid., p. 2, carried

AFPFL Executive Council and replaced by Pyawbwe U Mya and a Karen leader associated with the AFPFL, Saw Ba U Gyi, also was added to the council when it was enlarged, thus making it at the same time a more conservative and a more representative body. In addition, the Communist-inspired strikes gradually ended without coercion, and the local press reported that members of the Communist-sponsored All-Burma Trade Union Congress withdrew and joined the rival Socialist-run AFPFL affiliated trade union organization.[50] On November 1, the Supreme Council of the AFPFL confirmed the expulsion order.[51]

Despite this formal split, the AFPFL and the Communist Party did not wholly drift apart. Aung San and his colleagues in the Executive Council were successful in having the authorities lift the ban against Thakin Soe's Communist Party Burma, but this did not bring the two parties together. In the meantime the Soe faction refused to work within the limits of legal political action and was outlawed for a second time on January 23, 1947.[52]

Than Tun's Burma Communist Party remained a legal organization opposed to both the moderate leadership of the AFPFL and the conservative opposition of the revived prewar parties. Than Tun's group hoped that the British would balk at giving Burma its independence and that the AFPFL would have to adopt violent tactics and eventually have to reunite with the Communists. To its disappointment, this did not happen; in order to hold popular support and retain its public image as a nationalist party, it participated in the Resistance Day celebration in 1947 and allowed its members to contest the election for seats in the Constituent Assembly as individuals in areas where it was strong and where the AFPFL was not planning to make a vigorous fight.

---

Than Tun's rebuttal to the league in which he charged that during the police strike of the previous month the AFPFL sought to restrict its effects, whereas the Communists tried to expand them. See also *Burmese Review*, October 14, 1946, p. 8, for a broader discussion of this affair and also John F. Cady, *A History of Modern Burma* (Ithaca, 1958) for dates and votes that differ from the press accounts of the period.

50. *Burmese Review*, October 28, 1946, p. 8.
51. *Burman*, November 2, 1946, p. 1; it was reported that 99 of the 113 members attended the session; no vote count was made public.
52. By the Police Ii Branch, January 23, 1947.

The assassination of Aung San and his colleagues in July 1947 brought the Burma Communist Party to the support of the AFPFL against a potential threat from the right-wing prewar parties. With reservations, the Communists accepted the constitution and remained on friendly terms with the AFPFL until U Nu and Clement Attlee signed a treaty on October 17, 1947.[53]

The Communists used this Nu-Attlee treaty as the basis for a new attack on the AFPFL. They charged that it compromised the nation's independence by agreeing to accept a British training mission after independence and invalidated the socialist goals of the constitution by protecting British property and investment.[54] Nu responded to both charges and defended the treaty as not being a limitation on Burma's future independence.[55] Despite their public differences the Communists and the AFPFL entered into formal discussions on reunification but failed to arrive at an agreement. Talks were broken off in mid-November.[56] When the AFPFL met in its second All-Burma National Conference in December 1947, the Burma Communist Party was not present, nor was it ever again under the hegemony of the league.

Unlike the Communists, the Socialists remained inside the AFPFL and provided it with important leadership, ideas, and recruits. According to the "Report of the Secretary-General of the Socialist Party," the party remained inside the AFPFL after the first All-Burma AFPFL National Conference because its leaders realized that international and local conditions had changed, that the people wanted peace, and that "the method we use for the attainment of freedom must also be a peaceful one. We would win

---

53. Great Britain, *Treaty between the Government of the United Kingdom and the Provisional Government of Burma*, London, October 17 1947, Cmd. 7240 (printed prior to ratification) and Cmd. 7360 (printed after ratifications exchanged in Burma, January 4, 1948); hereafter Nu-Attlee Treaty Cmd. 7240.

54. Ibid., Art. 6; Annex, "Defence Agreement."

55. Nu, "Communist Allegations," in *Toward Peace and Democracy* (Rangoon, 1949), pp. 20–30; according to Burma, op. cit., p. 5, the Burma Communist Party pledged its support for the treaty, but U Nu's speech, together with the press accounts of the day, makes it clear that this was not the case.

56. *Times* (London), November 19, 1947, p. 3.

victory by mass organization method because the era of the power of the masses has begun."[57]

Organized on the basis of a Marxist ideology, the BSP sought to build an elite group of dedicated followers who accepted the principle of democratic centralism and strict discipline in the organization.[58] According to the party's analysis, the road to national leadership passed through three stages. The first was the defensive, wherein the Socialists organized and recruited quietly and drew as little attention as possible. This stage had ended on January 1, 1946. The second stage was called the hit and run, wherein the task was to build mass organizations and "transform masses into forces." During this stage the party would not attack other groups but at the same time would "brush aside all obstacles that lie in our way."[59] No time limit was set on this stage. In the third and final stage the party, having completed developing leaders and building mass support, would be ready to assume control of the state.

In reporting its success the secretary-general announced that by the end of 1946 it was organized in eighteen districts and had workers in nine others. To train its cadres it established classes in socialism in its Rangoon headquarters, and by January 1, 1946, it had successfully trained 228 students.[60] The BSP was very successful in carrying out its mass organization work. Four major social and economic groups were either formed or controlled by it: the All-Burma Peasants' Organization, the Trade Union Congress Burma, the Federation of Trade Organizations, and the Women's Freedom League. All were affiliated with the AFPFL "but actually organized and led by the Socialist Party."[61]

As the Communists lost their place in the League's leadership, the Socialists replaced them. Kyaw Nyein's election to the office of secretary-general of the AFPFL, together with Thakin Mya's role as close advisor to Aung San, marked the clear ascendancy of the

57. "Report of the . . . Socialist Party, December 1946," op. cit., p. 5.
58. Ibid., p. 7.
59. Ibid., p. 8.
60. Ibid.
61. Hla Aung, op. cit., p. 3.

Socialists over other groups. In the Constituent Assembly election, the BSP returned the largest number of representatives.[62]

The assassination of Aung San, Thakin Mya, and the others provoked a new situation. The AFPFL leadership passed to an independent, U Nu, but the basis of its strength came from two blocs, the Socialist Party with allied affiliate organizations and the now-leaderless PVO. Nu sought to combine the two into a new AFPFL subgroup called the Marxist League, hoping the PVO would lose its military character, surrender its hidden weapons, and find a new place in the political and social life of independent Burma. The formulators of the Marxist League idea hoped to attract all leftists away from the Communist Party leadership and bring them under the new banner.[63] The merger never fully materialized; fear among the PVO members that they would lose their identity and political power to the Socialists proved to be the main obstruction.

On the eve of the second All-Burma AFPFL National Conference, the Socialists were the dominant political group in the League despite the fact that technically, according to the constitution, they were not a constituent group. As the AFPFL met to celebrate the coming independence and plan the future, little attention was given to the revolutionary activity of the two communist parties, which marred the picture of political unity in Burma.

Most significant for the AFPFL as the party of national unity was the growth in the Frontier Areas of confederate and associate political and social groups resulting from two factors: direct contact among Aung San, his AFPFL colleagues, and the leaders of the frontier peoples, and the decisions of the British government

62. Burma, op. cit., p. 11.
63. New Times of Burma, October 10, 1947, p. 1; November 26, 1947, p. 1, named its Presidium as including Bo Let Ya, Bo Aung, Bo Sein Hman, Bo Taik Soe, and Bo Aung Nyunt representing the PVO and Ko Ko Gyi, U Ba Swe, U Kyaw Nyein, and Bo Aung Gyi representing the BSP; November 28, 1947, p. 1, includes a statement by Ko Ko Gyi on the political and social aims of the Marxist League, which called for a socialist economy including the nationalization of land and major industries.

embodied in the Aung San–Clement Attlee Agreement.[64] At the Panglong Conference in 1947, the Frontier Areas leaders organized themselves into the Supreme Council of the United Hill Peoples, the first formal unification of leaders from the Shans, Kachins, and Chins.[65] Though not formally affiliated with the AFPFL, it was associated through a common program and overlapping members.

At the conclusion of the Panglong Conference in 1947, the Shan *sawbwas* and leaders representing the people who were in contact with the AFPFL decided to organize the statewide Shan States Freedom League with the triple aim of unifying the masses, winning independence for the whole of Burma, and working for political and social progress of all the people. The seven-member Central Interim Council was formed, and eleven organizing secretaries were chosen.[66] In May the AFPFL headquarters announced that twenty-two delegates representing the Shan States Freedom League and including both *sawbwas* and popular leaders were accredited to attend the Constituent Assembly.[67] When the delegation arrived in Rangoon its spokesman, U Tun Myint, declared that the organization had enrolled over two hundred thousand members; he also pointed out that the Shan States Freedom League sent a delegation to the Constituent Assembly to cooperate with the Burmese and to demonstrate its complete support of the *Bogyoke's* resolutions on Burma's independence.[68]

In the area which was to become the Kachin State after independence, AFPFL branches were formed among the peoples of Bhamo. They presented their views on the future Kachin State before the Frontier Areas Committee of Enquiry.[69] In addition the Supreme Council of the United Hill Peoples was supported

64. Great Britain, *Conclusions Reached in the Conversations between His Majesty's Government and the Delegation from the Executive Council of the Governor of Burma*, Cmd. 7029, 1947.

65. "The Panglong Agreement, 1947," in Burma, *The Report of the Frontier Areas Committee of Enquiry 1947* (Rangoon, 1947), pt. 1, Report p. 16; pt. 2, Appendices, pp. 3–12. It sent representatives to testify before the Committee of Enquiry on April 21, 1947, after it had held public meetings March 18–25, 1947.

66. *New Times of Burma*, March 12, 1947, p. 2.

67. Ibid., May 18, 1947, p. 1.

68. Ibid., June 24, 1947, p. 2.

69. Burma, *Frontier Areas Committee of Enquiry*, op. cit., 2: 64–66.

by the Kachin chiefs, one of whom was both an official of the organization and a member of the Committee of Enquiry.[70] In an exchange between Sima Duwa Sinwa Nawng and a Burman before the Committee of Enquiry, the Kachin chief expressed the faith of his people in the words of Aung San and the leadership of the AFPFL: "We believe in Aung San because he is in the Government and he represents the AFPFL which represents the people."[71] Finally, there was the Kachin Youth League, which in 1947 reported a membership of fifteen thousand, that desired to unite with the All-Burma Youth Organization, at the time an affiliate of the AFPFL.[72] Thus, when the Constituent Assembly met, a vast number of the leaders in the proposed Kachin state were linked, either directly or indirectly, with the AFPFL or its affiliates.

With the exception of the Arakan Hills Tract, there is no evidence of any AFPFL organizations in the Chin Hills; the local chiefs and the few politically articulate people in this area, however, gave their full support to the Panglong Agreement and the leadership of the Supreme Council of the United Hill Peoples Organization. They supported the idea of an independent Burma and sent delegates to the Constituent Assembly. In the Arakan Hills Tract an AFPFL organization was formed, which had about three thousand members,[73] mostly Arakanese who sought to be linked closely with the peoples of Burma proper under AFPFL leadership.[74]

If to these groups in the Frontier Areas the Karen Youth League is added, the AFPFL in 1947 could claim to speak for most of the minorities as well as for the majority ethnic groups in Burma. No other organization in Burma could claim that kind of following.

70. The Kachin chief was Sima Duwa Sinwa Nawng; in 1949 he became the president of the Supreme Council of the United Hill Peoples' Congress; he already was the combined head and minister of state in the Kachin State and a loyal supporter of U Nu and the AFPFL.
71. Burma, *Frontier Areas Committee of Enquiry*, op. cit., 2: 70.
72. Ibid., p. 55.
73. Burma, *Frontier Areas Committee of Enquiry*, op. cit., 2: 97.
74. According to an interview with U Kyaw Min, M.P. from Akyab, on November 21, 1955, in Rangoon, the AFPFL was very widely supported in the Arakan region; its candidates won all the seats from the area to the Constituent Assembly; some ran uncontested.

On the eve of Burma's independence, the second National Conference of the AFPFL met in Rangoon. In conformity with the AFPFL constitution, the district AFPFL branches and the affiliate groups sent delegations to the conference and named their representatives to the Supreme Council. The latter chose U Nu to continue as the League's president.[75] Among the members of the Executive Committee were six BSP leaders, five PVO leaders, and at least one representative each from the All-Burma Muslim League, the Karen Youth League, and the All-Burma Youth Organization.[76]

This National Conference, unlike the previous one, was not marked by personal or ideological differences. The goals of the BSP were embodied in the numerous resolutions passed at the meeting. In particular, the fifth resolution called on the Union of Burma to adopt a national plan for state acquisition of all land and timber for distribution to the peasant and forest workers and for state ownership and operation of all natural wealth, transportation, water power, and industry. Resolution 6 expanded the ideas of state ownership of land and called for redistribution to cultivators, encouragement for the development of cooperatives, and "communal tenures [to] . . . be established in areas where this is possible." It ended by saying that those farmers who wished to remain independent ought to be able to do so.[77]

In the resolution on national defense, the AFPFL linked this problem with national unity. All ethnic groups must be trained and

75. *New Times of Burma*, December 23, 1947, p. 1; ibid., December 24, 1947, p. 1.
76. Ibid., December 24, 1947, p. 1; the following were chosen as members of the Executive Committee: U Nu, president, Independent; Bo Hmu Aung, vice-president, PVO; U Tun (New Light), treasurer, Independent; U Ba Swe, secretary-general, Socialist Party; Bo Sein Hman, PVO(?); Ko Ko Gyi, Socialist Party president; Bo Let Ya, PVO; U Nyo Tun, (?); U Mya (Henzada), Independent; Thakin Tin, Socialist Party; Bo Hmu Po Kun, PVO; U Than Myint, Burma Muslim League president; Mahn Win Maung, Karen Youth League president; U Kyaw Nyein, Socialist Party; U Ba Gyan, Youth League president; and the following were coopted members: Daw Khin Hla, Women's Freedom League president; Bo Aung Nyein, PVO; U Tin Nyunt, Labor Federation–Socialist; Thakin Pan Myaing, Federation of Trade of Organizations–Socialist; and Bo Taik So, PVO.
77. Ibid., December 23, 1947, p. 4.

must share the responsibility of protecting the nascent state.[78] The idea of national unity was also linked to the role of the AFPFL in the period of self-government. The league was proud to have achieved "unity under its flag of hitherto scattered forces represented by the impoverished worker and cultivator, the revolutionary middle classes, the forces of nationalism fighting against fascism and the diversified racial groups."[79] To maintain this unity, it said, the AFPFL must fight against corruption and continue to work toward greater harmony among groups. The conference also took note of the social and political unrest and revolutionary activity throughout the country and called on all AFPFL members to work for internal peace.[80]

President Nu's speech sought to explain the two main themes that exercised the AFPFL's leadership at that moment. The first was moral improvement. He called on the leaders to cease their jealousies, curb their appetites for power, and end their corruption: "We cannot let a great political organization which can give so much succour to the masses stink in the nostrils of the people merely because a few members of the League are rotten." His second theme was that the members of the AFPFL must help the government preserve internal order; as the only nationwide organization, it could and should work for domestic peace. The League, he argued, saved the "outworn state machinery" in the crisis caused by Aung San's death; it can and must play a major role in the current threats against the new state.

> Under present conditions, AFPFL is the best instrument for securing peace, for under its banner the Burmese masses are united as never before. Because of that unity, the ship of the AFPFL has weathered every storm, even the violent storm represented by the terrible assassination. . . . So long as the AFPFL can hold the Burmese masses, I am convinced that the danger of internal security cannot be serious.[81]

78. *New Times of Burma*, December 25, 1947, p. 1.
79. Ibid., December 27, 1947, p. 1.
80. Ibid.
81. Nu, "Toward a Lasting Peace," in *Towards Peace and Democracy*, op. cit., p. 41.

In many ways the AFPFL proved to be an ideal vehicle for the nationalist movement between 1945 and 1948. Its federated structure accommodated a variety of groups and leaders who supported a number of different goals and tactics. More important, it was an organization that could include the frontier minorities without their feeling overwhelmed or submerged. At a time when the minorities from these areas were beginning to become involved in national politics, the AFPFL structure gave them access to the nation's leadership while they pursued their particular ends in their own areas.

But if the AFPFL was a success in the struggle for national unity and national independence, it was a failure when independence made it necessary to bring all the people closer together to create a truly united state. The fact that units within the party remained intact made it possible for them to withdraw easily and take up an independent position quickly. Division among the national leadership on how to realize national unity, either through unity in diversity or through Burmanization permeated the organization and left it a loose coalition rather than a tightly knit national party.

The AFPFL was the right kind of organization to bring all the people together for a common end—independence—but it was not capable of reorienting itself for the new problems that came with independence. The insurrections of the late nineteen-forties and early nineteen-fifties and the party split in 1958 were the tragic ends for an organization that promised so much.

# 8

# The Constitution of 1947

Burma's formal solution to the double problem of national unity was outlined in the 1947 constitution and expressed in the political institutions it informed. The Constituent Assembly devised a solution to the problem of achieving ethnic unity by constructing a system of government that the Union's attorney general, U Chan Htoon, once described as federal in theory and unitary in practice.[1] To achieve political unity it devised a democratic system that attempted to protect the individual and at the same time permit the government to lead the nation toward the realization of a socialist state. Neither solution proved adequate nor was each universally accepted by the people. The failure stemmed in part from the conflicting ideas united in the constitution and in part from the absence of popular support for the constitutional-democratic process as a means for settling political disputes.

To answer the question of how to construct a union in which people who formerly were separated could be joined together so as to benefit from unity yet maintain nominal independence, the authors of the constitution constructed a unique federal system

1. *Nation*, July 2, 1952, p. 1; statement made in argument before the Supreme Court in a case that tested the legislative power of the Union.

that appeared to realize the goal of unity in diversity but in fact gave very little independence to the several states. The constitution made no mention of the words federal or federalism, but it is clear from an examination of the document that the founding fathers intended to divide authority between the states and Burma proper. It is also clear that they had no intention of creating a union of equals. Rather, they gave to each separate unit a minimum of power and those special concessions necessary to bring them into the Union of Burma. The federal solution as defended by Aung San in the early sessions of the Constituent Assembly was not a copy of any existing system in the world: "We have not tried to copy anything for the sake of copying. . . . Anything we have tried to utilize from modern constitutions of the world, we have selected . . . and thoroughly adopted to suit Burma's aspirations and Burmese genius."[2]

The federal solution was based on four principles: The people are citizens of the Union and residents of the states; state institutions are inferior to those of the Union, and the two are linked by the use of common personnel; states enjoy different rights and limitations because of their desires, particular background, and social composition; the institutions of the Union are also those of Burma proper.

---

The constitution made clear beyond doubt that "there is but one citizenship in the Union and there shall be no citizenship as distinct from the citizenship of the Union."[3] The constitution established three conditions for determining who was automatically a citizen of Burma: any person whose parents are members of an indigenous ethnic group; any person born in Burma who has at least one grandparent who is a member of an indigenous ethnic group or whose parents are citizens of the Union; and any person born in British Burma prior to independence who lived in the territory "not less than eight in the ten years immediately preceding the commencement of this Constitution or immediately pre-

2. *Burman*, May 30, 1947, p. 1.
3. *The Constitution of the Union of Burma* (Rangoon, 1948), Art. 10.

ceding the 1st January 1942" who intended to reside permanently in the Union and made this fact known in the prescribed way.[4] The constitution also provided for the naturalization of aliens and empowered the legislature to establish the conditions for carrying out that objective.[5] Accordingly the legislature, during its first provisional session, passed the Union Citizenship Act of 1948, which expanded the language of the constitution and described the conditions for naturalization. The law defined indigenous races as including the Arakanese, Burmans, Chins, Kachins, Karens, Kayahs, Mons, and Shans "and such racial groups as had settled in any of the territories included within the Union as their permanent home from a period anterior to 1823 A.D."[6] The act provided that an alien could be naturalized if he were over eighteen years old, had lived in the Union for more than five years, was of good character, could speak one of the local languages (Burmese, Chin, Kachin, Karen, or Shan), and planned to reside permanently in Burma.[7]

The benefits of citizenship, drawn largely from the Western political tradition, were numerous. The founding fathers provided that citizens should have equality before the law and equality of opportunity for public employment or the pursuit of a trade, profession, or business.[8] Further, citizens were guaranteed the rights of free speech and assembly,[9] the right to unite with others in an association or trade union, and the rights of residence anywhere and free mobility throughout the Union.[10]

In addition, both citizens and noncitizens were granted additional privileges. Women were entitled to equal pay for equal work.[11] Everyone was guaranteed freedom of religion. Ethnic and linguistic minorities were not barred from a state educational institution nor forced to accept religious instruction against their

4. Ibid., Art. 11.
5. Ibid., Art. 12.
6. *Union Citizenship Act*, 1948 [Act No. LXVI of 1948], Art. 3(1).
7. Ibid., Art. 7(1).
8. Constitution, Arts. 13, 14.
9. Ibid., Art. 16.
10. Ibid., Art. 17.
11. Ibid., Art. 15.

will.¹² Buddhism was permitted to enjoy a special position in the Union because it was "the faith professed by the great majority of the citizens."¹³ With limitations discussed below, everyone was entitled to the right to private property and the protection of the court against encroachment of enumerated rights either by government or by individuals.¹⁴ No person was subjected to ex post facto laws nor given a penalty for a crime "greater than that applicable at the time of the commission of the offense."¹⁵ Traffic in human beings and the involuntary servitude of individuals were also prohibited.¹⁶

As a counterweight to these rights, citizens and residents in the Union were subject to several limitations. The people were prohibited from using private property in a manner detrimental to the general public. The State was empowered to limit the amount of property any individual could hold and could expropriate property in accordance with the law.¹⁷ The Union, not the states, was declared the ultimate owner of the land and as such could regulate, alter, or abolish land tenure and "resume possession of any land and distribute [it] . . . for collective or cooperative farming."¹⁸

The Union, not the states, was paternally responsible for the protection of the workers' rights to organize, to obtain safe working conditions and holidays, and to promote "schemes for housing and social insurance."¹⁹ Clearly, the authors of the constitution intended the peoples of Burma to look to the Union for protection and identification, but at the same time, the authors gave the states a form and character that permitted them to make a claim on their residents and influence their way of life.

12. Ibid., Art. 22.
13. Ibid., Art. 21.
14. Ibid., Art. 25.
15. Ibid., Art. 24.
16. Ibid., Art. 19.
17. Ibid., Art. 23(2-4).
18. Ibid., Art. 18.
19. Ibid., Art. 31.

The second and third principles underlying the constitution are closely interrelated. To see how they are manifested, it is necessary to examine closely the structures, rights, and privileges of the states and to note how the states relate to the Union.

The Shan State was the largest in size outside of Burma proper and the most advanced in political organization and rights. The legislative body was the State Council. It had fifty members who derived their right to sit from the fact that they held seats in the Union Parliament.[20] There were no elections for state offices; all were derivative. So long as a person remained a member of the Union legislature, he could participate in the State Council. When the Union Parliament was dissolved, the State Council, too, was dissolved and could not be reformed until after new elections were held for the Union Parliament.

The State Council's powers to legislate and to tax were established in the constitution and defined in the annexes attached to it.[21] All legislative measures the council adopted were sent directly to the Union president for signature and promulgation. The president had a thirty-day suspensive veto; during that period he could ask the Supreme Court for an advisory opinion whether or not a state measure conformed to the constitution.[22] If the court said no,

20. Ibid., Art. 154(1). The constitution provides in Art. 154(2) that the Shan seats in the Union Chamber of Nationalities are reserved for Shan *saohpas* (chiefs) elected by a special constituency composed exclusively of chiefs. The *Constitution Amendment Act* of 1959 (second) repealed this provision, but the amendment did not become effective until after the next elected Union Parliament was dissolved, approximately in 1964; at that time all resident citizens would be eligible to compete in elections for these seats. The constitution did not specify the exact number of Shan State seats in the Union Chamber of Deputies. According to the apportionment made in 1951–1952, the state was allotted twenty-five on the basis of its population.

21. *Constitution*, Art. 92(2); 96(1); 155; Third Schedule, List 2; Fourth Schedule.

22. Ibid., Art. 156; 157(1).

the measure was returned to the state for redrafting; if the court said yes, the president had to sign the measure into law.[23]

The constitution authorized one annual session of the State Council but permitted the head of the state to call special sessions as frequently as necessary.[24] Practice during the first eight years of independence was to hold meetings twice yearly in February and August in order to coincide with the sessions of the Union Parliament.[25]

Administrative authority was delegated to the head of state, who was chosen by the Union prime minister after consultation with the State Council. The head of state had a second function, to serve at the pleasure of the Union prime minister as the minister for his state in the Union cabinet.[26] His duties included recruiting for and managing the state civil service;[27] keeping the State Council informed of the activity of state administration;[28] and preparing an annual budget for the State Council's approval.[29] To assist him, the State Council was authorized to elect from among its own members a state cabinet of ministers.[30] Practice during the first eight years of the state's existence had been for the State Councils to elect six ministers, whose task was to head the state ministries, convey decisions and views of the State Council to the head of state, and give advice and assistance to the chief administrator whenever called on.[31]

As the State Council depended on the Union Parliament both for its personnel and the length of its life, so too the combined

23. Ibid., Art. 157(2–4).
24. Ibid., Art. 159.
25. From an interview with U Saw Tha, secretary, Shan State Ministry, April 10, 1956, Rangoon.
26. *Constitution*, Art. 160; according to U Saw Tha, the head of state is in fact the agent of the Union in his state and, as such, his salary is paid by the Union government.
27. Ibid., Art. 161(2).
28. Ibid., Art. 163.
29. Ibid., Art. 164(1–2); the Union president is directed by the constitution to scrutinize the state budgets, approve them, and then have them incorporated into a consolidated Union budget.
30. Ibid., Art. 133.
31. Interview with Saw Tha.

head and minister of state depended on a Union official, the prime minister, for his appointment and duration in office. In his combined tasks his first responsibility was to the prime minister and not to the State Council. This peculiar arrangement depreciated his role as his state's chief administrator and at the same time lessened his effectiveness as his state's chief spokesman in the Union government. This situation led to many serious political and constitutional battles in the Kachin and Karen states. Thus this office provided the second example of state inferiority to the Union and of the unique interlocking of state and Union institutions and personnel.

The constitution also provided that the Union and the states share judicial powers. The Supreme and High Courts had review jurisdiction over any inferior courts established by the states.[32] No state system of courts was established under this constitution; instead the state councils passed resolutions directing the Union Parliament to regulate the administration of justice through an act of Parliament.[33] In 1953, the national legislature responded by passing the States Court Act, which permitted the minister of justice to establish a uniform court system throughout the states. Because of civil war, the absence of sufficient competent judges, and other problems, the act was never fully implemented in the Shan State.[34]

During the first eight years of state government, justice was administered chiefly under the preindependence judicial system of inferior courts that had been created under the Federated Shan States Law and Criminal Justice Order of 1926. In addition, the Shan chiefs were empowered to exercise very limited judicial authority under the Orders Modifying the Customary Laws in the Federated Shan States. Cases decided under the order of 1926 could be appealed in the High Court, and cases under the orders modify-

32. *Constitution*, Third Schedule, List II, Art. 3(3–4).
33. Ibid., Art. 92(3): "Any State Council may by resolution surrender any of its territory or any of its powers and rights to the Union."
34. *State Courts Act*, 1953 [Art. No. LII of 1953]; also information regarding the relationship of the Union and the states in justice administration from U Tin Naing, registrar, High Court, Rangoon, April 24, 1956, and subsequent correspondence.

ing the customary law could be appealed to the Resident of the district concerned.³⁵

At the local level the thirty-three Shan chiefs exercised administrative authority over their traditional domains. They enjoyed the right of taxation, and they raised extra revenue by controlling the gambling in their subdivisions. The people of the state could neither remove them nor alter the form of rule. In the five major towns in the state, administration was under Residents who, as state civil servants, were responsible to the head of state.³⁶

The structure of the Shan State was reproduced with modifications in the Kayah State.³⁷ The State Council of five members was composed of three members of the Union Chamber of Nationalities and two members of the Union Chamber of Deputies.³⁸

---

35. Interview with Saw Tha.
36. Ibid. On April 24, 1959, the Shan saophas signed agreements with the Shan State government to transfer "to and vest in the Government of the Shan State all his powers, authority and jurisdiction in relation to the Government of his state as from the 24th of April 1959," from *Agreement between Shan State Government and the Saophas*, Art. 1, which appeared in a photo reproduction in *Burma Weekly Bulletin*, n.s., 8(4) (May 21, 1959): 26–37. Four days later, on April 27, 1959, the Shan State Council passed in emergency meeting a motion introduced by the home minister recommending to the chiefs that they transfer "their respective administrative and judicial powers to the Shan State Government and that the Council shall approve in accordance with Section 161 (1) of the Constitution of the Union of Burma of such authority resting with the Head of the Shan State, or with whosoever may be appointed by him on his behalf for the exercise of such powers" *Burma Weekly Bulletin*, ibid., p. 26.
37. According to the constitution, the former name of the state is Karenni State; in 1951 the Union Parliament passed the *Constitution Amendment Act, 1951* [Act No. LXII of 1951], which changed the state's name to the Kayah State. Because this name remains and is the name by which the residents want their state to be known, it is used here and throughout.
38. *Constitution*, Art. 183(1); the three chiefs who hold the Kayah seats in this house are named in the constitution. In 1964 this article was to become inoperative; according to the *Constitution Amendment Act, 1959*, (second) the three members were elected from the total population of the state. On a population basis it was assumed that the state would not have sufficient representatives in the Chamber of Deputies; therefore, ac-

## THE CONSTITUTION OF 1947

From 1952 through 1956, the State Council operated with four members because one of the chiefs died and no successor was named.[39] To broaden the deliberative base of this legislative body, the State Council created in 1952 an advisory group of five members chosen from the recognized leaders in the state.[40] The act creating this body included no provisions or criteria for determining recognized leaders. The advisory body was permitted to discuss all matters before the State Council but had no power to vote.

Administration in the Kayah State, as in the Shan, was in the hands of a combined head and minister of state who was appointed by the Union prime minister.[41] The Kayah State Council did not create a state cabinet to assist the head of state even though it was authorized to do so. From 1948 through 1956 the head and minister of the state found that his duties as minister in the Union cabinet required his presence in Rangoon for the greater part of his time. He therefore appointed a Resident or administrative assistant to remain in Loikaw, the state capital, to act for him on the ordinary business coming to his office as head of state. In judicial matters, the state vested courts under the States Court Act of 1953.[42]

Government at the local level was under the administration of the chiefs and the head of state. In each of the subdivisions the chiefs enjoyed exclusive authority on matters governed by customary law; in all other matters the state civil servants acted for the head of state. The chiefs enjoyed local judicial and taxing power.[43] Unlike the chiefs in the Shan State, those in the Kayah

---

cording to *Constitution*, Art. 83(3), the Kayah State was entitled to representation on a higher ratio than used to compute representation in the other states.

39. Interview with U Myat Soe, secretary, Kayah State Ministry, on April 19, 1956, Rangoon.

40. *Kayah State Council Advisers Act*, 1952. No copy of this act was made available to the writer. All information regarding it came from the Kayah State Ministry in Rangoon and from interviews with U Myat Soe, secretary.

41. *Constitution*, Art. 189.

42. Interview with Myat Soe.

43. Ibid.

State did not surrender their powers immediately after the passage of the Second Constitution Amendment Act in 1959.

The Kachin State government, while outwardly similar to the structure in the Shan State, also had variations that resulted mainly from the ethnic composition of the population. When the state was in the process of being created, the local leaders and the members of the Frontier Areas Committee of Enquiry noted that the population, according to projections of the 1931 census and estimates made in 1947, would be almost evenly divided between Kachins and non-Kachins.[44] This fact was reflected in a number of ways in the political institutions and practices.

The State Council in the Kachin State had nineteen members, twelve who held seats in the Union Chamber of Nationalities and seven in the Union Chamber of Deputies.[45] The constitution provided that, although all the legislators must be elected from the resident population, six of the twelve chosen for seats in the Chamber of Nationalities had to be Kachins and the other six, non-Kachins.[46] There were no racial restrictions on who could hold the seats in the Chamber of Deputies. Ethnic rights and privileges enjoyed prior to independence were protected by the constitutional provision that any bill that prejudicially affected any of the rights or privileges enjoyed by any group during British rule could not become law unless a majority of State Council members representing the affected group gave their approval.[47] In all other matters the State Council had equal powers with its counterpart in the Shan State.

---

44. Burma, *The Report of the Frontier Areas Committee of Enquiry, 1947*, pt. 1, Report (Rangoon, 1947) pp. 3–4, gave the following population estimates:

| Ethnic groups | Bhamo | Myitkyina | Total |
|---|---|---|---|
| Kachins | 49,794 | 157,642 | 207,436 |
| Shans, Lolo-Moso | 36,765 | 76,586 | 113,351 |
| Burmans | 33,540 | 40,230 | 73,770 |
| Others | 8,901 | 23,542 | 32,443 |
| Total | 129,000 | 298,000 | 427,000 |

45. *Constitution*, Art. 166(1–2).
46. Ibid., Art. 166(2).
47. Ibid., Art. 167(1).

The office of head of state in the Kachin State was reserved for a person of Kachin ethnic origin.[48] To give ethnic balance, the constitution directed the State Council to elect no less than one-half the members of the State cabinet from among the non-Kachins.[49] Through 1956, the practice was to maintain a cabinet of three members, two of which were drawn from the non-Kachin members of the State Council.[50] Ethnic restrictions also applied to the state's civil service. The constitution provided that, in carrying out his functions as head of the civil service, the head of state had to consult with the non-Kachins before assigning or transferring a state employee to or from areas populated by a majority of non-Kachins.[51] In other respects the head of state and his cabinet had the same duties and limits as existed in the Shan State.

The States Court Act did become operative throughout the greater part of the Kachin State. Only in the hill areas, which were difficult to reach and had a transitory population, did the pre-independence Kachin Hill Tribes Regulations remain in effect. Under these a quasi-court system existed wherein a person charged with a violation was tried before a deputy commissioner who exercised power as a sessions judge. The deputy commissioner's decision was subject to review by the government of the Kachin State only.[52]

Local government varied with the locality; Myitkyina and Bhamo were considered municipalities with separate administrative and taxing powers. The rest of the state was divided into two districts administered by the deputy commissioners, who were responsible to the head of state. In the remote and backward plains

---

48. Ibid., Art. 173.
49. Ibid., Art. 175(3).
50. Interview with U Ba Maw, deputy secretary, Kachin State Ministry, March 28, 1956, Rangoon.
51. *Constitution*, Art. 174(2).
52. Interviews with Ba Maw and Tin Naing. *Constitution*, Art. 150: "Nothing in this Constitution shall operate to invalidate the exercise of limited functions and powers of a judicial nature by any person or body of persons duly authorized by law to exercise such functions and powers notwithstanding that such person or such body of persons is not a judge or a Court appointed or established as such under this Constitution."

area, local headmen were elected to govern the villages; in the hill areas the deputy commissioner appointed *duwas* (chiefs), most of whom were hereditary leaders, to govern their villages.[53]

Initially the Karen State provided a departure in the way its form of government was developed. Because the members of the Constituent Assembly were unable to get the Karens to agree on the size, location, and political organization of their state, the authors of the constitution made provisions for two types of government and left it to the people concerned to decide which to follow. According to the constitution if the Kayah State and the Salween areas, together with adjacent areas in which Karens were the majority ethnic group, decided to form a united territory, it was to be called the Karen State and was to "have the same status as the Shan State."[54] This suggestion was rejected by the people of the Kayah State, and the provision was repealed in the Constitution Amendment Act of 1951.[55]

The alternative option provided that a special region be created to include the Salween District "and such adjacent areas occupied by the Karens as may be determined by a Special Commission;" it was to be called Kaw-thu-lay. To administer the region the constitution provided for the creation of a Karen affairs council to be composed of all Karen representatives in the Union Chamber of Deputies and no more than five Karen representatives in the Union Chamber of Nationalities.[56] This council was empowered to advise and assist the minister for Karen affairs.[57] Parliament was authorized to alter the powers of the council by law if the need and desire arose.[58]

Administration of Kaw-thu-lay was placed under the control of the minister for Karen affairs. The Union prime minister was empowered to appoint the minister after consulting with the Karen Affairs Council. The minister's duties included general administration in the region, supervision and control of Karen

53. Interview with Ba Maw.
54. *Constitution*, Art. 180(1).
55. *Constitution Amendment Act, 1951*, op. cit., Arts, 2, 4.
56. *Constitution*, Art. 181(1).
57. Ibid., (4).
58. Ibid., (6).

educational and cultural institutions, and "all matters affecting the special rights of the Karens."⁵⁹ Chief among those special rights was the constitutional provision that gave the Karens reserved seats in the Union Parliament in proportion to their number.⁶⁰

The institutions never really took root because the territory of the special region became one of the main battlegrounds in the civil war that began in 1948 and continued throughout the life of the constitution. The Union government appointed the Regional Autonomy Enquiry Commission in September 1948 to examine, among other things, the Karen grievances about the proposed state, existent rights, and status in the Union.⁶¹ In its interim report the commission recommended that the Union government should act under the provisions of the constitution and form a new Karen state regardless of whether the Kayahs wished to join. The commission also recommended that, pending the formation of the new state, the area under the supervision of the Karen Affairs Council "be enlarged by including such areas adjacent to the Salween District as are predominantly inhabited by the Karens."⁶²

Acting on these recommendations the Union Parliament passed an amendment to the constitution and created the Karen State.⁶³ Under the amendment the state was limited to the territories of the Salween District and the adjacent areas in which the Karens were the dominant ethnic group.⁶⁴ According to the Karen State Ministry, the Karen State covered about 11,600 square miles and

59. Ibid., (3).
60. *Constitution*, Art. 83(1); Art. 87, Second Schedule. For a discussion from a Burman point of view of the special rights accorded the Karens, see Maung Maung, *Burma's Constitution* (The Hague, 1959), pp. 181–182.
61. *Burmese Review and Monday New Times*, September 6, 1948, p. 4; Nu, "Satisfaction to all Nationals," in *Towards Peace and Democracy* (Rangoon, 1949), pp. 156–158.
62. "Interim Report of the Regional Autonomy Enquiry Commission," February 19, 1949, Art. 4.7, in Burma, Ministry of Information, *Burma and the Insurrections* (Rangoon, 1949), pp. 28–30. Idem., *Burma's Freedom: The Second Anniversary* (Rangoon, 1950), p. 27, reproduces the recommendations only. The constitution provides for the creation of new states, Arts. 199, 200.
63. *Constitution Amendment Act*, 1951, op. cit.
64. Ibid., Art. 4(1).

included the areas known as Kya-in, Kawkareik, Hlaingbwe, Pa-an, and Thandawng in addition to the Salween District.[65] Its population in 1956 was estimated at 578,354.[66]

The amendment provided for the creation of a governmental structure similar to that which existed in the Shan State. A state council was created with a total membership of twenty-two, of which fifteen were members of the Union Chamber of Nationalities and seven were members of the Union Chamber of Deputies.[67] No seats were reserved for any ethnic group. Like the states previously discussed, the Karen State Council had power to legislate and tax according to the legislative and revenue lists attached to the constitution. Also, as in the other states, it could recommend to the Union Parliament legislation the council had no power to pass.[68] The State Council was authorized to meet at least once a year, but practice had been to hold sessions biannually at the same time that the Union Parliament was in session. All legislation had to be scrutinized and promulgated by the Union president and, if challenged, considered by the Supreme Court.[69]

The state administration was entrusted to the head of state, who, like his counterpart in the other states, had a second function, serving as the state's minister in the Union cabinet. He, too, was appointed by the Union prime minister after consultation with the State Council and was assisted by a state cabinet of ministers who were elected by the State Council from among its own membership.[70] Initially the cabinet included six, but when one resigned it was reduced to five.[71] The duties and relationships between the head and minister of state and the state cabinet were like those in the Shan State. The judicial power in the state was exercised by

---

65. Interviews with U Saw Butler, secretary, Karen State Ministry, and U Myint Tun, legal counsel, Karen State Ministry, on March 30, 1956, Rangoon. The new territories were added by an act of Parliament in 1952, the *Karen State Extension Act* [Act XIV of 1952].

66. Interview — Saw Butler, Myint Tun.

67. *Constitution Amendment Act*, 1951, Art. 4(180.2); interviews with Saw Butler and Myint Tun.

68. *Constitution Amendment Act*, 1951, Art. 4(180.4).

69. Ibid., (181.1).

70. Ibid.

71. Interviews with Saw Butler and Myint Tun.

local courts created under the States Court Act in 1953. The courts were under the administration of the Union minister of justice.[72]

Government at the local level was centrally administered. The state was subdivided into one district, three subdivisions, townships, towns, village tracts, and villages. The officials above the village tract level were civil service appointees; the village tracts and villages were governed locally by elected headmen who were responsible to the district commissioner.[73]

In terms of experience, the Karen State was the youngest. Because of the civil war and insurgency, the Karen State government did not assume responsibility for the areas added to it in 1952 until June 1, 1954.[74] A year later, on July 1, 1955, the Union president transferred power over the remainder of the territory to the state. Only small pockets in isolated areas remained under Union military jurisdiction because of the lingering insurgency.

Of all the separately administrated units in the Union of Burma, the Chin Special Division had the least characteristics of a state. It had a Chin affairs council, which was composed of fourteen members, eight having earned their place through membership in the Union Chamber of Nationalities and six through membership in the Union Chamber of Deputies.[75] Its only constitutional function was to aid and advise the minister for Chin affairs.[76]

The constitution did not provide for a head of the division; instead it called on the Union prime minister to appoint a minister for Chin affairs after consultation with the Chin Affairs Council.[77] Subject to the powers of the Union Parliament, the Chin minister was authorized to direct and control the division's administration, civil service, and "all matters relating to schools and cultural institutions in the Special Division."[78]

The Chins did not get a separate state equal in powers and

72. Ibid.
73. Ibid.
74. According to the Proclamation of June 1, 1954, the areas of Thandawng, Pa-an, and Hlaingbwe were transferred to state control.
75. *Constitution*, Art. 197(1); Art. 87, Second Schedule.
76. Ibid., Art. 197(5).
77. Ibid., (2).
78. Ibid., (3).

freedoms to the Shan and the other states because they did not want it.[79] In response to the Chin demands before the Frontier Areas Committee of Enquiry and the Constituent Assembly, their area became a special division of Burma proper. Article 198 of the constitution made clear that any alteration in the relationship between the division and the Union was the responsibility of the Union Parliament.

An examination of state institutions alone is not sufficient to make fully clear the unique structure of federalism in Burma. Also, certain rights and limitations on the states indicate how the basic principles underlying the constitution were manifest.

To meet the demands of the Frontier Areas peoples to contract out of the Union should it not serve their desires, the authors of the constitution provided a restricted right of secession. As defined in the fundamental law, this right applied only to those states not specifically excluded. The Kachin and Karen states were excluded; the Shan and Kayah states were the only two eligible to withdraw.[80] To exercise the right, a state would have to meet all the conditions established by the constitution and amplified by law.[81] First, they

79. Burma, op. cit., 2: 71–72. In a memorial to the committee, the Chin delegates requested that, "except for administration of internal affairs, the Chins have desired to unite with Burma proper in more subjects than the other Frontier Areas do."

80. *Constitution*, Arts. 201, 178; Constitution Amendment Act, 1951, Art. 10. It was the belief of the informed that the Kachin and Karen states were excluded from the right of secession because the states were created out of territory that was originally part of Burma proper (interviews with Saw Butler and Myint Tun). Maung Maung, *Burma's Constitution*, op. cit., pp. 193–194, gives substantially the same reasons as the Karen State Ministry.

81. *Constitution*, Arts. 202–206. For a detailed examination of the right of secession and the Shan State, see Josef Silverstein, "Politics in the Shan State: The Question of Secession from the Union of Burma," *Journal of Asian Studies* 18(1) (1958): 43–57. See also *Memorandum Submitted by the Constitution Revision Steering Committee Shan States*, February 22, 1961 (mimeo) for Shan criticism of the constitution and their demands for change. For a general discussion of the question of secession, see Lee G. Buchheit, *Secession: The Legitimacy of Self-determination* (New Haven, 1978).

would have to wait ten years from the day the constitution became operative before attempting to exercise their right. It was hoped that within that initial decade unity between the eligible states and the remainder of the Union would be so firmly established that no state would desire to withdraw. Second, if, after the waiting period, a state still wished to withdraw, its state council would have to pass a resolution of secession by a two-thirds majority. Third, the resolution would then have to be sent to the Union president, who would then appoint a plebiscite commission to oversee a plebiscite to "ascertain the will of the people concerned." The Union Parliament never legislated who should vote and what majority was necessary to express the people's will. No state made a formal attempt to apply this right. In 1961 the Shans sought to change the relationship between their state and the Union and, failing that, to secede from the Union.

In a legal sense there was no way for the states to communicate with each other. The constitution provided the ministers for the states and the Chin Special Division with direct links only through the Union government. To bridge this gap an informal practice developed. Beginning about 1952, the Kayah State Ministry suggested to the other state ministries that it would be useful to find a means to exchange ideas and discuss common problems. As the result of this inquiry the States Affairs Committee came into being. Without any legal sanction the secretaries of the ministries met informally and irregularly to discuss common problems such as forestry, judicial affairs, and the writing of state constitutions. From these meetings the state ministries suggested the writing of a uniform States Court Act, and the suggestion was adopted in 1953.[82] There was no representative from Burma proper at these meetings.

Although all the states were permitted to raise money through taxation, no state was self-supporting; all depended on the Union Treasury to augment their funds with annual grants. U Myat Soe, secretary of the Kayah State Ministry, claimed the arrangements in effect in 1956 were not sound, for there were no established principles nor was there uniformity in apportioning aid. In 1956 the Kayah State was capable of meeting only one-seventh of its budgeting

82. Interviews with Myat Soe, Saw Butler and Myint Tun, Saw Tha, Ba Maw.

requirements.[83] The Union minister of finance and revenue sponsored a state aid board to consider state annual requests and to make recommendations, but the board did not devise any satisfactory method for apportioning annual aid. U Ba Maw, deputy secretary of the Kachin State, revealed that there was no coordination between the states and the Union in planning state expenses and that the Union government did not consider state needs in making its grants. Up to 1956, the Union government set aside a lump sum for the states and then distributed it on a 5-3-2-1 basis to the Shan, Kachin, Karen, and Kayah states.[84] Early in 1959, the Union government moved to correct the situation by appointing an inquiry commission to investigate the complaints of the states about inadequate funds and "to recommend ways and means by which the Centre may be able to satisfy demands for the various State Governments for increased monetary grants."[85] The commission was headed by the auditor-general, and it included representatives from the states and the Ministry of Finance.

83. Interview with Myat Soe.
84. Interview with Ba Maw. This was later confirmed by U Myat Soe of the Kayah State. An example of actual distribution of the Union contribution:

| State | 1957/1958 | 1958/1959 | |
|---|---|---|---|
| Shan | 27,966,000 | 12,500,000 | |
| | | 10,900,000 | (special control) |
| Kachin | 7,000,000 | 7,500,000 | |
| Karen | 3,800,000 | 3,800,000 | |
| Kayah | 2,000,000 | 2,000,000 | |

The higher figure in both years for the Shan State is due to the proposed payment to the Shan chiefs for surrendering their right (letter to author from Kin Mae Wynn, second secretary, Embassy of the Union of Burma, June 24, 1959, who drew the figures from the Embassy copy of the budget).

85. *Nation*, January 18, 1959, p. 1; this was not the first such Union action. In 1952, for instance, the Union government sponsored a Union conference in order for the states to air their grievances. At that meeting the finance minister promised to consult all heads of state in the future before preparing the annual budget; see *Nation*, June 22, 1952, p. 1. In 1957 the New National Planning Commission, the successor in name to the Economic and Social Board, promised to create an inquiry commission to investigate financing, taxes, and fiscal policy in the states; see *Nation*, November 25, 1957, p. 1.

The fourth principle underlying the constitution was that the institutions of the Union are also those of Burma proper. This can be seen initially from an examination of Burma proper, the largest political unit in the Union of Burma. Burma proper had no separate and distinctive political institutions of its own. Its parliament, administration, judiciary, and local government were those of the Union. This made Burma proper a unitary state with the interesting exception that representatives from the other states participating in the Union Parliament and holding portfolios in the Union government shared the decision making and administrative function of Burma proper with its own representatives. Thus no state in the Union was autonomous; all were linked and united by innumerable threads.

A close examination of the powers of and limitations on the states suggests that the line separating the Union from the states was badly blurred in many places and nonexistent in others. To begin, the constitution established the supremacy of the Union over the states. While a state could elect to surrender its rights, powers, or territory to the Union, a converse power did not exist for the Union.[86] In a proclaimed state of emergency the Union Parliament was empowered to legislate for any state on any subject regardless of the separate Union–state legislative lists attached to the constitution.[87] Under a presidential proclamation of a state of emergency, the Union army did reorganize local government in the areas under their jurisdiction.[88] When the proclamation became void in 1954 and power was returned to local civilian officials, the new system of government introduced by the army remained in effect.[89] At all times state laws were inferior to Union legislation regardless of whether or not the law in question was enacted before the national law.[90]

In 1952, a case involving Union–states relation in regard to

86. *Constitution*, Art. 92(3).
87. Ibid., Art. 94(1).
88. Proclamation, issued by the president of the Union, took effect on December 11, 1952, lasted until August 1954, and applied to twenty-two of the thirty-three state subdivisions in the Shan State.
89. Interview with Saw Tha.
90. *Constitution*, Art. 94(2).

legislation was argued before the Supreme Court. In *States v. Union of Burma* the question before the court was which had the power to legislate—the Union or the states—on subjects delegated to both. The case arose over the extension of the Land Nationalization Act of 1948 to the states. Mr. Basu, arguing in behalf of the states, said that in forming the Union the states did not surrender their proprietary rights, only their exclusive right to legislate. The constitution granted land legislation rights to both the Union and the states; in particular, the Union was given the right to legislate on the regulation of land tenure. Basu claimed that because the Land Nationalization Act abolished land tenure in many cases it did not come under the aforementioned Union legislative category. Finally, he argued that, given the states' right of secession, the application of this piece of legislation to a state that later decided to secede would put the state in "the absurd position that secession would be made without the land."[91]

The rebuttal of the attorney general centered about the following points: The Union had power to legislate in areas not expressly enumerated in the state list; where both the Union and the states share legislative power, the authority of the Union was paramount; and on matters of national interest and importance, the Union had power to legislate even though "it trenches on any of the matters enumerated in List II."[92]

The court ruled in favor of the Union by holding that it, not the states, was the ultimate owner of all the lands. It also ruled that the law did not abolish land tenure altogether; by providing that certain categories of people—nonagriculturists—should not own land, the effect of the law was to regulate land tenure, not abolish it.[93] The ruling of the court provided an important precedent for the ascendancy of the Union's legislative power over that of the states.

These conditions—dependence on the Union for protection of individual rights; membership in state councils being determined by prior election to the national legislature; selection of state administrative heads by the Union prime minister, with states neither

91. *Nation*, June 25, 1952, p. 1.
92. Ibid.
93. *Nation*, July 10, 1952, p. 1.

paying for their services nor having the authority to remove them; dependence of the states on the Union Treasury to meet annual operating costs; and scrutiny of state legislation by the Union president and, if he so desired, by the Supreme Court as well before it could be promulgated—all taken together make it clear that the federal structure was more nominal than real. The solution met the exigencies of the situation prevailing in 1947 and proved adaptable to the demands of some of the Karens a few years later. It did not prove satisfactory to the minorities in Burma proper such as the Arakanese and the Mons, whose leaders thought their people did not have equal rights and status with the other minorities in the Union. The Constituent Assembly omitted a definition of federalism and did not establish the states on any principle of administrative efficiency or decentralization; instead it used the idea of divided political authority to guarantee ethnic and cultural diversity. As a result there was confusion between politics and culture, which undermined national unity among the nation's ethnic groups.

# 9

# The Politics of Contradiction

The moment of national unity passed quickly as the politics of contradiction took over. Within three months after independence, Burma was convulsed by a series of rebellions and widespread insurgency that began with the Communists seeking to seize power and displace the national government. There followed a PVO split with one faction joining the Communists in revolt and the other remaining loyal to the government. Within a few months elements of the Karens, Mons, and other minorities revolted, either in league with each other or separately; all pursued a nearly common objective: to secure territory of their own and the right to determine the political and cultural future of their people. The other ethnic groups did not join the revolt; the Shans, Kachins, and Chins for nearly a decade remained loyal to the national government. Their leaders continued to believe that the promises made at Panglong and later embodied in the constitution would be honored. They showed their loyalty to the nation by standing firm with its leaders, and they permitted military units drawn from their communities to fight against the political and ethnic rebels. But as the years passed their support weakened and in some cases turned to open hostility as neither warfare nor words solved the problems of national unity. Throughout the constitutional period, neither the Burmans nor the minorities were strong enough to impose a permanent solution on the other, either through battle or election.

At the root of the problems that divided the peoples of Burma was the government's inability to devise a policy or policies to bridge the social and political gaps between communities and its failure to make known its real intention on the issue of national unity. It could be argued that the national leaders supported unity in diversity; it could also be argued, and even more forcefully, that they paid lip service to that ideal while working steadily toward political nationalization and cultural Burmanization. These contradictions were evident at all levels and in all issues. Ultimately the failure to resolve them provided the pretext in 1962 for the seizure of power and the displacement of the constitutional system by dictatorship.

---

During the fourteen-year era of constitutional government, many steps seem to have been taken that strengthened unity in diversity. Education in the states through the first four standards was conducted in local languages and dialects. This was extremely important because the areas were predominantly rural and most people did not leave their villages or the general areas of their birth. Thus, education in local languages and dialects insured the widespread use of these local tongues in the home, the marketplace, and the fields. Through these languages local culture passed from the old to the young and remained strong and secure in its areas of origin.

The national government also gave dramatic national recognition to the diverse groups who composed the nation. The anniversary date of the Panglong Conference—February 12—became a national holiday called Union Day, marked by a pageant wherein a stream of runners, representing all the races of Burma, carried a lighted torch from the Shan State to Rangoon. Celebrations of the day were observed throughout the nation; representatives of the varied races wore local dress and participated in a series of activities meant to remind the people of Burma that the nation was multinational, all freely joined in political union, and that all were equal in independent Burma.

The promise of unity in diversity was also marked by the rotation of the Union presidency from a Shan, who served as the first president, to a Burman, and then to a Karen.[1] One of the main functions of the president and an important one for the prime minister, too, were the visits they made to the states, during which they donned local dress and took part in the rituals and celebrations of their hosts.

Supporters of the idea of unity in diversity could find further evidence of its existence in the fact that each state enjoyed its own holidays in addition to the national ones and was free to work toward the revival of local arts and crafts without interference from the Union government. If all this is added to the fact that the state governments were in the hands of local officials, a good case could be made for the argument that the national leaders were indeed living up to the promises of Panglong and the constitution.

Yet despite these and other signs of the acceptance of unity in diversity as the basis of the political union, there was even more evidence to suggest a slow process of political nationalization and cultural Burmanization that threatened to overwhelm the rival concept of unity and become the ideological and cultural basis of the state. The nationalization of the population and the Burmanization of culture did not progress as the result of a well-thought-out plan originating in Rangoon or elsewhere, and it did not follow a precise timetable. It progressed haphazardly, in most cases as the result both of the constitutional contradictions and the particular efforts of national leaders on the one hand and of peculiar local conditions on the other.

The most obvious example of political nationalization resulted from the threat of foreign invasion. Newspaper reports in 1956 that troops of the People's Republic of China (PRC) were encamped on what was thought to be a portion of Burmese territory in the Kachin State electrified the nation.[2] Regardless of where

1. Just prior to the coup of 1962, it was announced that the fourth president of the Union of Burma would be a Kachin, Sima Duwa Sinwa Nawng.

2. See the Nation, July 3, 1956, for the first report of the situation. For the next six months all the newspapers in Burma followed and reported the story in detail as it unfolded both in Burma and China.

people lived or of their ethnic identity, they participated in demonstrations and protests as though the invaded land were their own and called on the national government to take steps to remove the intruders and restore Burmese territory to the nation. It mattered not that the problem was localized in a remote area of one of the states; it was seen as a threat to the whole nation. The protests were as loud and demanding in the South as they were in the middle and northern parts of Burma.

This was not the first time since independence that Burmese territory had been invaded by Chinese forces. A few years earlier, from 1950 onward, remnants of the Chinese National Army (Kuomintang or KMT) who refused to surrender their arms and be interned entered Burma in their efforts to escape from their PRC pursuers. Burma, then fighting several insurgent groups, could not force the KMT to comply with its demands, so the Chinese were able to settle in the Shan State, where they became involved in local politics, rebellion, and the opium trade. Through their public statements and those emanating from Taiwan, the KMT justified their presence in Burma as a regrouping for their planned invasion of China. To remove this unwanted force that posed a potential threat to Burma's relations with the new government of China, the Burmese, in 1953, took the problem to the United Nations.[3] Eventually several member states of the world body joined in helping to remove a portion of the unwanted intruders. Although the nation generally supported its government as it worked to eliminate this threat, popular feeling was much less aroused than it was by the later invasion threat and varied according to whether the protesters were located in Rangoon or one of the outlying areas.

The 1956 intrusion of PRC troops was immediately perceived as a national threat throughout Burma and was taken far more seriously. Public protests throughout the nation were immediate and nearly uniform in their demand that the Chinese get out. The government of Burma dealt with the problem through diplomacy. Its discussions with the Chinese led the latter to agree to accept

3. Burma, Ministry of Information, *Kuomintang Aggression against Burma* (Rangoon, 1953). This includes the documents and other evidence Burma offered to the United Nations at the time it presented its case.

most of Burma's version of their common border conditional on certain small adjustments requiring the transfer of strategic territories in the Kachin State to the PRC. According to Burma's constitution, any change in a state's boundary required the agreement of the state government concerned.[4] Once the terms became known, the burden for making sacrifices and approving the requested transfer shifted from the nation as a whole to the Kachin State government, which was subjected to national pressure coming from the press, political leaders, and the Burmese public to accede to China's demands. Here, national interests collided with those of a member state. While it was everyone's intention to avoid war, it was the Kachin State that was being asked to make the sacrifices. With pressure coming from all sides the members of the Kachin State Council were faced with maneuvering by their leaders and realignments among themselves aimed at producing a majority favoring the transfer of a portion of their state to a foreign country. In the Kachin State, as in the nation at large, the debate between national and local interests was dominated by those who supported the former; this caused a minority of the Kachin leaders to resent the national pressure on them to sacrifice to save the nation.

This issue, which seized the nation for four years, contributed greatly toward a sense of nationhood, the feeling among the people that it was the nation, not just the residents of a particular state, that was involved. Whereas a minority of state and national opinion leaders attempted to pose the issue as a local one, the newspapers, most national leaders, and the general public saw it as a national issue; and the distinction between Kachin and Union of Burma territory was blurred and obliterated as they debated, maneuvered, protested, and wrote about the problem. It was clear that when security of the nation or any part of it was involved, national interest took precedence over the territorial sovereignty of one of the member states.

External threats were not the only basis for the nationalization of politics; some internal events, such as the multiple revolts by

---

4. *The Constitution of the Union of Burma* (Rangoon, 1948), Art. 92(3).

political and ethnic groups in 1948 and 1949, came to involve all of the people regardless of where they lived. The fighting over these revolts took place throughout the nation and involved people whether or not they were members of the groups in revolt. In many ways the loyalty of those minorities who stood by the national government provided the added strength that saved the Union.

An even more important crisis arose in 1958 when the AFPFL leaders split the party and nearly brought the nation to civil war as they fought among themselves to be the successors of the once-united organization. This struggle, which centered in Rangoon between rival Burman leaders, was confined neither to the Burmans who fought each other for power nor to Burma proper. It quickly transcended both, drawing in state leaders whether or not they were members of an AFPFL affiliate in their local areas, so that some were forced out of their local offices for supporting one side or the other.[5] When U Nu, who had precipitated the split and fought to hold the prime minister's office, decided to allow the Union Parliament to resolve the issue of which faction of the AFPFL would govern Burma, he sought support from both the Burman representatives and the minority representatives from the states. On the eve of the vote Nu forced all his ministers and parliamentary secretaries to promise their vote to him or resign from the government. Because the combined ministers and heads of state from the Kachin and Karen states favored his opponents, Nu dismissed them and replaced them with leaders who pledged their loyalty to him. These replacements did not have a majority of supporters in their state councils because Nu took his action without consulting the state councils as required by the constitution.[6]

---

5. For details of the split in the AFPFL and the day-to-day exchange of charges and countercharges, see any of the local press, either in English or Burmese. For a detailed description of the third National Conference of the AFPFL, where the long simmering feud became public, see *Burma Weekly Bulletin*, n.s., 6(43) (February 6, 1958). For a good overview of the split from the perspective of the Ba Swe–Kyaw Nyein faction, see Sein Win, *The Split Story* (Rangoon, 1959).

6. *Constitution*, Art. 160; *Nation*, June 7 and 8, 1958.

During this crisis no state escaped the effects of the split. In the Shan State the United Hill Peoples' Congress, a supporter of the original AFPFL, called on the rivals in Rangoon to end their quarrel and unite the party. In the Kachin State, following Nu's replacement of the combined minister and head of state, two members of the local AFPFL joined the opposition and made it impossible for Nu's appointee to muster a majority in the State Council. The Chin and Karen leaders also split their local organizations; the national crisis over who would govern the Union of Burma transcended all local issues. Thus when Parliament assembled on June 5, 1958, the issue was no longer one of intraparty rivalry in Burma proper; it had become one of national and political unity involving all the people through their elected representatives. The vote of no confidence, which would have unseated Nu and given power to his rivals, failed by eight votes. Nu's majority was provided by the support he received from the representatives of the minorities and from the former opposition parties. Most AFPFL representatives from Burma proper gave their votes to Nu's rivals.

The political divisions between the two factions, both in Burma proper and in the states, were so deep that Nu was unable to govern for long. In October, when the Parliament was required to pass the budget, rather than continue in office as the leader of a fragile coalition with no real chance of survival, Nu called on Gen. Ne Win to form a temporary caretaker government to calm the nation and create the conditions for new elections. The crisis demonstrated again the predominance of national over local politics. It also showed how the national leaders were able to extend their personal struggles to the states and disrupt the political life there, forcing local leaders to choose sides and pay a political price in local and national politics if they chose the wrong side. This crisis more than any other led to the emergence of an informal centralized political system overlying and displacing the constitutional federal arrangement. It also provoked new revolts among the minorities, especially among those who a decade earlier had stood firm in defense of the Union of Burma. By 1960, the caretaker government extended Burman penetration into state politics, and the contradictions grew sharper as the minorities sought ways to reverse the trend and protect their local interests.

The nationalization of politics was not the result of large dramatic issues only; its growth over fourteen years was incremental and was aided and abetted by local conditions and by apparent contradictions in the constitution itself, such as the ambivalent role and source of authority of the combined ministers and heads of state. Other contributing conditions did not come to light until particular issues arose to reveal their existence.

If at the outset of the Union of Burma, state leaders looked to the Burman-led AFPFL for guidance and instruction because they were inexperienced in self-government, they learned quickly and soon tried to free themselves from their tutors and carry on their politics in their own way. They found, however, that this was nearly impossible. For one thing, the states were not financially independent. Although all the states were permitted to raise money through taxation, no state was self-supporting; all depended on the Union Treasury to augment their funds with annual grants. The national government took steps neither to make the states self-supporting nor to distribute aid on a rational basis. Instead it appropriated a lump sum annually for distribution to the states and, in an arbitrary fashion, divided it roughly on a 5-3-2-1 basis, the Shans receiving the most and the Kayahs the least. The Chins had no independent budget because as a special division they were treated for financial purposes as part of Burma proper. Because all state budgets had to be passed by the national legislature as part of the national budget, the Union government was in a powerful position to influence local politics, and it did not hesitate to use this power when it served its purposes.

Another means of national manipulation of state politics was through state branches and affiliates of the AFPFL, who sometimes had greater influence than their actual size because rival parties representing the ethnic minorities were too divided to govern by themselves. Take, for example, politics in the Kachin State, where the population was divided nearly equally between Kachins and Burmans, each having an equal number of seats in the Chamber of Nationalities. While the Kachins supported two or more rival ethnically based parties, the Burmans generally were united and supported the local AFPFL. As a result no Kachin group could govern without allying itself with the Burmans to form a majority in the State Council. In theory that should have had the positive result of forcing the rival ethnic communities to sink their difference to produce a workable majority; in fact it meant that, for one or the other of the Kachin parties to form a coalition with the Burmans, it was they, not the Burmans, who made the compromises in exchange for local AFPFL support. Thus, because the local AFPFL was under the dominance of the national parent, Rangoon's influence, and at times its dictates, led to open charges of national AFPFL interference in local matters. The Kachins came to resent this intrusion and to despise their dependence on the Burman minority in their state, who demanded compromises and changes in programs and leaders in return for their support. By 1959, a small element among the Kachins went into open revolt in the hope of separating their state from the Union and winning the autonomy they came to believe had been denied to them.

It was the Shan State that faced the greatest amount of interference from the national government and the governing party. As one of the two states with the theoretical right to secede and as a state with entrenched traditional feudal leaders whose powers were guaranteed in the constitution, the Shan State was the greatest threat to those in Rangoon who sought to nationalize politics in the Union.

Almost from independence there were forces both in and outside the Shan State who worked to end feudal rule and replace it with a more democratic form. A group of Shans who were not members of the local nobility appealed to Rangoon to help bring about constitutional changes in their state; but because the multiple insurrections elsewhere posed the most direct threat to the Union, the Rangoon leaders devoted their limited resources to suppressing those rather than taking up the issue of constitutional change in the Shan State. Because the insurgency spilled over into the Shan State and the capitol, Taunggyi, was for several months under the control of the Karen National Defence Organization (KNDO),[7] the Union government sent the army into the Shan State to drive out the intruders. But the military did more than that; it used its

---

7. Burma, Ministry of Information, *Burma's Freedom: The Second Anniversary* (Rangoon, 1950), pp. 30–31. Taunggyi was held from August 3 to November 23, 1949.

authority to effect important political and social changes while it carried out its military mission. The popular reaction to the army was mixed. Initially the rural population was hostile and feared and mistrusted the soldiers because the army was composed largely of Burmans. The image of an arrogant, conquering army was reinforced by individual cases of brutality, rape, and other criminal acts reported to have been committed on the local residents. In areas not under direct military rule, the Shan leaders who were not members of the local nobility welcomed the occupation because it suspended sawbwa rule and permitted the introduction of political and social reforms. When martial law ended in 1954, both supporters and opponents had hardened in their attitudes, one group seeing it as a vehicle for change; the other, as an unnecessary intrusion on the rights and privileges of the people.[8]

Even as these events were taking place, the government in Rangoon mounted its own pressure for change in the Shan State. As early as 1952, the Union government established an inquiry commission, the Shan State Administrative Enquiry Commission, to find answers to three questions: Was it necessary to abolish sawbwa rule? If so, what sort of government should replace it and what political forms were necessary?[9] The commission did not finish its work because of the deteriorating political situation inside the state. A year later the national AFPFL leaders chose a new tack: to unite all political parties in the Shan State into a single organization under AFPFL leadership. The Shan chiefs opposed this and it was dropped. When martial rule ended in the Shan State in 1954, the Union government renewed its efforts to bring about political change by entering into discussions with the sawbwas about what they would insist on receiving in exchange for the surrender of their hereditary and constitutional rights.[10] Their demands were so high that the issue was again dropped, only to be revived

---

8. See Josef Silverstein, "Politics in the Shan State: The Question of Secession from the Union of Burma," *Journal of Asian Studies* 18(1) (1958): 51–52.

9. *Nation*, March 6, 1952.

10. The Union government was unaware that on August 18, 1951, the Shan chiefs had decided secretly to surrender their administrative powers; they took no steps following the decision to implement it.

two years later, in 1956, but the national government then found the Shan chiefs no longer interested in discussing the issue. They had begun to call for their state's secession from the Union. In 1957, the secessionists organized a new party, the Shan State Unity Party, to lead them out of the federation. Shortly thereafter, a second movement developed among a portion of the Shans. On May 21, 1958, a group of the dissident Shan chiefs formed the *Noom Sukhan*, "the Shan States Independence Army" (SSIA), which "aimed at not merely freeing Shan State from Burman domination but also building a united, independent and democratic Shan State."[11] In March, less than a year later, it launched its first attack on the Union army.

When the caretaker government took power the Shans found the military a tougher and more demanding opponent than their constitutional and elected predecessors. In his Union Day address, Gen. Ne Win gave special attention to the Shan threat to secede from the Union and to other matters that threatened the stability of Burma. This signaled the beginning of a new campaign to end *sawbwa* rule and draw the state more tightly under Rangoon domination. Under the pressure of the military, the Shan State Council voted in March to end feudal rule in the state and supported an amendment to the constitution that would give legality to its decision. The Union Parliament then quickly passed the amendment, and it was signed by the president and became part of the law. In April 1959, 33 Shan chiefs signed separate agreements with the state government to exchange their administrative authority and legislative rights for a fixed compensation and the retention of their titles and personal property.[12]

The caretaker government also took steps to gain control over the most backward areas in the Shan and Kachin states by creating the Frontier Areas Administration. Under the leadership of Col. Saw Myint, commander of the Seventh Brigade, and with assistants

---

11. *First Manifesto of the Shan State Independence Organization* (April 29, 1959) (mimeo), p. 5.
12. *Burma Weekly Bulletin*, n.s. 8(4) (May 21, 1959): 37. This measure applied to the hereditary chiefs in the Kayah State as well.

drawn from the Shan and Kachin state ministries, territory and population on the border areas came under Union control. To make this a legal change, the state councils passed resolutions empowering the Union government to take direct authority in their states and to exercise its rule on the inhabitants for an initial period of seven years, with a proviso that the period could be extended.[13] Unlike the transfer of Kachin State territory to China, there was no national pressure on the Shans and Kachins to surrender their authority; instead the pressure came from the presence of the Union army in the states, the actions of the caretaker government, and the growing insurgency in both states.

A third example of political nationalization took place among the Karens, both in and out of the Karen State. As noted in chapter 8, the Constituent Assembly could not agree on the territorial and population composition of this proposed state and left it to a special inquiry commission to make the final recommendations. In the meantime a secessionist movement under the KNDO emerged and proved to be the most serious challenge to face the new nation during its first two years of life.

Although the Union government's immediate response to the KNDO revolt was to suspend Karens from the police and military while taking the field and seeking to defeat the insurgents, U Nu sought to treat the insurrection as the result of political dissidents acting as "bad" citizens, maintaining that their behavior should not reflect on the "good" citizens who were loyal and supportive of the Union. Once the threat of the KNDO movement began to pass, Nu took steps to demonstrate the government's trust in the loyal Karens. In 1951, the Rangoon Police Department reinstated ninety-one Karen officers who had been suspended when the KNDO insurrection broke out; a year later, the Union army reinstated three Karen captains to rank and organized a new formation, the Fourteenth Burma Regiment, its membership drawn from Karen soldiers who had proven their loyalty to the Union.[14] Later other Karen military formations followed. Nu's attitude toward the

13. Nation, December 29, 1959.
14. Ibid., February 2, 1952.

Karens and his leadership in their reincorporation into Burmese society helped ease the emergence of a Karen State in the Union and the acceptance of the Karens as loyal members of the nation.

Politics within the Karen community felt the strong influence of the AFPFL. To offset the KNDO insurrection and its effort to separate the Karen State from the Union, the national government and the AFPFL worked among Karens and helped organize a political movement both inside the state and outside among the Karens who lived intermingled with Burmans and Mons and who held the reserved seats assigned to their community under the original constitution. During the 1951/1952 election a triparty system emerged, with two parties under AFPFL influence. Outside the Karen State the United Karen League (UKL) was formed; it was the successor organization to the old Karen Youth Organization, an original member of the AFPFL. It was led by U Win Maung, the future third president of the Union of Burma, and it worked closely with the AFPFL and the national government. Inside the Karen State, a rival party, the United Karen Organization (UKO), also backed by the AFPFL, was created. The two refused to merge because their popular bases differed and because each sought to be the spokesman for the Karens and the channel between their community and the national leadership. Opposing the two was the Karen Congress (KC), which drew together Karens who supported neither the AFPFL nor the KNDO. It held power for a short while in the Karen Affairs Council, but after the 1951/1952 election it lost popular backing and withdrew from political contests to become the unofficial opposition in the state.

Between 1952 and 1956, the UKL and UKO contested for leadership; and as the latter consolidated its hold on the Karen State population, the former lost influence. The AFPFL came to depend on the UKO on matters within the state and on the UKL for influence among Karens living outside the state. In 1956, when the second national election was held, the AFPFL convinced the UKL that, with the loss of reserved seats in the forthcoming national parliament, it would be best to dissolve its party and urge its members to join the AFPFL as direct members. To make this solution palatable, it offered UKL leaders support as AFPFL candidates in Karen-dominated areas in Burma proper. With the dissolution of the UKL, the UKO, now under the leadership of Dr. Saw Hla Tun, became the uncontested leaders of the Karens in their state and as such worked closely with the national AFPFL until its split two years later. On March 9, 1956, the UKO merged with the AFPFL in the Karen State. Thus within eight years the AFPFL had managed to create a viable rival Karen leadership both within and without the Karen State; and once the two Karen parties were accepted by their separate support groups, the national party was able to absorb both within its web and assure itself that the KNDO and its efforts to lead the Karens out of the Union would be challenged politically both in its goals and in its claims to speak for the Karen peoples.

These events in the Shan, Kachin, and Karen states provide examples of the ways in which political nationalization went forward. They demonstrated how national interest transcended local interest and how the Union government and the national AFPFL eroded the guarantees and provisions of the constitution and the promises that underlay that document regarding the political autonomy of the peoples residing in the states. From the viewpoint of the Union government it was trying to create a political unity where none had existed before, and in trying to save the Union, it had to step in and play a variety of roles in local affairs. From the viewpoint of the minorities it was not a question of helping progressive interests triumph over reactionary forces; it was illegal involvement by the Burman-dominated government and the army in affairs supposedly excluded to it. For many in the states, the only real alternatives were to leave the Union or see themselves absorbed in a centralized state.

More examples could be offered from the experiences of the other states and those of the Mons and Arakanese, who did not have states but who sought statehood or greater autonomy in their historic areas. As the political nationalization process moved inexorably forward, it created resentment and rearguard resistance to its progress. With no government, elected or appointed, willing to develop and express a clear and forthright policy on political nationalization versus unity in diversity, the contradictions between promises and practices kept the nation divided and in turmoil.

The Burmanization of the nation's culture also contributed to the perpetuation of national disunity. It could be said, as many Burman educational and political officials did say, that the nation could ill afford an equal development of all the languages and cultures of Burma. Given the fact that an overwhelming majority were Burmans, it seemed natural to those in power who came largely from this community that Burmese should be the lingua franca of the nation; and while they did not say it, implicit in the idea of the language of the majority as the national language was the concomitant idea that Burman dress, manners, and religion should also take precedence over all others. Yet the constitution and the promises at Panglong seemed to have assured the minorities that their languages, culture, and beliefs would coexist and that they need not be Burmanized in order to participate in the life of the Union of Burma. Although the national government acknowledged this at least within the states, wherever Burmans and minorities met, it was with Burmese they communicated; and it was in Burman areas that the minorities received their higher education and found urban jobs in government and business. In order not to seem different and stand out, representatives of the minorities when living in Burma proper, for whatever reasons, gradually adopted Burman dress, lifestyle, religion, and speech.

In some respects the process seemed deliberate. The Burmans, after all, had led the nationalist movement; they were the most numerous and they perceived themselves as the most advanced group in the nation. Thus to imitate them was to be modern and part of the mainstream of Burmese life and culture. One alternative to adopting the language and ways of the Burmans might have been to retain the British language and culture, but that was never a real alternative, for it was seen by all concerned as alien and imposed by a colonial situation that none wanted to bring back or perpetuate. During colonial rule all local cultures and languages suffered. The thinking was that for the nation to recover its true identity and unite the people it was necessary to choose the local language most widely used—Burmese—update it, and make it the basis of education, government, business, and everyday life. While varieties in dress and customs were interesting, they did not have the same kind of unifying pull that a single national culture had. This unity did not have to be everywhere—it was possible to use local languages and follow local customs in the areas of their origin—but for a nation to grow there had to be a common identity all could share. Thus, it was possible for unity in diversity to coexist with a national culture. This thinking created a twofold problem: Policy was never clearly and fully debated, and the advance of Burmanization seemed to most of the minorities to come at the expense of local diversity.

Consider education, for example. For a bright student whose parents were able to encourage his advance beyond the fourth standard, it was necessary to become fluent in Burmese in order to progress up the educational ladder; further, he had to leave his local home area to advance his education because secondary schools were located in the cities and larger towns and the universities were situated in Burma proper. More important, he had to overcome the language advantages of native speakers because all education beyond the fourth standard was in Burmese or English.

By moving to Rangoon or Mandalay for his higher education, a student became part of Burman culture; and in order not to stand out or to be treated as a rustic, he tended to modify his dress, speech, and living pattern so that he fit in. Thus language and higher education combined to Burmanize the elite of the minorities while leaving the remainder of young people in their home areas, outside this growing mainstream. The system not only divided the minorities from their natural leaders; it also separated them physically and nearly permanently, as many of the Burman-educated minorities found jobs and new homes in the centers of Burman culture—Rangoon and Mandalay.

If Burmese language was important to government and education, it also was important to the military. Initially, the army was organized like the Indian army, along ethnic lines. After 1949, when several Karen units defected and joined the KNDO, however, the army quietly reorganized with Burman officers placed in charge of new or reorganized Burmese units. By 1951, the military adapted Burmese to code for use in signaling; and two years later, in 1953, the Parliament passed the Defence Services Academy Bill, which created an officer's training college. Its stated purpose was to train officers in a "way to eliminate any tendency toward minority disunity in ideological concept among the Armed Forces and thus to ensure the enduring security of the Constitution. . . ."[15] To ensure the Burmanization of the new officers, it linked the academy with the University of Rangoon, where the curriculum was Burman oriented, with history, political science, sociology, and literature reflecting the heritage and traditions of the majority group. The Burmese armed forces under the nationalized and Burmanized leaders was remarkably stable with no important defections, even though it spent most of the time fighting local ethnic and political dissidents, groups with which the officers had ethnic or political ties.

Burmanization also was to be seen in the growing urban culture. Films, literature, and the press were devoted to Burman themes, culture, and problems. With no competing centers of culture outside Burma proper, Burman culture emanating from Rangoon and Mandalay slowly spread throughout the nation.

Next to language, religion was the most important vehicle of Burman culture. Although an overwhelming majority of the people of Burma are Buddhists, there are also significant minorities of Christians, Hindus, Muslims, and animists. Of greater importance is the fact that these minority religions were most widespread among the ethnic minorities. As noted earlier, while the constitution gave Buddhism a "special position," the State recognized the other faiths. All were protected by the provision that "all persons are equally entitled to freedom of conscience and the right freely to profess and practice [their] religion. . . ."[16] During the first twelve years of independence, Buddhism's "special position" led to the passage of legislation giving support to the faith, creating of the Ministry of Religious Affairs, sponsoring a Buddhist celebration that lasted for two years and in which Buddhist leaders of other nations were invited to participate, sponsoring Buddhist missionary activity among the backward hill tribes where animism was the traditional faith, and promulgating Buddhist holidays as national holidays.[17]

15. *Burma Weekly Bulletin*, n.s., 2(27) (October 7, 1953): 212.
16. *Constitution*, Arts. 20, 21.
17. For a detailed discussion of Buddhism and the state, see Donald

The clear ascendency of Buddhism and its patronage by the Union government led to conflict with the other religious groups in Burma. Dissatisfaction, particularly among Muslims, developed over the fact that Buddhism was taught in the public schools. When U Nu sought to widen religious instruction to include other faiths, the Buddhist monks objected. To avoid conflict, religious education was temporarily dropped, but this action too excited the Buddhist monks and new protests resulted. Nu finally reinstated religious instruction in the schools and made provision for instruction in other faiths if there were a sufficient body of non-Buddhist students.[18]

The most serious problem that arose in conjunction with religion occurred when the government, in 1961, sponsored an amendment to the constitution making Buddhism the State religion. U Nu had vowed to accomplish this as early as 1954; however it was not until the election of 1960 that he made its passage a campaign issue. On August 17, 1961, he fulfilled his long-standing pledge by introducing the proposed amendment and permitted debate to take place without party restraints. Despite protests from non-Buddhists in and out of the AFPFL, the measure passed with an overwhelming majority.[19] During the debate Nu and his co-leaders came to realize that the amendment might be more divisive than unifying; and to remedy the situation, his government quickly introduced a second amendment that guaranteed to all non-Buddhists the right to teach, as well as practice and propagate, their faiths, thus insuring the survival of all religions in Burma.[20] This move infuriated the Buddhist clergy, and shortly after its passage, serious religious conflict between Buddhists and Muslims occurred in North Okkapala, a suburb of Rangoon. Before that conflict

---

Eugene Smith, *Religion and Politics in Burma* (Princeton, 1965), especially chaps. 5–8; E. Michael Mendelson, *Sangha and State in Burma*, ed. John P. Ferguson (Ithaca, 1975), chaps. 5, 6.

18. For the details of the controversy, see *Burma Weekly Bulletin*, n.s., 3(24) (September 15, 1954): 178; ibid., 3(26) (September 29, 1954): 194, 198–200.

19. Ibid., 10(18) (August 31, 1961): 137–140.

20. See Mendelson, op. cit., pp. 352–353, for a discussion of this amendment.

could spread further or new ones could arise, the military leaders seized power and religion no longer had its patron in government.

Lastly, the government in Rangoon sought to Burmanize through the revival and propagation of a national culture, which in fact was Burman culture. Government policy proceeded from two assumptions: that there was in the cultures of all the indigenous peoples of Burma a basic unity that underlay the apparent ethnic and political disunity and that the mainstream of Burmese culture was Burman in origin, making it right and proper for the government to give it the largest amount of attention.

In 1952, the government established the Ministry of Culture to take charge of reviving interest in indigenous culture and help recover the lost cultural treasure of the nation. To accomplish its tasks, the ministry sponsored archaeological surveys to recover remnants of earlier civilization, classify artifacts, and preserve them. It also opened the National Museum and Art Gallery, where it displayed everything from the artillery and palaquins of the pre-British period to the furniture and belongings of Aung San. In Mandalay it opened the National Library, which gave particular emphasis to Burman culture, history, and arts.

The Ministry of Culture also made an effort to recognize the cultural legacy of the minorities by establishing the Union Library and Museum in Moulmein, where books—in Burmese, Mon, and English—on the ancient Mons were collected along with Mon palm-leaf inscriptions. In 1954, it also began to make a systematic collection of photos, pamphlets, and curios of all the other indigenous peoples of Burma.

At the University of Rangoon the Department of Anthropology focused its research on the Burmans and Mons. It had plans to study the other peoples of Burma, but the unrest caused by the insurgency prevented it from sending research teams to the disturbed areas. In the other departments of the university, little or no interest was shown in the minorities of Burma.

Through the Mass Education Movement the national government sought to broaden basic education and strengthen national unity. The idea for this movement emerged as early as 1948 and it was originally to be called the Scheme for Social Education. The then–minister of education suggested that the government create a fundamental education corps of young people who would work in the hinterlands and teach basic health and sanitary techniques, reading, and other nationalizing subjects, which would help the more backward peoples into the mainstream of Burmese civilization. Once the Mass Education Bill was passed, the government appointed a supervising board of fifteen to direct the new agency's affairs. The original appointees included none from the states, but a year later the board was reorganized and the omission was corrected. The first trainees were appointed in 1949; after six months of instruction they were sent to various mass education centers in Burma proper and the Chin Special Division. Their initial success prompted the Shan and Kayah states to request the establishment of similar centers in their areas.

The mass education instructors went to villages and sought local support by instructing inhabitants on improving sanitary conditions. Once rapport was established, the instructors opened reading rooms and community centers and gave instruction in a variety of subjects. Probably their most controversial activity was their effort to open classes in religion. According to one of the early program directors, U Aung Min, "they have not missed taking full advantage of the religious renaissance among the people" as they sought to revive interest in "the existence of a tradition for a purer way of life."[21]

Despite its originality and the high hopes placed in it by the government, the Mass Education Movement faced problems stemming largely from poorly trained corpsmen, who were arrogant and indifferent. Although it was possible to overcome these and other such problems through better recruitment and training, the movement failed to realize its potential because of the suspicion its officers created among the minorities, especially through efforts to propagate Buddhism and to teach Burman manners and ways. By the mid-nineteen-fifties the movement declined as the government turned to other means of raising the educational levels and Burmanizing the more backward peoples both in Burma proper and the states.

21. Burma, Ministry of Information, *Burma: The Fourth Anniversary* (Rangoon, 1952), pp. 41–43.

The caretaker government also addressed itself to the problem of national unity. It created the National Solidarity Association. This new political organization drew its initial recruits from the military, both active and retired, which proved to be its greatest weakness, for it failed to attract a wide popular base. Its objective was to build national consciousness among the people and unite them behind the government in its fight to end insurgency and lawlessness, to support the constitution, and to build unity among the peoples of Burma.[22] It was intended to replace the old united AFPFL as the national organization; it sought to transcend political divisions and identities so that nonpartisans, members of the armed forces, and civil servants, could join with the ordinary citizens and work for common national goals. Although in theory it seemed a logical solution to the political and ethnic rivalries that divided the nation and nearly brought it to civil war, in fact its military leadership, its hierarchical organization, and its conservative ideology discouraged all but military personnel and civil servants from joining. In the states it was seen as a new means for Burman domination and was rejected almost universally.

---

With the return to elected government following the election of 1960, U Nu embarked on a program that, among other things, was intended to remove the causes of national disunity. To accomplish this end he had promised, during the political campaign, to see the establishment of separate states for the Mons and Arakanese, if there was genuine support for statehood among the members of the two groups. Following the victory of his party, Nu formed an inquiry commission to examine the statehood question. In the parliamentary session of the fall of 1962, Nu introduced an Arakan statehood bill; but on the advice of the opposition leaders (his former colleagues in the old united AFPFL), who feared that such a bill at that moment might aggravate, rather than calm, the growing racial tension in the Union, he withdrew the measure before it came up for debate, thereby alienating the

22. "The National Solidarity Association," *Nation*, November 2, 1959; *Burma Weekly Bulletin*, n.s., 8(29) (November 12, 1959): 281–288.

Arakanese and Mon leaders, who had supported him from 1958, when he was locked in battle with his former allies over control of the government.

The growing tensions among the minorities did not decrease; they grew sharper among the Shans and, to a lesser extent, the Kachins, Kayahs, and Karens. Nu was aware of the Shan discontent, which had been building over the years. He also was aware of the serious efforts by some Shans to lead the state out of the Union. There were Shans who wanted to remain in the Union, but under different terms. As a last effort to avoid civil war and secession, thirty-three Shan leaders met in Taunggyi in February 1961 to form the Constitutional Revision Steering Committee, and they drew up a memorandum, which they laid before the Union government in the hope that real changes in the relations between the Shan State and the Union of Burma might follow and that the political and communal tensions might subside.[23]

Among the things the Shans complained of in their memorandum were the inequality among the states, the dependence of the Shan State on Burma proper and the Union government for approval in undertaking many actions that properly belonged to the states, the absence of state control over lands located in the states, and the control of funds by the national government, the lack of control by the state over the movement of peoples in and out of the states. The memorandum called for the creation of a union of coequal states; separation of Burma proper from the national government and for Burma proper to be treated as a separate and coequal state with the others; the two chambers of the national parliament to be made equal in power so that the Chamber of Nationalities could protect the interests of the states; and the complete separation of the Union government from that of the states, the latter to have sufficient power and a large enough financial base to manage their own affairs. Following this assembly the Shan leaders met with U Nu, and out of their discussions grew the idea of calling a federal seminar wherein all the leaders of the Union of Burma would assemble and discuss changes in

23. *Memorandum Submitted by the Constitution Revision Steering Committee Shan States* (Taunggyi, February 22, 1961) (mimeo), 33 pp.

the constitution together with changes in attitudes among national and state leaders so that a new basis for national unity and harmony might be found.[24]

The seminar met at the end of February 1962, and newspaper accounts indicated that full and frank discussions were in progress. It never completed its work because the military, on March 2, 1962, seized power, arrested all the national leaders, dismissed Parliament, and took the first steps toward the establishment of a military dictatorship. There can be no doubt that the military feared the outcome of the seminar because they were uncertain how far U Nu might go in granting some or all of the demands of the minorities. Brig. Aung Gyi, speaking for the new Revolutionary Council a few days after the coup, said in its defense that it was necessary because "we had economic, religious and political crises with the issue of federalism as the most important reason for the coup."[25]

---

In assessing the sweep of events, decisions, and contradictions of the constitutional period, a case can be made that as a nation Burma began life with deep political, cultural, and geographic divisions that were not closed despite the best efforts of all those who wanted the Union to grow strong and united. There is no way of measuring the loss of Aung San to the new nation. It was he who had won the minorities to join the new Union of Burma, and with his death there was no one strong enough to carry on his ideas and put them into effect. But even in his day there were leaders among the Burmans who saw Burma's possibility of developing into a strong nation as dependent on the unification of the people into a Burman state, and they never fully understood or shared Aung San's outlook. Therefore it was not surprising that the men thrust into leadership when Aung San and those closest to him were murdered were less committed to his ideals and goals

---

24. For U Nu's version of the events leading up to the federal seminar and what took place at that meeting, see Nu, *U Nu: Saturday's Son* (New Haven, 1975), pp. 338–342.

25. *Guardian* (daily), March 8, 1962.

# The Politics of Contradiction

than he was. Besides, they quickly had to face a series of insurrections that nearly tore the nation apart. Given this history it is not hard to understand why Burmanization and nationalization became the dominant ideal whether spoken or implied. But, as those minorities who were loyal to the new state watched the implementation of these policies, they had good reason to believe that there was contradiction between word and action. The breakdown in communication and trust was the result of these contradictions. The contradictions, then, between what the government said and did, between what the minorities expected and received, were too great to overcome in the short period of constitutional government, especially in the environment in which they had to root and flower.

It is this legacy that the military inherited when it seized power on March 2, 1962. The military is proving to be a better heir to U Nu than to Aung San in the way in which it has tried to solve this problem.

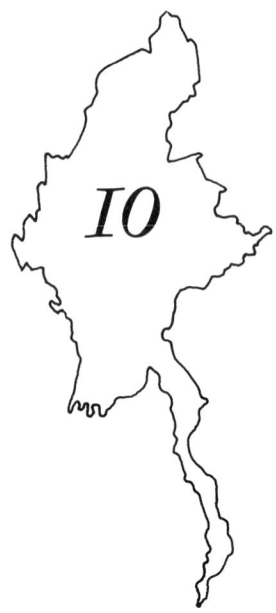

# 10

## Military Rule and the Future of National Unity

In form and style, the period of military rule differs markedly from the constitutional period and even from the brief interlude of military rule during the period of the caretaker government. It was then that Gen. Ne Win, standing before the Parliament in order to gain its approval for the office of prime minister, said,

> I wish deeply that all Members of Parliament would hold as much belief in the Constitution and in democracy as I do. I wish deeply that all Members of Parliament would sacrifice their lives to defend the Constitution as I would do in my capacity as Prime Minister, as a citizen and as a soldier.[1]

He did not repeat these words when he and his fellow officers seized the government, displaced the constitution, dismissed Parliament, and substituted a dictatorship for democracy.

Despite their rhetoric the military rulers expressed goals not really different from those of their civilian predecessors. This was particularly true on the issue of national unity. They attempted to be

---

1. "Text of Address by Prime Minister General Ne Win to Parliament, October 3, 1958," in Director of Information, *Is Trust Vindicated?* (Rangoon, 1960), p. 547.

the true interpreters of Aung San's thought while, in fact, they departed further from his ideas than the civilians they replaced. They, too, repeated the ideal of unity in diversity while they moved the nation along the road to Burmanization and nationalization.

---

Among the first things the Revolutionary Council (the ruling body of the coup government) did after consolidating its power was to proclaim its goals and the steps it would take to realize them. Entitled *The Burmese Way to Socialism* (BWS), the declaration of the coup leaders announced that they, together with the people, would "march unswervingly . . . toward the goal of socialism."[2] To achieve their ends, the leaders said it was necessary to eliminate the existing administrative system—which they called a "stumbling block"—and replace it with a new one based on their ideas of socialist democracy.[3] The military leaders also said they intended to unite the people and create a viable nation. Cloaking themselves in the words of Aung San, as the elected leaders had done before them, they published a passage, from one of his speeches, that emphasized the primacy of the nation over its parts and the source of nationhood as the shared experiences of all the people and not their individual identity: "Though race, religion and language are important factors it is only their traditional desire and will to live in unity through weal and woe that binds a people together and makes them a nation and their spirit a patriotism."[4]

With a commitment to change both institutions and goals, the Revolutionary Council wasted little time getting started. On May 9, 1962, a few days after announcing the *BWS*, the council replaced the existing political and administrative system in both Burma proper and the states with a new centralized hierarchy of administrative councils, called the Security and Administration Councils (SAC), which radiated from Rangoon to the borders of the nation.[5]

2. Revolutionary Council, *The Burmese Way to Socialism* (Rangoon, 1962), p. 1.
3. Ibid., p. 5.
4. Ibid., p. 6.
5. The forerunners of the Security and Administration Councils were established selectively in the states during the caretaker government. When

Under a single head, the Security and Administrative Central Council, the councils descended through two parallel hierarchies, one for Burma proper and the other for the states. To make way for the new system the Revolutionary Council abolished the offices of head and minister of state, the state councils, and the various state administrations. In their place they established for each state a new State Supreme Council responsible directly to Rangoon, and a number of inferior councils—the lower one responsible to the one immediately above—which together were responsible to it. For the first time in Burma's history the country had a centralized administration under a single ruling authority with power to make the system work.

The SACs, at all levels both in Burma proper and the states, were composed of representatives from the military, the civil service, and the police; in the higher councils, the chairmanship was reserved for the military representative. It was not until 1972 that the Revolutionary Council made any changes in the composition of the councils. Then it decreed that there should be civilian representatives added, to be drawn from the government-sponsored Burma Socialist Program Party (BSPP), the People's Peasant Council, and the People's Workers Council.

With all the nation now under its direct control and with all the legal and natural leaders of the minorities either in prison or inactive, the military rulers turned their attention to ending the various insurgencies and rebellions through negotiations. On April 3, 1963, the Revolutionary Council made its first gesture of conciliation by announcing a general amnesty to all citizens, including insurgents, for all crimes except murder, rape, and the destruction of property, if they surrendered before July 1. The offer did not extend, however, to people detained by the military government either during or after the coup: the members of U Nu's government and the leaders of the minorities.

By itself this gesture was not new; the elected leaders had offered

---

U Nu and his party came to power in 1960, these councils were terminated; but as insurgency and lawlessness increased, his government established law-and-order committees with roughly the same composition but less power; see Burma Weekly Bulletin, n.s., 9(52) (April 27, 1961): 463.

amnesties in the past. The approach of the Revolutionary Council differed from previous ones, however, in that it did not stop at this point; a short time later (June 11) it made a second gesture of conciliation by inviting all groups in revolt, both political and ethnic, to Rangoon to discuss their grievances and the ways they might be solved. No preconditions for the talks were laid down; the insurgents did not have to surrender and they could hold their weapons; further, they were promised safe passage to and from the meetings regardless of their outcome. The Revolutionary Council also extended the amnesty for an indefinite period and withdrew all offers of reward for the capture of insurgent leaders. The public welcomed these moves and hoped that they would lead to peace and the end of internal warfare.

Between the time of the announcement and November 14, when the talks broke off, representatives of the various political and ethnic groups came to Rangoon and held discussions with the spokesmen, including Ne Win at times, of the Revolutionary Council.[6] During the talks, the Burma Communist Party, the Karen National Union, the New Mon State Party, the Karenni National Progressive Party, and the Chin Presidium Council joined together as the National Democratic United Front (NDUF) and negotiated, at times on a collective basis, at other times individually. The talks ended abruptly because there was no agreement on the definition and implementation of a ceasefire as the first step toward ending all insurgency. The military rulers claimed afterward that the "Revolutionary Council had come to realize the danger of the country being split into two by allowing the NDUF to try to set up a parallel government."[7] The NDUF countered by saying that it only wanted to continue to exercise power in the areas it claimed to hold. It wanted to continue the talks and left Rangoon reluctantly. Only a small group of Karen

---

6. For detailed transcripts of the talks between the Revolutionary Council and representatives of the insurgents, see Revolutionary Council, *Internal Peace Parley* (Historical Documents, no. 1) (Rangoon, 1963) (mimeo). There were two other groups that had contact or direct talks with the military rulers in addition to those included in this document: the Karen Revolutionary Council and the Communist Party of Burma.

7. Revolutionary Council, *Internal Peace Parley*, op. cit., p. 155.

insurgents, the Karen Revolutionary Council, remained and entered into an agreement with the government to end their insurgency.

The negotiations demonstrated several things about the problem of national unity. They showed that it was not possible to solve it by a single gesture of goodwill and understanding. Some of the rebels had been fighting for so long it was nearly impossible to define the terms for halting their armed opposition, let alone for solving the problems that caused it in the first place. A careful study of the transcripts of the discussions also shows that the military, too, was highly suspicious of everything the rebels said, promised, or questioned because they had been at war with the insurgents for so long they had little trust in their enemies. In many ways the discussions were unreal because they focused on one aspect of national disunity—the insurrections—and included only a portion of the opposition—the illegal groups and their leaders. Those leaders among the minorities who represented the peaceful members of their societies and had sought to solve the problems through legal means were excluded. Therefore the majority of the members of the ethnic groups involved were unrepresented.

The negotiations broke down on technical military grounds without ever getting to the root causes of why portions of the minorities went into and remained in revolt. In contrast, in the meetings held between the former elected government and the legal leaders of the minorities at the 1962 federal seminar just prior to the coup, the discussions centered on the fundamental issues of disunity. The seminar also might not have been able to produce lasting results had it been able to conclude its discussions, but it did manage to engage both sides in frank and open discussion for first time since the Panglong Conference in 1947.

The apparent unity among the insurgent ethnic and political groups disguised the deep cleavages that existed between them. Over the years individual groups cooperated and fought with one another as well as with the government. The creation of the NDUF was a temporary alliance. It continued after the talks broke down and even gained the cooperation of the Kachin Independence Army and the Shan State Independence Army for a few years, but the latter two never joined the NDUF and eventually separated from it. The

Communists, too, gave their support as long as the NDUF served their interests. With little basis other than a common enemy for a firm bond between rebel groups, the NDUF broke up in the early nineteen-seventies, as the ethnic and political groups united and separated like pieces in a kaleidoscope.

If the negotiations were a failure, it did not daunt the military from looking for other ways to unite the various peoples of the Union. On Union Day 1964, Gen. Ne Win issued a new policy statement entitled, a "Declaration of the Conviction of the Revolutionary Council on the Question of Union Nationalities." Like the legislative lists of the displaced constitution, wherein the rights and duties of the Union and the states were set forth, the new declaration identified the areas of activity in which all nationalities together would share responsibility and also those areas that each nationality, under circumstances peculiar to itself, would carry out individually and independently. Economic development and social welfare of the Union were tasks for all nationalities, whereas the development of national language, literature, culture, religion, and customs were the tasks of the various nationalities. There was a proviso that no independent actions should be taken if they proved to be politically and socially divisive or if they affected the welfare of another nationality.[8] As before, this new policy elevated the Burmese nation above its member states and placed the common good before particular rights.

To implement the policy and build national unity, the Revolutionary Council moved forward on two tracks. One was the creation of the Academy for the Development of National Groups. Although it was hailed as a new idea, it proved to be an updated version of the old Mass Education Movement, which U Nu and the AFPFL developed in the early years of independence. The new academy was located in the heartland of Burman culture, Sagaing. Its purpose was to recruit and train representatives from all ethnic groups to preach the new ideals of socialism and national unity, to be teachers of basic health and social and educational subjects for the

---

8. "A Report on Ten Years of Social Revolution in Burma," *Working People's Daily*, March 2, 1972, p. 6.

peoples living in the remote and isolated areas of the states, to assume leadership of the peoples with whom they worked, and to help them to improve their standards of living.[9]

Despite the wide publicity given to the academy and the funds appropriated for its activities, it proved to be no better at achieving its ends than its predecessor. U Tun Aye, the chairman of the Shan State Supreme Council, speaking in 1971 at a seminar on the working of the academy, pointed out that it was failing to realize its mission because of the poor recruitment of trainees. Most were drawn from urban youth and relatives of the military rather than from minorities. More important, the recruits refused to serve in the remote areas after their training was completed, thus defeating the very purpose for which the academy was created.[10] Despite these and other criticisms the academy continued, but its goals were never achieved.

The other track followed by the Revolutionary Council was to give attention to the minorities in much the same way as the elected government did before it was overthrown. Union Days were major celebrations; instead of holding them only in Rangoon, they were held in other cities and large towns throughout the Union. The high point continued to be the flag march from Panglong in the Shan State to the capital and then to the city of the celebration. The military rulers also encouraged nationwide celebrations of ethnic national days and published the folklore of certain minorities as well as historical and anthropological studies of the various peoples of the Union. Brig. San Yu, at the Union Day 1965 celebration, declared that the culture of one nationality was part and parcel of the culture of the whole nation.[11] But these and other gestures were never seen as evidence that the military was any more interested in furthering unity in diversity than U Nu's governments were before them.

New programs and superficial attention to minority pride and identity did not bring the peoples of Burma together. At each of the Union Day celebrations from 1965 onward, the leaders—Ne

9. Ibid.
10. *Guardian* (daily), January 1, 1971.
11. Ibid., February 13, 1965.

Win and others—spoke out vigorously on one failure or obstruction or another that prevented the achievement of internal peace and national unity. In 1966, the theme of the Union Day celebration was the continued existence of racial prejudice and the government's efforts to overcome those who were disrupting national unity. A year later Ne Win complained, "In spite of the obvious need for united action, certain dissident elements are holding fast to narrow racial outlooks with misguided extremist policies, carrying on their disruptive work, hindering progress of development projects and imperiling national unity."[12] In 1968, Col. Hla Han repeated the earlier criticism made by Ne Win and went one step further. He linked the failure of the minorities to cooperate and unite with foreign influence: "They are trying their best to sabotage our plans and it is not difficult to see the traitors of our flesh and blood are acting as stooges for foreign powers. . . ."[13] His remarks must be considered against the fact that Burma–China relations were at a low point owing to the riots in Rangoon a few months before, the recall of ambassadors over the extension of China's Cultural Revolution into Burma, and China's open appeal to the Burmese to overthrow the Ne Win government.

The 1969 Union Day celebration saw no real improvement in the racial problems of Burma. Again Hla Han returned to the theme of foreign influence on racial relations in Burma. He also saw the minorities divided between those who wanted unity, peace, and security and those who wanted to destroy unity and continue the various insurgencies that had plagued Burma since independence.

Given the continued disunity among the people and the failure of the Revolutionary Council's efforts to bring the majority and the minorities together through one dramatic gesture or another, and taking into account the threat Burma felt from the open hostility expressed by China and the aid China was believed to be giving the minorities and political groups in revolt, the Revolutionary Council chose yet another approach to the problem of national unity. In 1968, Ne Win invited thirty-three former political and ethnic leaders, many of whom had been his prisoners for five or

---

12. "A Report on Ten Years of Social Revolution," op. cit., p. 6.
13. Ibid.

more years, to participate in a new committee, the Internal Unity Advisory Body. This group was asked to "submit ideas on means of establishing internal unity that would effectively and directly benefit the working people of the Union of Burma politically, economically, socially and ethnically."[14] The report was due by May 31, 1969.

Given the diversity of the membership of the committee, it is not surprising that it could not agree on a single report. A majority of eighteen favored a return to the old constitution with amendments as necessary to make it serve the needs of the public. A minority of eleven rejected the idea and asked instead for the creation of a national unity congress, the formal retention of a federal structure, the creation of an all-inclusive single political party, and the adoption of socialist democracy as its ideology; its position was similar to that outlined over the years by the military rulers.

On national unity the majority group called for a return to the old federal system with the possibility of creating new states where they were necessary and when the proper criteria for establishing them was defined. Three of the members of the majority group rejected this solution and called instead for the establishment of a unitary state with cabinet representation for all ethnic groups. The minority suggested that a new federal system be created with autonomous territories both in and outside the states for the smaller ethnic groups.[15] Its ideas reflected the suggestions Aung San had made more than twenty years before at the AFPFL preconstituent assembly meeting. With no agreement among the former leaders, Ne Win felt free to continue along his own path, a path that now led to the writing of a new constitution.

Before turning to the second period of military rule, which began with the implementation of the new constitution in 1974, it is useful to sum up the first twelve years of military dictatorship. The Revolutionary Council, like the civilian elected leaders before it, worked on two levels in dealing with the issue of national unity.

14. Proclamation nos. 72, 74, Forward 7(9) (December 15, 1968): 2; see also Josef Silverstein, "Political Dialogue in Burma: A New Turn on the Road to Socialism," Asian Survey 10(2) (February 1970): 133–141.
15. Working People's Daily, June 5, 1969.

Through the SACs it was able to have more effective control over the minorities in areas where there were no insurgents or where insurgents held little or no power over the people. With no ethnic leaders who opposed the military in positions of authority, the hierarchy of councils was able to extend the policies emanating from Rangoon more effectively than any previous government had been able to do. While the military leaders, like their civilian predecessors, spoke in ways that seemed to lend support to the ideal of unity in diversity, they pursued a variety of policies that led to the assimilation of peoples into a common culture and a common loyalty. Thus they emphasized the nationalization of the society and the Burmanization of its culture.

There was one area wherein they differed with their civilian predecessors. The state was no longer the patron of Buddhism; the numerous religious days that became holidays after the faith was declared the state religion (Ne Win once complained that there were 209 holidays in a 365-day year) were ended abruptly; so too were the restrictions on animal slaughter and other proscriptions sanctioned by the Buddhist faith. More important, proselytizing among the non-Buddhist minorities almost came to a complete halt. The Revolutionary Council's policy of treating all religious groups equally and not subjecting any group to the values and laws of another was a return to the very early policy of the AFPFL government in the nineteen-fifties, before the state became the patron of the Buddhist faith, and it was consistent with the constitutional guarantee of equality for the citizens of Burma.

The minorities responded as before. Some accepted their fate and saw no way to reverse the present course of social history; others joined the rebels—ethnic and political—and fought to bring about changes that would allow them to pursue their own ends in their own way. But with the military enjoying a monopoly of power and willing to use force to achieve its ends, the Revolutionary Council was able to hold tightly to most of the country and extend its rule over most of the people; only in the border areas, particularly Burma's frontiers with China, Laos, and Thailand, was there a kind of no-man's-land where the few residents faced dual pressure coming from the military and from dissident political and ethnic groups. When the new constitution came into effect, the nation was no closer to national unity than it was when the military seized power; some, in fact, said it was further from that goal.

---

When the military turned to the writing of a new constitution, the problem of national unity was given a great deal of attention. As early as 1969, Ne Win launched the process by giving an extensive criticism of the old constitution and suggesting some guidelines for a new one.[16] The general saw part of the problem as stemming from British influence on the minorities in 1947, which resulted in a constitution that separated the peoples of Burma along ethnic and geographic lines. It also resulted in a serious compromise with democratic principles when it reserved the seats in the Chamber of Nationalities to the Shan *sawbwas* and gave them administrative power in the state. Ne Win also saw the problem as growing out of the peculiar arrangement wherein the prime minister of the Union had the power to effect state administration through the appointment of the combined head and minister of state. The new constitution must remedy these and other defects, he said, by creating a new union that would embody at least two new principles: The territory of the entire nation must be open to all to live and settle wherever they will without regard to race, language, and historical origin; and the Burmans and minorities must grow closer to one another and help each other.[17] "Our Union is just one homogeneous whole. A Chin, for instance, can go wherever he likes within the Union and stay wherever he likes. So too, a Burmese. Everyone can take part in any of the affairs, whether political, economic, administrative or judicial. He can choose his own role." When this has been achieved, Ne Win concluded, "we will not need to have separate governments within the Union."[18] Clearly the new constitution would emphasize assimilation and nationalization at the expense of unity in diversity.

16. BSPP, *Address Delivered by General Ne Win, Chairman of the Burma Socialist Programme Party, at the Opening Session of the Fourth Party Seminar on 6 November 1969* (Rangoon, 1969), pp. 7, 26–27.
17. Ibid., pp. 28–29.
18. Ibid.

Two years later, the machinery for writing the new constitution was created. The BSPP Congress, meeting in 1971, declared itself responsible for writing the new fundamental law. To carry out its work it created the State Constitution Drafting Committee of ninety-seven under the leadership of Brig. San Yu. Sixty-four of its members represented social classes, ethnic groups, political leaders from the past, and legal experts; the remainder of the committee were drawn from the military. The congress also drew up six guidelines, of which two referred specifically to national unity. One principle held that the new constitution must insure racial equality and national unity in good times and bad; the second held that the people shall have both democratic and personal rights within the framework of a socialist democracy and duties and obligations toward socialism and the state.[19]

The writing of the new constitution took two years, went through three drafts, and finally, in 1973, was offered to the people in a referendum. Although 90.19 percent of the total vote cast favored it, people in the states were less supportive.[20]

Under the new constitution the nation was renamed the Socialist Republic of the Union of Burma. It was federal in name but unitary in practice.[21] Although the territory of the Union was redivided into fourteen states and divisions (seven divisions and two states were created out of Burma proper), it was united administratively by four tiers of councils: the national assembly at the top, and state or division, township and ward, and village tract councils below, with the lowest responsible to the one immediately above. In the new system the size, shape, and name of any state or division could be changed after ascertaining the wishes of the people living in the particular area. The states no longer belonged to any ethnic group; consistent with the principle enunciated five years earlier, the states

19. *Guardian* (daily), December 3, 1971.
20. *Asian Research Bulletin* (Singapore) 3(9) (February 1974): 2453–2454; in the Shan State it was approved with a 66.4 percent margin; in the Kachin State, with a 68.8 percent margin; and in the Kayah State, with a 71.01 percent margin.
21. For a detailed analysis of the 1974 constitution, see Josef Silverstein, *Burma: Military Rule and the Politics of Stagnation* (Ithaca, 1977), pp. 120–134.

and divisions in the Socialist Republic of the Union of Burma belonged to their residents. Inasmuch as all people were free to move and live where they chose, emphasis on local culture, language, and history gave way to national culture, language, and history. Because all citizens shared the territory of the nation, there was no longer any need for the inclusion of the right of secession. In a technical sense the new constitution solved the problem of national unity by emphasizing the equality of all as Burmese and not as representatives of separate and distinct groups. They would, in Ne Win's terms, share the "weal and woe" of the nation together, and whatever differences once divided them now were decreed to have ended.

But in fact the problems persist. Although the various councils that govern in the states are closely supervised by the national assembly and the various levels of administration in the states carry out the directives they receive from above, the sense of nationhood and unity has not become a reality. The various minority insurgencies persist, and warfare has become a way of life both for them and for the government forces they face. More important is the fact that the Burma Communist Party (BCP), with whom they sometimes cooperate, holds sizable territory on the border between China and Burma. It receives material help from its fraternal allies inside the People's Republic and propaganda support from the transmitters located somewhere in Yunnan. While the BCP is still considered a political threat to the Union government, its composition has altered over the years so that today its main recruits come from the minorities whereas its leaders are predominantly Burman. Although most observers believe that so long as its main recruits are from the minorities it cannot be a real alternative to the Burman-dominated government in Rangoon, nevertheless its growing multiracial character makes it easier for it to cooperate with the ethnic insurgents and keep the struggles alive.

There is yet another element in the disunity equation. The border areas of the Shan and Kachin states are a major source of opium, which finds its way onto the world illegal market. The revenues from its sale by the various insurgent groups and the Burmese Communists who control parts of it keep their movements well-financed. Because much of the opium or the roughly refined heroin passes through its neighbor states on the way to consumers around the world, the issue of opium has become a major irritant in Burma's foreign relations. The Burma government cannot, by itself, control the growth and sale of this important narcotic. Recently the government turned to the United States for equipment—helicopters and other items—with which to stem the trade and control the people who grow the poppies.[22] Despite the original promises that this equipment would only be used to control opium, it is in fact also being used to fight against the insurgents and Communists. This never-ending warfare in the border areas of the states has kept the military in semioccupation in the disputed areas, and this has not eased relations between the ethnic minorities and the government in Rangoon. Also the fact that the minority insurgents can keep their struggle alive and continue to recruit new members to replace those who have fallen or deserted suggests that the socialist government in Rangoon has not "won the hearts and minds" of the minorities to their idea of a Burmese nation. As the decade of the nineteen-eighties begins, the problem of national unity seems no closer to solution than it was nearly two decades before when the military seized power.

---

More than thirty years have passed since the original constitution was written and adopted, and more than a half a decade since the new constitution was approved and put into practice. It is time to ask why the solutions embodied in them have failed. If one considers the original constitution, many answers have been offered. Burmans have argued that the minorities did not wish to merge their land and people with the majority, whereas Shan spokesmen have responded by saying that the Burmans never intended to live

22. U.S. Congress, House of Representatives, Ninety-Fourth Congress, First Session, *Hearings before the Subcommittee on Future Foreign Policy Research and Development of the Committee on International Relations House of Representatives: Proposal to Control Opium from the Golden Triangle and Terminate the Shan Opium Trade.* In January 1979, Congressman Lester Wolff visited Burma and the Golden Triangle. When he was told at a news conference that the helicopters were being used against the ethnic minorities as well as the opium trade, he said there were no objections, as this did not violate the terms of sale.

by the agreements embodied in the fundamental law.[23] A case can be made for an absence of good faith on both sides, but that does not answer the question.

The problem was insoluble from the outset because neither the leaders of the Union of Burma nor their counterparts among the ethnic minorities defined the problem in a common way and offered solutions the other side could trust and accept. So long as the Burmans spoke in the language of Aung San and offered solutions based on the idea of unity in diversity, a majority among the ethnic groups were willing to give the constitution and the new state a chance to make good on its promises. When some of the initially loyal minority members saw practices that were leading toward the creation of a unitary state in which they feared the Burmanization of their language and dress, religion and culture, they felt betrayed and willing to take up arms and join those already in revolt. The initial aspect of the problem was lack of a common understanding of what each side meant by the terms of the constitution and a general agreement on how to realize those objectives.

Consider the question of the safety valve for most of the minorities, the right of secession—a promise with which all minorities identified even though all but the Shans and Kayahs were deprived of the right. The Shans recognized very early that the right offered no escape hatch; instead the union was to be indestructible, and the Burmans and some of the smaller groups of ethnic minorities were willing to fight to preserve it. For the majority community, there was never any question but that the union, once formed, would be permanent; and they never could attach the same importance to the right of secession as did the Shans and some of the other minorities. By moving militarily against the dissidents, the government took the road of political and ethnic dominance, which found its logical counterparts in the language and education, economic and social policies that in the long run would blend the people together and create a Burmese society in which the heritage of the Burmans would be dominant.

23. See *Memorandum Submitted by the Constitution Revision Steering Committee Shan States* (Taunggyi, February 22, 1961) (mimeo) for the case of the Shans against the Burmans and the Union of Burma.

Along with the idea of the right of secession as a promise of escape, the idea of ethnic-oriented states seemed to offer institutional protection of diversity, but that idea was based on a false premise. No state was ethnically pure; all contained minorities as protective of their own identity and heritage as the group for whom their state was named. Despite the obviousness of this fact only the Kachin State faced it clearly and made provisions for it. In Burma proper the Burmans enjoyed a numerical superiority on the basis of total population; yet in small areas broken up in checkerboard fashion, Mons and Karens were dominant.

In dealing with this problem the Burmans were unwilling to find a solution like that of the Kachins. One was adopted as a stopgap in order to present a completed document to the Constituent Assembly; but when a permanent recommendation for a Karen state was made, the Karens were faced with the loss of reserved seats in Burma proper. Even the physical unit to be known as the Karen State was limited to territory that was contiguous and in which the Karens were in the majority; thus, the large cities or major market towns that traditionally served the Karens were separated and excluded from the new state. In a smaller way the Mons made a similar case, but their numbers were fewer and their determination to fight was weaker. The Arakanese, a third minority in Burma proper, still lived in their traditional area, compact and away from the major centers of Burman population, which assured them of the possibility of electing Arakanese to represent them and of working together to protect their interests. Thus, despite being a minority in Burma proper, effective collective action was more possible for them without resorting to arms than for the Karens or Mons.

What was true in Burma proper was also true in the hill areas, but on a much smaller scale. As a result, insurrection against the Burmans provoked insurgency in the Shan State among the Pa-Os against the Shans. In similar ways, ethnic groups fought with each other because the constitution did not make proper provision for unity in diversity either in the nation as a whole or in the states. Here, then, the problem was not the promise but the implementation.

It could be argued that the promises, specific and implied, about unity in diversity could have been avoided and that the goal of a centralized Burmanized state could have been imposed directly by the nationalist leaders. At least then everyone would have known where he stood. Because Great Britain was unwilling to take up arms to protect the minorities and was equally unwilling to carve out separate states for those minorities unwilling to live under Burman dominance, that solution might have seemed an obvious one; but it was never seriously considered by Aung San and the AFPFL at any time. From the earliest days, during World War II, it was the nationalists' objective to bring the minorities into an independent union with Burma proper through voluntary means. This was stated over and over again in party documents, speeches of the leaders, and proposals and plans actually offered. In such a free association, the nationalists hoped that the more backward and underdeveloped areas and their peoples would look to the more developed and advanced Burmans for guidance and advice and would model their institutions, laws, and society on those the Burmans were in the process of creating. They hoped that through national policies on language and education, on economic, political, and social improvements the peoples of Burma would blend together and create a Burmese society in which the heritage of the Burmans would be dominant. But there was no clear and uniform understanding of what Aung San meant when he argued for unity in diversity, and there was less commitment to it among those who succeeded him. It is clear that a widely held misunderstanding, both in idea and implementation, about the nature of the relationship of the several peoples was a major cause of the persistence of the problem despite the agreements and the constitution.

The failure of the first constitution was also a product of time. There was not enough time between 1946 and 1948 to educate both the Burmans and the minorities to the meaning of unity in diversity as expressed in the key documents and agreements and to its implications for all concerned. Had there been a longer constitution-making process, or had there been fuller discussion of the implications of the Panglong Agreement, the peoples as well as their leaders might have foreseen some of the contradictions in such a policy and moved in ways to modify it or tailor it to fit the specific situation in Burma. But time was not on the side of the Burmese. The demand for an end to colonial rule was in the air. The events in India, Indonesia, and the Philippines were known and discussed in Burma, and there was no time to discuss the peculiar situation in Burma and seek a solution that might have stood the shock of controversy and revolt.

To the men and women attending the Constituent Assembly, who had lived through the assassination of Aung San and those who died with him, the constitution they brought forth seemed like the solution they were seeking. Rather than test it in severe debate or allow it to incubate while the peoples of Burma became familiar with its provisions and had time to think about how they would be effected, its drafters were willing to adopt it unanimously and test it in action, believing that it could be amended or changed if the need arose.

Finally, it was the time factor that robbed the Burmese of a chance to draw up a better solution to the divisions among the many peoples who populated the land. Given the time and the pressures to arrive at a solution, it is no wonder that they left their convention believing that they had found a meaningful solution. With hindsight, it is not easy to judge them wrong.

What of the second constitution? It was not born in haste; it was not the result of bargaining, and it was not written against a background of monumental changes in the world outside. It was the product of a few disguised as the work of many. A careful examination of the three drafts and of the pages of public comments solicited after each version was made public suggests that the authors already knew what they wanted and were going through the motions of engaging in dialogue with the people about its content. There was no equivalent of the Panglong Conference. Only the insurgents were invited to talk about the future in 1963, and only the old politicians were asked for their ideas in 1969. In the first instance the discussions never went beyond the gesture of dialogue, as neither side trusted the other and each seemed to seek an advantage from the process. In the second instance the variety of ideas offered were dismissed with finality by the general as he outlined his own ideas for a united Burma. When the people were given a chance to speak during the hearings on the drafts of the constitution, it was the ordinary farmer and laborer who spoke without the guidance of an educated natural leadership because the latter had been separated from the people and silenced over the years of military rule. Given the Burmese propensity to accept authority from those in power and able to impose it, there was no dialogue between the people and the representatives of the Revolutionary Council despite the two years of discussion.

Whatever merit derived from the dialectic of different peoples and cultures clashing and working together to hammer out a national culture and identity wherein all would contribute and share, it was dismissed by the authors of the second constitution as they imposed their doctrines and procedures for realizing them. The people were assigned a place; all would be equal in their obligations to carry out their assigned tasks and all would be faithful to the imposed ideology. In a society where a Buddhist ethic prevails, man knows that all in this world is impermanent and subject to change. The Burmese, regardless of their cultural and ethnic antecedents, seem to have adopted a resigned attitude toward the new constitution and the men who have imposed it, knowing that, like the constitution and leaders who were displaced, the present document and its champions, too, will pass from the scene.

But, imperfect and impermanent as it may be, does the second constitution provide a basis for Burma to realize national unity? Here the answer must be found in the slow progress of Burmanization and assimilation begun by the AFPFL and continuing in the present, regardless of the constitution that governs the state. The forces opposing this trend are on the defensive, and the present constitution provides them with no outlet to halt or temporarily deflect its progress. But this progress is not without some illegal opposition. The insurgents, both ethnic and political, keep old identities and ideas alive. More important, many are supported either by foreign governments or by the profits the insurgents realize from the illegal trade in narcotics and other products they transport abroad. There also are thousands of educated Burmese living outside Burma who would like to return if the system were less authoritarian and predetermined in its present course. Whether these expatriates attempt to mount revolt from abroad, as U Nu did in the late nineteen-sixties and early nineteen-seventies, or just keep alive their cultures and identities and continue to communicate them to their relatives and friends still in Burma, they pose a threat to the present government and impede its march toward the nationalizing goals it has set.

The constitution embodies the confidence and righteousness of the men who wrote it. Ne Win and those who share his power can defend it in the words Thakin Mya expressed in his inaugural address to the 1947 Constituent Assembly after he was chosen president of that body:

> Though we may see some superficial differences when we look at one another, yet in essence we are just one. There is hardly any other nation more homogenous than the people of Burma. Economically and geographically our country is an indivisible unity. In our affinity of race and language, unity of culture and historical traditions, we have all the characteristics of a strong and united nation.[24]

But claiming unity without demonstrating it to the satisfaction of all is no answer, and the continuation of the armed struggle seems to bear that out. Three decades of struggle over this problem has hardened all sides, and it will take a new generation of Burmese to find a new basis for unity. Many say the die is cast and there is no turning away from the nationalization and Burmanization in progress. Others think that the peoples of Burma could return to the idea of unity in diversity as expressed during the struggle for independence between 1945 and 1948 and find a new answer that eluded their parents. Until a common solution is found, there will be struggle and unrest in Burma.

---

24. Burma, Ministry of Information, *Burma's Fight for Freedom* (Rangoon, 1948), p. 92.

# Selected Bibliography

Ba Maw. *Breakthrough in Burma: Memoirs of a Revolution, 1939–1946.* New Haven, Yale University Press, 1968.
Banks, David, ed. *Changing Identities in Modern Southeast Asia.* The Hague, Mouton Publishers, 1976.
Ba Than, Dhammika U. *The Roots of the Revolution.* Rangoon, Director of Information, 1962. Reproduced from the *Guardian*, March 27, 1962.
Ba, U. *My Burma: The Autobiography of a President.* New York, Taplinger, 1958.
Burma. *Burma and the Insurrections* (Government of the Union of Burma Publication). Rangoon, 1949.
———. *The Constitution of the Socialist Republic of the Union of Burma.* Rangoon, Printing and Publishing Corporation, 1974.
———. *Constitution of the Union of Burma.* Rangoon, Superintendent, Government Printing and Stationery, 1954, in Burmese and English.
———. *Enquiry Commission for Regional Autonomy: Report.* Rangoon, Superintendent, Government Printing and Stationery, 1952, in Burmese and English.
———. *The Report of the Frontier Areas Committee of Enquiry, 1947,* pt. I, *Report,* and pt. II, *Appendices.* Rangoon, Superintendent, Government Printing and Stationery, 1947.

———. *Some Public Utterances 1942–1945 of His Excellency, the Governor of Burma, Sir R. H. Dorman-Smith.* Rangoon, Superintendent, Government Printing and Stationery, 1945.

Burma. Director of Information, *Forward* (fortnightly).

———. *Is Trust Vindicated?* Rangoon, Director of Information, 1960.

———. Mass Education Council, *Mass Education, Burma.* Rangoon, Union Printing Works, 1954.

———. Ministry of Information. *Burma's Fight for Freedom: Independence Commemoration.* Rangoon, Superintendent, Government Printing and Stationery, 1948.

———. Ministry of Information. *Burma Weekly Bulletin.* New Series issued since 1951.

Burma Socialist Program Party. *Address Delivered by General Ne Win, Chairman of the Burma Socialist Programme Party, at the Closing Session of the Fourth Party Seminar on 11th November 1969.* Rangoon, 1969.

———. *Address Delivered by General Ne Win, Chairman of the Burma Socialist Programme Party, at the Opening Session of the Fourth Party Seminar on 6th November 1969.* Rangoon, 1969.

———. *The Specific Characteristics of the Burma Socialist Programme Party.* Rangoon, 1964.

———. *The System of Correlation of Man and His Environment.* Rangoon, 1964.

———. Central Organising Committee, *Party Seminar 1965.* Rangoon, 1966.

Cady, John F. *A History of Modern Burma.* Ithaca, Cornell University Press, 1958.

Chakravarti, N. R. *The Indian Minority in Burma.* London, Oxford University Press, 1971.

Christian, John L. *Burma and the Japanese Invader.* Bombay, Thacker, 1945.

Crosthwaite, Sir Charles. *The Pacification of Burma.* 1912. Reprint. London, Frank Cass, 1968.

Furnivall, John S. *Colonial Policy and Practice.* New York, New York University Press, 1956.

Great Britain. *Burma: A Statement of Policy by His Majesty's Government, May 1945.* London, His Majesty's Stationery Office, 1945. Cmd. 6635.

———. *Conclusions Reached in the Conversations between His Majesty's Government and the Delegation from the Executive*

Council of the Governor of Burma. London, His Majesty's Stationery Office, 1947. Cmd. 7029.

———. Treaty between the Government of the United Kingdom and the Provisional Government of Burma. London, His Majesty's Stationery Office, 1948. Cmd. 7240 and 7360.

Guardian (daily and monthly). Nationalized in 1964.

Hall, Daniel G. E. Burma. London, Hutchinson's University Library, 1950.

Harvey, Geoffrey E. History of Burma from the Earliest Times to 10 March 1824: The Beginning of the English Conquest. London, Longman's Green, 1925.

Htin Aung, A History of Burma. New York, Columbia University Press, 1967.

India. Census of India, 1931, vol. 11, Burma, pt. I, Report, and pt. II, Tables. Rangoon, Superintendent, Government Printing and Stationery, 1933.

Kunstadter, Peter, ed. Southeast Asian Tribes, Minorities, and Nations. 2 vols. Princeton, Princeton University Press, 1967.

Leach, Edmund R. Political Systems of Highland Burma. London, Bell, 1954.

Lehman, Frederick K. The Structure of Chin Society: A Tribal People of Burma Adapted to a Non-western Civilization (Illinois Studies in Anthropology, no 3). Urbana, University of Illinois Press, 1963.

McAllister, John T., Jr. Southeast Asia: The Politics of National Integration. New York, Random House, 1973.

Marshall, Harry. The Karen Peoples of Burma: A Study in Anthropology and Ethnology. Columbus, Ohio State University Press, 1922.

Maung Maung. Burma's Constitution. The Hague, Martinus Nijhoff, 1959.

Mendelson E. Michael. Sangha and State in Burma: A Study of Monastic Sectarianism and Leadership, ed. John P. Ferguson. Ithaca, Cornell University Press, 1975.

Mi Mi Khaing. Burmese Family. Calcutta, Longman's Green, 1946.

Morrison, Ian. Grandfather Longlegs. London, Faber & Faber, 1947.

Mountbatten, Louis. Report to the Combined Chiefs of Staff by the Supreme Allied Commander, South East Asia, 1943–1945. London, His Majesty's Stationery Office, 1951.

Mya Sein, Daw. The Administration of Burma: Sir Charles Crosthwaite and the Consolidation of Burma. 1938. Reprint. Kuala Lumpur, Oxford University Press, 1973.

Nation (daily). Forced to shut down in 1964.

Nu, Thakin. *Burma under the Japanese*. London, St. Martin's, 1954.
———. *U Nu: Saturday's Son*, trans. U Law Yone and ed. U Kyaw Win. New Haven, Yale University Press, 1975.
Pe Maung Tin and Gordon H. Luce. *The Glass Palace Chronicles of the Kings of Burma*. London, Oxford University Press, 1923.
Pye, Lucian W. *Politics, Personality and Nation Building: Burma's Search for Identity*. New Haven, Yale University Press, 1962.
Saimong Mangrai, Sao. *The Shan States and the British Annexation*, (Data Paper no. 57). Ithaca, Cornell University Southeast Asia Program, 1965.
Sangermano, Father. *A Description of the Burmese Empire*. Reprint. London, Susil Gupta, 1966.
Sarkisyanz, E. *Buddhist Backgrounds of the Burmese Revolution*. The Hague, Martinus Nijhoff, 1965.
Scott, J. George, and J. T. P. Hardiman, eds. *Gazetteer of Upper Burma and the Shan States*. 5 vols. Rangoon, Superintendent, Government Printing and Stationery, 1900–1901.
Sein Win. *The Split Story*. Rangoon, Guardian, 1959.
Shway Yoe [J. George Scott], *The Burman: His Life and Notions*. 2 vols. 1882. Reprint. London, Macmillan, 1910.
Silverstein, Josef. *Burma: Military Rule and the Politics of Stagnation*. Ithaca, Cornell University Press, 1977.
——— ed. *The Political Legacy of Aung San* (Data Paper no. 86). Ithaca, Cornell University Southeast Asia Program, 1972.
Slim, William. *Defeat into Victory*. London, Cassell, 1956.
Smith, Donald Eugene. *Religion and Politics in Burma*. Princeton, Princeton University Press, 1965.
Spiro, Melford E. *Buddhism and Society: A Great Tradition and Its Burmese Vicissitudes*. London, Allen & Unwin, 1971.
Thompson, Virginia, and Richard Adloff. *Minority Problems in Southeast Asia*. Stanford, Stanford University Press, 1955.
Tinker, Hugh. *The Union of Burma*. London, Oxford University Press, 1957.
Trager, Frank N. *Burma: From Kingdom to Republic*. New York, Praeger, 1966.
Woodman, Dorothy. *The Making of Burma*. London, Cresset, 1962.
*Working People's Daily* (in Burmese and English). Official newspaper of Burma since its founding in 1963.

# Index

Academy for the Development of National Groups, 235, 236
Act of 1935, 29, 31-32, 97
Ahmudan, 11
Alaungpaya, King, 22
All-Burma Gurkha League, 115
All-Burma India Youth League, 131
All-Burma Muslim Congress, 171, 172, 182
All-Burma Peasant's League, 136
All-Burma Peasant's Organization (ABPO), 170, 178
All-Burma Students' Union, 136
All-Burma Trade Union Congress, 175, 176
All-Burma Youth League, 171
All-Burma Youth Organization, 57, 181, 182
Anglo-Burmans, 89, 95, 119, 141; unity with Burmans, 89, 95-96
Anglo-Indians, 28
Animists, 21, 222
Anti-Fascist People's Freedom League (AFPFL), 60-63, 64, 66-67, 70, 72, 116, 117, 118, 119, 126, 127, 128, 130, 131, 133, 145, 146, 152, 155, 158, 161, 162, 218, 219, 223, 226, 235, 239, 246; affiliate groups, 163,

Anti-Fascist People's Freedom League (AFPFL) (continued)
164, 165, 167, 168, 211; All-Burma National Conference (1946), 165, 172, 173, 177; All-Burma National Conference (1947), 173, 177, 179, 182; All-Burma National Conference (1958) 157; Executive Council, 75, 76, 77, 82, 95, 140, 165, 175, 176, 182; financial base, 167; impact on federal structure, 213-216; Instrument of Instructions, 75-76, 77; mass organizations in, 164; opposition to Dorman-Smith, 68-69, 74-75; party of national unity, 170-181; policy on unification, 94-95, 99-100; political objectives, 66-68, 69-70, 96; pre-constituent assembly convention, 120-125, 142, 143, 238; Provisional Rules of the Supreme Council of AFPFL, 163-164; relations with Frontier Areas, 83-89, 95, 179-181; reorganization, 169; sources of power, 80-83; sources of strength, 77-79; split in, 172-177, 211-212; structure, 163-169; subgroups in, 165, 166; Supreme Council, 75, 76, 77, 86, 98, 120, 163,

# INDEX

Anti-Fascist People's Freedom League (AFPFL) (continued) 164, 165, 166, 169, 174, 175, 176, 183
Arakan Hill Tract, 110, 181
Arakan State, 150
Arakanese, 8, 13-14, 48-49, 61, 181, 187, 205, 219, 227, 245
Arakanese National Congress, 67
Assimilation under Burman kings, 25
Athi, 11
Attlee, Clement, 93, 96-97, 98, 100, 102, 103, 177
Auchinleck, Gen. Claude, 82
Aung Gyi, Brig., 228
Aung Min, U, 225
Aung San, U (Bogyoke), 52-53, 54, 59, 60, 61, 73, 78, 80, 81, 83, 84, 91, 93, 95, 98, 99, 100, 101, 105, 106, 118, 119, 120, 127, 134, 136, 137, 138, 145, 146, 147, 148, 150, 151, 152, 155, 168, 169, 170, 171, 172, 174, 175, 176, 178, 180, 181, 224, 228, 229, 231, 238, 244, 246; assassination of, 126, 132, 177, 179, 183, 247; on church and state, 143-144; concept of nationalism, 139-140; on national unity, 140, 144; self-view, 138-139; on socialism, 143; source of federal ideas, 142-143; speech to AFPFL pre-constituent assembly, 121; symbolic use of, 135; unity in diversity, 140-141
Aung San-Attlee Agreement, 101-102, 104, 105, 108, 109, 116, 117, 120, 131, 138, 180; debate in Parliament, 102-103; opposition to amongst Burmese, 103
Aung San-Attlee meeting, 100-102
Aung Sein, U, 172
Aung Zan Wai, U, 91

Ba Gyan, U, 56, 171
Ba Hein, Thakin, 137
Ba Khaing, Mahn, 78, 128
Ba Maung, Saw, 59
Ba Maw, Dr., 42, 47, 53, 56, 57, 58, 98, 118, 124, 126, 137, 145; criticism of AFPFL constitutional ideas, 124-125

Ba Maw, U, 202
Ba Pe, U, 73, 99, 164, 172, 173
Ba Sein, Thakin, 98-99, 101, 103
Ba Sein–U Saw–Ba Maw coalition, 99
Ba Shin, U, 56
Ba U, Sir, 73, 78
Ba U, U, 41
Ba U Gyi, Saw, 78, 88, 176
Baptists, American, 17, 44
Basu, Mr., 204
Bayinnaung, King, 22
Bernard, E., Mr., 95
Bogyoke, see Aung San, U
Bohmu-mintha, 19
Bose, Subhas Chandra, 55
Bottomley, A. G., 104, 105, 108
British Administration in Burma, 26-29; in Frontier Areas, 29-32
British Conservative Party, 102
British Labour Party, 78
British Military Police, 53
British policy for post-World War II Burma, 65
British response to AFPFL demands, 96-98
Browderism, 173
Bu, U, 43
Buddhism, 14, 25, 147, 153, 156, 188, 222, 223, 225, 239, 248; Burmans adopt, 10; political activity, 37
Buddhist–Muslim conflict, 223
Buddhist State, 123, 143
Burma Army, 80-81, 222; see also Burma National Army
Burma Census of 1872, 7; of 1931, 7, 8-9
Burma Chamber of Commerce, 27
Burma–China relations, 237
Burma Communist Party (BCP), 155, 156, 170, 171, 178, 179, 206, 233, 235, 242; expelled from AFPFL, 169, 172-177, 243
Burma Defense Army (BDA), 53
Burma Frontier Service, 31, 43
Burma–Great Britain Treaty of 1947, 133
Burma Independence Army (BIA), 50-51, 52, 54
Burma Independence Preparatory Committee, 54

Burma–India, relations under British rule, 32–33
Burma National Army (BNA), 53, 56, 57, 60, 62, 67, 80, 169
Burma Parliament of 1922, 28
Burma proper, 90, 104, 106, 111, 112, 113, 131, 150, 203, 205, 211, 219, 220, 221, 225, 227, 232, 241, 245
Burma Rifles, 53
Burma Round Table Conference, 38, 42, 43
Burma Socialist Party, 61, 67, 155, 169, 170, 171, 175, 178, 179, 182
Burma Socialist Program Party (BSPP), 232, 241
Burma Trade Federation, 175
Burma Trade Union Organization (Trade Union Congress Burma), 170, 178
Burma Translation Society, 154
Burman–British Land and Agriculture Committee Report, 41
Burman Empire, 6, 23–25; lack of stable bureaucracy, 24
Burman–Indian relations, 40–43, 51
Burman–Karen Central Organization, 58
Burman–Karen relations, 47–48, 50–51, 58–59
Burman nationalism: under British rule, 35–44; early political activity, 36–37; issues, 40–43; sources of, 38
Burmanization, 24–25, 43, 123, 184, 207, 208–211, 220–226, 229, 231, 239, 246, 248
Burmans, 10–12, 42, 44, 46, 48, 50, 85, 86, 87, 113, 114, 129, 142, 150, 172, 187, 207, 208, 211, 213, 214, 215, 220, 224, 228, 240, 242, 243, 244, 245, 246; kingship, 23–24; religion and culture, 10, 12, 221; society, 9–12
Burmese, 105, 128, 129, 144, 152, 218, 220, 248
Burmese military: cooperation with Allies, 53; participation in AFPFL, 61; wartime origins, 50–54
Burmese Resistance Movement, 51, 57, 60–63, 80; Ba Maw's government compared with, 62–63; British support of, 62; formation of AFPFL, 61; membership in, 61

Burmese Review, 88
Burmese student movement, 37
Burmese Way to Socialism (BWS), 231
Butler, R., 102
Bwe (Karen subgroup), 15–16

Cady, John, 3, 16, 47, 48
Caretaker government, 158, 212, 216, 226
Carnegie, Dale, 146
Central Karen Board, 58
Central Karen Organization, 88
Chamber of Deputies, 192, 194, 196, 198, 199
Chamber of Nationalities, 122, 123, 129, 192, 194, 196, 198, 199, 227, 240
Chan Htoon, U, 185
Chin Affairs Council, 199
Chin Hills, 110, 122, 129, 181
Chin Presidium Council, 233
Chin Special Division, 199–200, 201, 225
Chinese, 28, 61, 141, 209
Chinese invasion of Burma, 208–211
Chinese Nationalist Army (Kuomintang), 209
Chins, 20, 22, 61, 84, 86, 95, 105, 111, 113, 115, 129, 131, 150, 180, 187, 199, 200, 206, 212, 213
Chit, Thakin, 175
Chittee, Saw, 111
Christians, 123, 222
Church and state relationship, 123, 143–144, 153–154
Churchill, Winston, 97–98, 99, 103
Collis, Maurice, 70, 76, 77, 78, 138
Commonwealth of Nations, 97–98
Communal representation, 28, 41–43, 46
Communications between states, 201
Communist Party of Burma (CPB), 61, 67, 117, 119, 121, 132, 133, 137, 172–173, 174, 176
Conrad, Joseph, 146
Constituent Assembly, 1, 4, 5, 93–97, 110, 111, 116, 120, 125–133, 143, 144, 146, 151, 176, 178, 179, 180, 181, 185, 186, 196, 200, 205, 217, 245, 247, 249; seat allotment in, 116, 119

# INDEX

Constitution Amendment Act of 1951, 196
Constitution of 1947, 1–2, 127, 160, 208, 210, 220, 226; Article 198, 200; Buddhism's special position, 188, 222; citizenship, 186–187; civil rights, 187, 188; federal system, 185–186, 200; human rights, 187; Ne Win's criticism of, 240; powers of president, 189–190; protection of workers, 188; reasons for failure, 243–247
Constitution of 1974, 241–242, 247–249; National Assembly and councils, 241; preparation for, 241; states and divisions, 241, 242
Constitution Revision Steering Committee, 227
Constitutional democracy, 157, 158, 230
Constitutional dictatorship, 238–240
Craddock scheme of reforms, 45
Criminal Justice Order of 1926, 191
Crosthwaite, Sir Charles, 18, 19, 29, 30
Cultural Revolution (China), 237
Cumberland (HMS), 70, 73

"Declaration of the Conviction of the Revolutionary Council on the Question of National Minorities," 235
Defence Services Academy Bill, 221
Democratic centralism, 163, 164, 178
Democratic National United Front (DNUF), 98–99, 117, 118
Dobama Asiayone, 38–40, 53, 57, 58, 91, 99, 136, 137, 145, 172
Dobama-Sinyetha Party, 57–58
Dominion status, 100
Dorman-Smith, Reginald H., 68, 70, 79, 81, 84, 87, 138, 174
Dorman-Smith's administration, 74–79; policy statement, June 20, 1945, 70–72
Driberg, T., 103

East Asiatic Youth League (EAYL), 56, 60, 171
Education, 207, 221
Election of 1947, 116–120; parties boycott, 117–119; results, 119

escalator clause, 97–98
Europeans, 28, 42, 86, 142
Executive Council, government of Burma, 78, 79, 84, 87; under Hubert Rance, 91–92, 96, 99, 100, 102, 103, 105, 106, 108, 109, 112, 119, 128; mission to London, 99

Federal Council of Shan Chiefs, 30
Federal seminar, 227–228, 234
Federated Shan States, 110, 111, 122
Federated Shan States Law, 191
Federation of Trade Organizations (FTO), 178
Feudal rule, 216
Forum, 175
Fourteenth Burma Regiment, Burma Army, 217
Free Indian Movement, 55
Freedom Bloc, 136, 137
Freud, Sigmund, 146
Frontier Area Councillors, 109
Frontier Areas, 65, 71, 74, 79, 80, 83, 87, 90, 91, 93, 94, 95, 99–100, 102, 104, 106, 108, 110, 113, 127, 128, 129, 140–141, 150, 170, 180, 200; Part I (Act of 1935), 31–32; Part II Areas, 32; unification with Burma proper, 43–44
Frontier Areas Administration, 75, 216
Frontier Areas Committee of Enquiry, 109–116, 118, 122, 180, 181, 194, 200; recommendations, 110, 113; testimony before, 111–116
Furnivall, John S., 2, 3, 6, 10, 14, 35, 147

General Council of Burmese Associations (GCBA), 36, 37
General strike, 90–92
Germany, 63
Glass Palace Chronicle of the Kings of Burma, 14
Great Britain, 246
Green, J. H., 8, 9

Gumlao, 21
Gumsa, 21
Gurkhas, 115

Hall, D. George E., 10, 13
Hall, H. Fielding, 12
Harvey, Geoffrey, 2, 9, 13, 20, 34
Head-minister of state, 190–191, 195, 198
Heho, 58
High Court, 191
Hindu influences on Burman culture, 11
Hindus, 222
Hla Han, Col., 237
Hla Pe, U, 58
Hla Tun, Dr. Saw, 219
Hlin Maung, U, 105
Htin Aung, U, 3
Htoon Aung Gyaw, U, 76, 78

Imperial Affairs Committee, Conservative Party, 67
Independence, 100
Independents, 119
India, 247
Indian Army, 221
Indian Congress Party, 33, 39
Indian immigration under British rule, 32–33
Indian National Congress, 137
Indians, 41, 42, 52, 61, 95, 130–131, 141, 144
Indirect rule, under Burman kings, 24
Indonesia, 247
"Instrument of Instructions," for British governor, 29
Internal Unity Advisory Body, 237–238

Japanese occupation, 137; areas outside Burma, 55; Ba Maw government, 51, 55, 57–60, 145; Ba Maw's Declaration of Independence, 61; British Executive Administration, 53–54; Burma Baho government, 53; Burma independence under, 54; Burman-Karen relations, 58–59; Burmese political party, 57–58; policies of, 51–53, 56–57; policies toward Frontier Areas, 54–55; relations with Indians, 55–56
Judicial powers, 191
Judson College, 56

Kachin, criticism of AFPFL, 85
Kachin Hill Tribes Regulations, 195
Kachin Hills, 111, 122
Kachin Independence Army, 234
Kachin Manao celebration, 83–84, 85
Kachin State, 112, 113, 129, 180, 181, 191, 194–196, 200, 202, 208, 210, 211, 212, 213–214, 216, 217, 219, 242, 245; State Council, 210, 213
Kachin Youth League, 181
Kachins, 20–21, 55, 61, 84, 85, 86, 95, 105, 112, 113, 128, 129, 132, 150, 180, 181, 187, 194, 206, 212, 213, 214, 217, 227; attitude toward Europeans, 44; political organization, 21; relations with Burmans, 21–22
Karen Affairs Council, 196, 197, 218
Karen Central Organization, 67
Karen Congress, 218
Karen National Defence Organization (KNDO), 214, 217, 218, 219, 221
Karen National Union (KNU), 109, 112, 114, 115, 117, 118, 172, 233
Karen nationalism, 44–48
Karen political organization, 44–45
Karen response to British reforms, 45–46
Karen Revolutionary Council, 234
Karen State (also called Kaw-thu lay), 130, 150, 151, 191, 196–199, 200, 202, 211, 217, 218–219
Karen Youth League (KYL), 119, 171, 182, 218
Karen Youth Organization (KYO), 78, 109, 171, 218
Karenni, see Kayahs
Karenni Area, 110, 122
Karenni National Progressive Party, 233

# INDEX

Karens, 14, 15–18, 28, 34, 41, 44–48, 50, 52, 61, 62, 84, 86, 87, 89, 95, 102, 109, 111, 112, 114, 115, 118, 119, 123, 124, 130, 132, 133, 144, 150, 151, 152, 172, 187, 196, 197, 205, 206, 208, 217, 218, 219, 227, 245; conversion to Christianity, 17; goodwill mission to London, 88–89; idea of an independent state, 46–47; political organization, 16–17; relations with British, 17, 88–89; relations with Burmans, 16, 58–60; subgroups, 15–16
Kaw-thu-lay, see Karen State
Kayah State, 130, 192–194, 196, 200, 201, 202, 225; State Ministry, 201
Kayahs, 20, 22–23, 30, 41, 86, 100, 113, 150, 187, 213, 227, 244; relations with British, 20–21; relations with Burmans, 20–21
Khin Maung Gale, U, 109
Khin Maung Pyu, U, 59
Komin Kochin Party, 39
Ku, Saw T. Po, 111, 112
Kya Doe, Col., 62
Kyaw Myint, U, 56
Kyaw Nyein, U, 109, 119, 137, 175, 178
Kyaw Thet, U, 2, 3

Land Nationalization Act, 1948, 204
Land of Pagodas, 123
Laos, 239
Leach, Edmund, 3, 21
Ledwidge, W. B. J., 109
Leftist Unity Plan, 155
Lehman, Frederick, 4
Lewisohn, Chief Secretary, 46
Leyden, John, 105
Lieberman, Victor, 3
Loo-Nee, Sidney, 45, 88
Luce, Gordon, 10
Lun, U, 78

Mahabama Party, 117, 118
Man, the Wolf of Man, 147

Mao Tse-tung, 146
Marshall, Harry, 16
Martial law, 215
Marx, Karl, 146
Marxism, 39, 136, 137, 147, 178
Marxism and the National and Colonial Question, 142
Marxist League, 179
Mass Education Movement, 154, 224–226, 235
Maung Maung, Therrawaddy, 78
Military, 199, 203, 214, 215, 216, 217, 221, 222; Burmanization of, 221–222
Military coup of 1962, 4, 158, 228
Military rule, 231–242; amnesty offer, 232–233; meeting with insurgents, 233–235; oppose state religion, 239; policy toward minorities, 235–238
Military under British rule, 34–35
Min, Saw Johnson D. Po, 115
Ministry of Culture, 224
Ministry of Finance, 202
Ministry of Religion, 143
Ministry of Religious Affairs, 223
Minkyinyo, King, 22
Mon–Burman War of 1740–1757, 3
Mon State, 150
Mons, 14–15, 46, 48–49, 152, 187, 205, 206, 218, 219, 224, 227, 245
Montagu, E. S., 27, 36, 45
Moral Re-Armament, 153
Morley–Minto reforms, 27
Morrison, Ian, 62
Mountbatten, Louis, 62, 80, 81, 82
Mountbatten Report, 77
Muslims, 123, 222, 223
Mya, Henzada U, 77
Mya, Pyawbwe U, 175, 176
Mya, Thakin, 58, 59, 60, 91, 99, 120, 121, 123, 125, 127, 128, 137, 169, 170, 178, 179, 249
Mya Bu, Sir, 54
Mya Sein, Daw, 11
Myat Soe, U, 201
Myint Thein, Saw, 109
Myochit Party, 39, 77, 91, 99, 117, 172
Myoma National High School, 144–145
Myothugyi, 10–11, 24, 26

Naga Hills District, 110
Nagas, 86
National Day, 38, 95
National defense, 182
National Democratic United Front (NDUF), 233, 234, 235
National Karen Association (NKA), 44–46
National Library, 224
National Museum and Art Gallery, 224
National schools movement, 37
National Service Organization, 60
National Solidarity Association (NSA), 226
National unity, 126, 134–135, 140, 154, 207, 230; Ba Maw's contribution to, 57–60; before British rule, 6–7; under Burman Kings, 23; problem of, 4–7; sources of wartime cooperation, 51; theories of, 2–4
Nationalism amongst minorities, 48–49
Nationalization, 207, 208–219, 229, 231, 239
Nay-thu-yain Theater, 82
Ne Win [Naywin], General, 67, 158, 212, 216, 230, 233, 235, 236–237, 238, 239, 240, 242, 249
Nepali Association, 115
New Mon State Party, 233
*New Times of Burma*, 124–125
Nicholson, G., 102
Nu, Thakin [U], 1, 59, 84, 85, 109, 114, 117, 130, 132, 134, 144, 177, 179, 183, 211, 212, 217, 223, 226, 227, 228, 229, 232, 235, 236, 248; attitude toward politics, 146; Buddhist influences upon, 147; on civil servants, 158–160; criticism of dictatorship, 156–157; differences with Aung San, 155, 160–161; education, 145; idea of national unity, 148–152, 158–160; idea of socialist state, 156; ideas on Marxism and Buddhism, 147; ideas on military, 160; intellectual influences on, 146–147; on minority rights, 151; on national culture, 154–155; on political unity, 155; president of AFPFL, 146, 182; on religion, 152–154; social background, 144; on socialism, 155–

Nu, Thakin [U] (*continued*)
156; splits AFPFL, 157–158; style of communications, 148; support for democracy, 157; vice president of AFPFL, 145–146; wartime activity, 145

Opium and insurgency, 242–243
Orders Modifying the Customary Laws in the Federated Shan States, 191
Ottama, U, 37

Palaung, 61
Panglong Agreement, 107–108, 110, 113, 122, 181, 206, 208, 220, 246
Panglong Conference (1946), 84–85; (1947), 102, 104–108, 110, 140, 180, 207, 234, 247
Pa-O, see Toungthus
Patriotic Burmese Forces (PBF), 66, 80, 81
Paw Tun, U, 76, 78
People's Peasant Councils, 232
People's Republic of China (PRC), 208, 209, 210, 217, 237, 239, 242
People's Revolutionary Party, see Burma Socialist Party
People's Volunteer Organization (PVO), 80, 81–83, 155, 156, 169, 171, 179, 182, 206
People's Workers Councils, 232
Phayre, Arthur, 13
Philippines, 247
Po, San C., 45, 46, 47, 54, 59
Po Chit, Saw, 88
Political unity, 185
Prime minister, 196, 198, 199, 204
"Problems for Burma's Freedom," 141, 144
Provisional Parliament, 151
Pu, U, 43; and 1945 governor's council, 78
Pwo (Karen subgroup), 15–16

Rance, Hubert, 87, 90, 93, 132, 175
Rance administration, 90–92

# INDEX

261

Rangoon Police Department, 217
Rangoon police strike, 89–92
Rangoon Trade Association, 27
Rangoon University Students' Union, 137
Red Flags, see Communist Party of Burma (CPB)
Rees-Williams, D. R., 109, 118
Referendum on constitution, 1973, 241
Reformed Legislative Council of 1909, 27
Regional Autonomy Enquiry Commission, 197
Religious freedom, 153
*Report of the Frontier Areas Committee of Enquiry, 1947*, 21
"Report of the Secretary-General of the Socialist Party," 177
Resident, 192, 193
Resistance Day, 117, 176
Resistance Movement, 137
*Review of the First Stage of the New Order Plan*, 56–57, 58–59
Revolt and insurgency, 206, 210–211
Revolt on the frontier, 242
Revolutionary Council (RC), 228, 232, 233, 235, 237, 238, 239, 248
Riot Inquiry Committee, 41
Rural Self-Government Act, 32
Russia, 63, 156

Saimong Mangrai, Sao, 3, 106
Salween District, 110
San Yu, Brig., 236, 241
Sangermano, Father, 15
*Sangha*, 25
Sankey, Saw, 109
Saw, U, 78, 84–85, 98, 99, 103
Saw Myint, Col., 216
Saw Yi, U, 112
*Sawbwa*, 19, 84, 215, 216, 240
Saya San Revolt, 37, 47
Scheme for Social Education, 224
Scott, J. George, 10, 11, 13
Seagraves, Dr. Gordon, 84
Secession: right of, 113, 200–201, 214, 244; threat of, 4, 216

Security and Administrative Central Council, 232
Security and Administrative Councils (SAC), 231, 232, 239
Sein Fein, 39
Service Corps, 58
Seventh Brigade, Union Army, 216
Sgaw (Karen subgroup), 15–16
Shakespeare, William, 146
Shan Association, 67
Shan State, 129, 189–192, 193, 194, 196, 198, 200, 202, 207, 209, 212, 214–216, 217, 219, 225, 227, 236, 242, 245
Shan State Administrative Enquiry Commission, 215
Shan State Council, 216
Shan State Independence Army (*Noon Sukhan*), 216, 234
Shan State Unity Party, 216
Shan States, 75, 140
Shan States People's Freedom League (SSPFL), 104–105, 180; Central Interim Council, 180
Shans, 29, 30–31, 42, 54, 59–60, 61, 86, 87, 95, 104, 105, 106, 129, 132, 142, 150, 180, 187, 201, 206, 208, 213, 216, 217, 227, 244, 245; chiefs' powers under 1947 Constitution, 192; culture, 18–19; dissidence, 227–228; origin of, 18; relations with Burmans, 18–20
Shaw, George Bernard, 146
Shwe Thaike, Sao, 1, 132, 133
Shwedagon Pagoda, 82, 117
Shwegyin Karen Association, 114
Shwin, Saw Marshall, 114
Simon Commission, 40–44, 46; Report, 38
Sinwa Nawng, Sima Duwa, 105, 108, 128, 181
*Sinyetha* ("Poor Man's") Party, 39, 57, 91, 137, 172
Slim, Gen. William, 138
Socialism, 143, 155–156
Socialist Republic of the Union of Burma, 241, 242
Socialist State, 121

Soe, Thakin, 137, 172–173, 174, 176
Stalin, Josef, 142, 146
Standing Committee of Federal Council (Shans), 30
State Constitution Drafting Committee, 241
State Council, 189, 190, 192, 193, 194, 195, 198, 212
State governments, structure (1947), 189–190, 192, 193, 194, 195, 198
State of emergency, 203
State religion, 239
State Religion Bill (1961), 223
State Supreme Council, 232, 236
Statehood proposal for Mons and Arakanese, 226–227
States, power to tax, 201
States Court Act (1953), 191, 193, 199, 201
*States v. Union of Burma,* 204
Steavenson, H. N. C., 75, 84, 86
Student strike (1936), 145
Supreme Council of the United Hill Peoples, 113, 180, 181
Supreme Court (1947), 189, 191, 198, 204, 205

*Taikthugyi, see Myothugyi*
Taiwan, 209
*Talaings, see Mons*
Tantabin Affair, 83, 174
*Taungya,* 21
*Teza, Boh, see Aung San, U*
Tha Din, Saw, 88
Tha Htoo, Thra, 112, 114
Thailand, 239
*Thakins,* 38–39, 53, 117, 147
Than Tun, U, 59, 60, 61, 73, 80, 81, 82, 137, 169, 173, 174, 175, 176
Thein Pe [Thein Pe Myint], 91, 173, 174, 175
Thin, San Po, 59, 62, 119
*Thugyi,* 26
*Times* (London), 79, 84–85, 88, 90, 98–99, 119, 120, 130
Tin Tut, U, 88, 91, 99, 105, 109, 114
Tinker, Hugh, 34
Toungthus, 16, 245

Trade Union Congress Burma (TUCB), also Burma Trade Union Organization, 170, 178
Trager, Frank, 3
Tun Aye, U, 236
Tun Myint, U, 180

Union Citizenship Act of 1948, 187
Union Day, 207, 216, 235, 236, 237
Union financial aid to States, 202
Union flag (1947), 132
Union government, 202, 203, 208, 213, 214, 215, 217, 223, 227, 242
Union Library and Museum, 224
Union of Burma, 86, 130, 133, 159, 186, 199, 210, 212, 213, 220, 227, 228, 238, 244
Union Parliament, 189, 197, 198, 199, 201, 203, 211, 212, 213, 216, 228, 230
Union president, 198, 199, 201, 205, 208
Union-state legislative lists, 203, 204
Union-state relations, 129, 202, 213
Union supremacy, 191
Union Treasury, 201, 205, 213
United Hill People's Congress, 212
United Karen League (UKL), 218, 219
United Karen Organization (UKO), 218, 219
United Nations, 74, 96, 209
United States, 243
Unity in diversity, 140–141, 184, 207, 208, 221
University Act, 37, 136
University of Rangoon, 56, 136, 222, 224

Village autonomy under Burman kings, 24
Village Regulation Act of 1887, 26–27
Vum Ko Hau, 108

Wavell, Gen. Archibald Percival, 82
Wavell Plan, 68

Webb, Sir Charles, 46
White Paper of May 17, 1945, 65, 68, 71, 72, 73, 74, 84, 86, 97
Whyte Committee, 46
Win Maung, Mahn, 172
Wisara, U, 37
Women's Congress, 175
Women's Freedom League (WFL), 171, 178
Women's League, 67

World War II, 5, 246; see also Japanese occupation
Wunthanu Athin movement, 36–37

Yan Aung, U, 78
Young Men's Buddhist Association (YMBA), 36, 45
Young Men's Christian Association (YMCA), 36
Youth League, 67